THE PROFESSIONAL WRITING (

THE PROFESSIONAL WRITING GUIDE:

Writing Well and Knowing Why

ROSLYN PETELIN AND MARSHA DURHAM

Businesss & Professional Publishing

© First published by Woodslane Pty Limited 1992
This edition first published by Allen & Unwin in 2003.

Allen & Unwin
83 Alexander Street
Crows Nest, NSW 2065
Australia
Phone: (61 2) 8425 0100
Fax: (61 2) 9906 2218
E-mail: info@allenandunwin.com
Web: www.allenandunwin.com

National Library of Australia
cataloguing-in-publication data:

Petelin, Roslyn.
    The professional writing guide.

    Includes index.
    ISBN 978 0 58287 181 6

    1. Authorship. 2. Business writing. 3. English language –
    Rhetoric. I. Durham, Marsha. II. Title.

808.042

Designed by Jan Schmoeger/Designpoint
Set in 11/12 pt Goudy
Printed in Australia by McPherson's Printing Group

14 13 12 11 10 9 8 7 6 5 4

CONTENTS

Acknowledgements

We wish to acknowledge the support we received from our respective institutions in writing this book: the Communication Centre in the Faculty of Business at the Queensland University of Technology and the Faculty of Humanities and Social Sciences at the University of Western Sydney. We also wish to thank Robyn Penman and David Sless at the Communication Research Institute of Australia, who gave us valuable feedback.

We are grateful to our publisher, Robert Coco, for his cheery patience and for providing us with two such excellent professionals—our editor, Elizabeth Watson, and our designer, Jan Schmoeger.

As much as possible we have attributed the sources of our material. But, like most long-term educators, we have examples in our files which were often passed on to us, unidentified. We would welcome claims for acknowledgement in future editions of the book.

PREFACE

In our experience, the business community and the public both desire high-quality writing—writing that is clear, complete, authoritative, compelling, human, and error-free. It is generally acknowledged that writing that does not fulfil these criteria can detract from a company's image and can result in expensive mistakes.

Who is this book for?

This book is for professionals whose jobs require them to write, but who were not trained as writers, nor hired as writers, nor consider themselves to be writers. It is also for those who already write competently but who would like to enhance their strategies for writing more efficiently and effectively. This book is for those professionals whose only guidance has been: 'This is how we do it here' (as someone hands them a model document or style manual to follow) or 'See what you can come up with'. Although it is designed for middle- and upper-level management, writers entering the organisation at lower levels will find the strategies usable and reliable. Rarely are school-leavers or graduates capable of producing the kind of writing that their organisations desire.

Increasingly, highly-developed writing skills are recognised as having a strong impact on career advancement. There is also a growing tendency to test the writing competence of job applicants who will spend much of their working time engaged in writing and writing-related activities. At least one-third of an executive's time is spent writing. Companies hire staff—and wrongly assume that they are highly-skilled writers. When they are subsequently revealed to be poor writers, who perhaps neither enjoy writing nor feel motivated to improve their writing skills, both parties feel cheated.

Organisational writers write to think, to understand, to convey information, to explain, to request information, to record, to develop and enhance business relationships, to identify their own competence, to generate opportunities, to 'get things done'. Much organisational writing is badly-organised, full of inappropriate jargon, and boring. This is the kind of writing produced by writers who lack the basic knowledge and strategies that successful writers have and practise—the principles and strategies that we cover in *The Professional Writing Guide*.

How is this book different from other 'business-writing' books?

It is different in two main ways.

First, it is based on the recent upsurge in research on writing—primarily in the US workplace—attention that was previously given almost exclusively to academic and creative writing. What questions have writing researchers been asking?

- How do readers read/comprehend/remember?
- How can writers cater for different readers' abilities and needs?
- Can using computers to write help corporate writers produce 'higher quality' documents faster, more efficiently, and more cheaply?
- How are other new technologies changing writing?

Our book is based on this research and on our extensive consulting to Australian organisations. In fact, the original impetus for the book came from endless requests from our corporate clients for a comprehensive guide to the management of writing within organisations. Because we were unable to recommend one, we decided to write our own.

Second, we do not present the unsubstantiated folklore, 'quick tips', and 'textbook rules' usually found in writing guides, because we have found them to be either too vague or too prescriptive for untrained writers faced with complex stylistic decisions. Instead, we have based this book on a distillation of the principles that underlie effective writing.

Another issue that we have stressed throughout the book is that writing always exists in a context. We go beyond the simplistic rules into the situational context of professional writing, using examples based on our direct experience of the organisational environment. The skilled writer goes beyond knowledge of the appropriate format and mechanical correctness, to the way in which the document will be used in the larger communication context of the organisation.

Although writing is a mainstream activity in most organisations, up until now management has too often dismissed its importance until there is a crisis such as a deadline for a crucial report or proposal. As we move through the nineties there is no doubt that writing will increasingly be vitally important within organisations, as more and more people will need to be kept more fully informed. Writing extends the possibilities for thinking, and advances in technology to date have offered no evidence that machines can think and write for themselves the way humans can.

Finally, we would like to caution readers not to assume that our advice is eccentric merely because it occasionally varies from what is commonly taught in Australian classrooms. Writing the book engendered a great deal of discussion between us because of our different backgrounds. Our editor comes from a different background from either of us. We hope that the end result practises what we have advocated.

CHAPTER 1

WRITING IN THE BUSINESS ENVIRONMENT

Organisational writing is specialised. To be an effective writer in the business environment, you need to have excellent general writing skills and to understand the complex communication choices involved. Knowing how writing is structured in an organisation and what is acceptable helps you to shape your writing so that it communicates successfully.

WHAT CAN GO WRONG?

If you are like most writers in organisations, you have sufficient skill in writing to escape being labelled a poor communicator. To write effectively, however, you should be aware of how your writing is affected by the organisation itself, operating as a writing environment. This writing environment is complex: some writing researchers estimate that it takes up to three or four years for an employee to gain the needed organisational skill to produce successful documents (Paradis and others, 1985, p. 302).

Part of this complexity stems from organisational writing being both socially-oriented and task-oriented. As an organisational writer, you are writing messages to link with others (social) to undertake some action (task), for example, to provide answers, explain a problem, co-ordinate an activity, or persuade others about a choice. Whether these messages become communication (that is, your reader picks up your intended meaning) depends on how well you handle a range of complex choices associated with the document, the reader, and the organisation itself.

Your chance of communicating successfully is lessened when problems crop up in any of these three areas. For example, even a simple written request from a supervisor asking staff to comment on a new piece of equipment can fail because of any one of the following problems (see Figure 1.1).

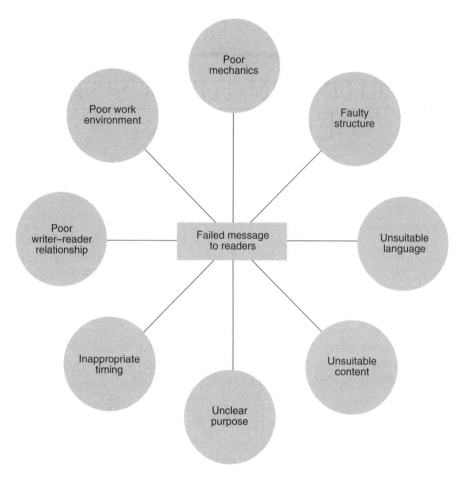

Figure 1.1 Problems which can lead to a failed message to your readers

- **Poor mechanics**—poor punctuation or spelling can frustrate readers by making them re-read to understand the message.
- **Faulty structure**—poor sentence structure can confuse or mislead readers. For example, a misplaced clause may force readers to recast the sentence mentally for it to make sense.
- **Unsuitable language**—difficult words, for example, may cause readers to 'turn off'.
- **Unsuitable content**—too many trivial or irrelevant points can cloud the subject and confuse readers.
- **Unclear purpose**—readers may miss a document's communication if its purpose is not made clear soon enough.
- **Inappropriate timing**—timing can affect a document's success, and even give a message which contradicts that of the document. For example, if staff receive a memo after the requested return date they will believe their views are not valued.

- **Poor writer–reader relationship**—a poor relationship between the writer and his or her readers increases the chances of the document being 'mis-read' or ignored.
- **Poor work environment**—if the general work environment is not conducive to effective communication, staff may be less inclined to act on a document. Communication can be adversely affected by physical elements (noise, overcrowding, poor lighting and ventilation) as well as emotional elements (a repressive organisational climate).

'SATISFICING' AS AN ORGANISATIONAL WRITER

Effective business writers solve many of these potential problems and produce successful documents by **satisficing**. This term, coined by organisational theorist Herbert A. Simon, describes practical decision-making based on probabilities. Because it is impossible to gather complete information, writers can never write with full knowledge of an issue. Organisational writers do not have the time or the resources to explore all possibilities and test all alternatives. Instead, they 'satisfice' by selecting the most satisfactory solution according to their knowledge of the present conditions and influences within the organisation.

Efficient organisational writers are adept 'satisficers' who can create an effective document for particular readers in the time given. They can do so because they understand the organisation's culture and the effect of this culture on communication.

LEARNING AN ORGANISATION'S COMMUNICATION ETIQUETTE

Part of knowing an organisation's writing environment lies in your ability to see it also as a culture, with some things being acceptable and others being taboo. The accepted communication in the organisational culture makes up what is known as its communication 'etiquette'. Just as you may kiss goodbye in one culture and shake hands in another, how you write is affected by your sense of an organisation's etiquette.

The etiquette is not only what is written down in a company's style manual. Communication etiquette deals with the often unspoken agreements about when and how you write, and to whom. Your acceptance and success in the organisation can be influenced by your knowledge of this etiquette, that is, your understanding of 'what is worth communicating, how it can be communicated, what other members... are likely to know and believe to be true about certain subjects, how other members can be persuaded...' (Faigley, 1985, p. 238).

Part of the communication etiquette which new employees must grapple with includes

- who they should or should not write directly to

- when writing is preferred over speaking face-to-face or telephoning
- what tone is appropriate in memos and letters
- and when and how they represent the organisation to the outside world.

Writers new to the corporate world lack experience with communication etiquette and thus face three major writing problems: developing ideas, acknowledging readers, and meeting deadlines.

Problem one: Trouble developing ideas

New organisational writers may have problems developing their ideas into documents. They may not be familiar with the organisation's usual format or structure for specific documents, such as proposals. They may not know what is commonly included or how much they are expected to research, that is, to check sources, read, and ask questions. Successful ideas are usually those that fit in with the organisation's plans and directions, so, to become effective, these new writers must also become knowledgeable about what is going on in the organisation and develop their writing within this context.

Problem two: Not acknowledging readers

Juggling not only what to write but how to write to a specific reader can be difficult for new writers, because selecting incorrectly can be highly embarrassing. Inexperienced organisational writers may find it difficult to understand the organisational status or role of their reader. For example, Susan, when asked by her director during a morning tea-break to comment on a topic, replied to what she thought was an informal request with an equally informal, handwritten memo. She was shocked when it was distributed at a formal meeting for senior staff.

Problem three: Not meeting deadlines

Inexperienced organisational writers may have little idea of the importance of deadlines. They may not fully understand that missing a newsletter's copy deadline means a 'hole' in page three or that not getting a report to the secretary in time means that their material is not distributed for a board meeting.

THE ETIQUETTE OF COMMUNICATION FLOWS

To understand the communication etiquette of your own organisation, you need to know how it can be influenced by the directional flow of communication within your workplace.

Communication etiquette is partly determined by the hierarchical structure of an organisation. Communication flows through the hierarchy in different directions: upwards, downwards, and across. Each direction presents potential problems for organisational writers. We describe some of these problems below and suggest strategies used by effective communicators to handle them.

Handling upward communication

Your chances to communicate upward, above your immediate superior, are limited. Few organisations condone open communication throughout. For example, you may contribute much at one organisational level but be effectively barred as a 'major player' at higher levels because you do not receive the necessary information to participate. Access to information, organisational roles, and duty statements suggest to us our place in the organisation's communication flow.

Some organisations, however, suppress upward communication more openly. They may rule that communication above one's immediate manager is forbidden. Or they may ignore staff's attempts to communicate upward. An excellent example of this is how the suggestion box is used in two different organisations. In one, employees get no information about how suggestions are handled, so the box is ignored. In the other organisation, replies to the suggestions are posted. Because employees see that their communication is attended to, they use the box. Both organisations seem to provide a means of upward communication, but the communication etiquette shows that only one supports it.

Organisational writers may not only be denied access to those higher up, but also find that their documents move upward without their knowledge, sent on by the intended reader. Not knowing who else 'higher up' will read your document makes it more difficult to choose what and how to write.

To effectively communicate upward, you must find the acceptable way to do so within your organisation. Two main variables affect your success: your superior's attitude to you and your expertise on the topic. If you have a good relationship with your superior, you have more chance of your document being forwarded to others—unaltered, with your name on it! You must also have something to communicate. Look for opportunities to write with not only your immediate readers in mind, but also a possible reader higher up in the organisation. Often it is all in the focus. If you are writing a report of a business trip, for example, you can make it a simple diary of events or highlight what is most relevant to the organisation. Which has a better chance of being sent from your manager to his or her superiors? Effective organisational writers weigh up the chances of any document being sent upward and plan it accordingly.

They also understand the peculiar etiquette of filtering in an organisation. Filtering is the selection of what information to make known to your manager. It is generally assumed that staff filter out 'bad news' and focus on what is good when communicating upward. They may sometimes not even commit themselves to writing, as it creates a permanent record of their decisions, whether right or wrong. The staff member knows how to filter appropriately and when to choose writing over face-to-face communication when communicating upward.

Handling downward communication

Downward communication can present problems when the amount is inappropriate, the content is irrelevant, or the information is distorted.

The amount of written communication that an employee must cope with is increasing. No longer is it assumed that subordinates need to know only whatever is pertinent to their immediate duties. They are often expected to read more and more and, as a result, they may respond by leaving unread much of the material which crosses their desk or shows up on their computer screen.

Staff trying to cope with too much to read may, paradoxically, suffer from information 'underload' if too many of the documents are about trivial matters. For example, one organisation sent out three messages about the revised date of a minor social function but only one short, incomplete memo about a major funding proposal. This lop-sided flow of downward information is common in many organisations.

As in any other flow, downward communication can suffer from distortion, especially when too many people are involved in preparing the document. Accidental distortions are common. 'Gatekeeping', in which some people manage or control communication, creates power flows within the organisation which can then further distort communication.

The effective writer copes with these problems of downward communication by being sensitive to how much people will read, and attempting to balance the need to restrict the amount of information sent downward with the problems of distorting information as a result.

Handling horizontal communication

Horizontal communication flows across the organisational structure, between people at the same level. Communicating effectively with colleagues requires skill and a certain amount of intuition. There seem to be fewer established etiquette rules for horizontal communication than there are for upward or downward communication. This is not because horizontal communication is more simple. Communicating with others at the same hierarchical level includes making choices such as how colleagues should be addressed, what communications others should receive, how much background information they need, and when a written message is more appropriate than a spoken one.

Make the wrong choice and you might alienate or even lose a possible ally. For example, when Renee wanted the same newly-vacant office as her colleague, Colin, she was told to come to an agreement with him. Instead, she chose to move in without consulting Colin and tried to deflect his possible anger by sending him what she thought was a humorous memo. The result? Colin was upset not only about Renee's action but also about what he interpreted as a 'proprietary', smug note. Renee won her office, but lost her colleague's support.

Handling informal communication

Upward, downward, and horizontal directions comprise the formal flows of organisational communication. But communication also flows informally within the organisation, in a network pattern, as people connect with others whom they consider to be good sources for information. Networks cross the formal hierarchy of the organisation, for these connections rely on people's friendship or common interests.

Much has been written about networking, the art of developing your informational network of professional contacts. The network is usually regarded as being made up of spoken communication, but effective communicators do not neglect writing. For example, a thank you note may be treasured far more than a telephone call. Verifying conversations, especially agreements, with written messages is also common. The informational network within an organisation has been helped, interestingly, by the advent of photocopiers, for they have made it easier for people to spread information. Unless a document is marked 'strictly confidential'—and even this is no guarantee—its potential readers can be innumerable.

WRITING TO MEET A CHALLENGE

Many potential writing problems can be avoided by planning the writing task, that is, deciding why you are writing. The first step in planning is to acknowledge that you are writing to make something happen. This 'something' is often called the writing problem that you need to solve. We prefer the term 'writing challenge', as it has more positive connotations.

You may not think that straightforward business writing presents a writing challenge. However, consider the example of Harry, an office manager who wants to raise staff morale. He is writing a memo to encourage his staff to attend the annual Christmas party. If the memo is not effective, he will not gain his goal, that is, to make staff interested and gain their co-operation.

Harry's first attempt incorporates essential information like the time and place, plus a cartoon to give the idea of 'fun'. He includes this statement: 'Cost $20–$25 includes food and wine'. When he realises that staff have not responded to the memo, he asks around and discovers that the light drinkers are complaining that the set price means that they must 'subsidise' the heavy drinkers. Harry tries again, with a second memo that reads in part: 'Cost $15 per head—for the banquet (payable in advance). Drinks are to be ordered and paid for individually'. When the response is still low, he follows this memo up with a third one, which reads in part

The basic charge for the meal will be $15. This money will be collected before the meal and individuals and/or groups will order and pay for their drinks over and above this charge. It will make settling up the final account easier and avoid quibbling over the variation that alcohol consumption will cause to the basic price.

In this example, the writer finally meets the writing challenge by thinking through not only what he wants the message to contain, but also what result he wants it to have. The emphasis is on communicating to others, not just creating a message. To communicate effectively in the corporate setting, you must understand the particular situation and your readers. To think through a writing challenge, use the questions commonly asked by journalists, that is, 'How?' and 'Who?', 'What?', 'Where?', 'When?', 'Why?' (the H and five Ws).

Consider the writing challenge presented to Jean, an investment counsellor who advises public servants on the verge of receiving substantial superannuation payouts. The legislation is complex and changeable, and she has been spending too much time explaining details in the initial interview with potential clients. The answer seems to be to construct an explanatory letter which the potential client can digest at leisure. The communication challenge for Jean is to inform potential clients and encourage them to go ahead with the investment. How can this be done? Imagine that you are preparing this letter and ask yourself the H and five Ws.

How?

How to meet the communication challenge comprises many choices, from stationery to tone. (These are taken up in later chapters.)

Organisation

How will you organise the information? Most readers appreciate a document that is structured from their individual perspective. However, this does not mean that all writing should be individualised. If most of your potential clients need the same information, you can boilerplate some parts of the letter (that is, use the same information).

Word choice

How will you handle terminology? Thinking of your readers in this example, can you avoid terms like reasonable benefit limits and annuity escalation rate? If not, do you need to provide a glossary of terms? Word choice also contributes to the tone of the document.

Appearance

The letter to your potential client communicates through its appearance, from the logo design to the colour, type, and weight of the stationery itself. The letter's layout also gives a message, as seemingly minor choices such as margins and punctuation can suggest certain qualities to your reader.

Amount

Writers can provide too much or too little information to their readers. In this example, giving too much information can create problems both for your reader (who may tire or become confused) and yourself (who may be giving away too much free information). Think what the reader has requested or expects and adjust the amount of information accordingly.

Who?

Who are your readers? In this example, the primary reader is a specific potential client, someone who has already been to see you. You can assume a bond between you, as you know some of the person's specific interests. Remember that your reader probably has an attitude not only to the subject matter but also to you as the originator. Predicting this attitude can help you choose your material and your method of presentation.

Other potential readers who influence what and how you write could include other financial advisers in your company or your counterparts in other companies.

What?

What do your readers want to know? What do they need to know? In this example, some of your readers may want more financial details and even computer projections of their investment options. Others may expect you to make decisions for them. A clear idea of the 'what' of the task is essential to help you make appropriate communication decisions.

Where?

Where will you get your information? In this case, someone in your position would have a great deal of knowledge about the subject matter. You may still need to supplement this with discussions with colleagues and government personnel, as well as information you pick up in specialist books or the financial pages of newspapers and magazines.

When?

When is your deadline? If you have suggested a response in your initial interview, assess when you can realistically complete this required work and send the letter. If you work with multiple deadlines or large projects, using a time and task chart can help you schedule sub-deadlines for your writing tasks. You can develop the chart as a flow chart (see Figure 1.2) or a Gantt chart (see Figure 1.3). The Gantt chart allows you to show overlapping duties. For example, in Figure 1.3, the writer is planning two activities, editing a draft and consulting Person X, on the same day, 11. 9. Whichever chart you use, the important point is to start from your deadline and work backwards, writing in all the tasks that you need to finish and the time that these will take.

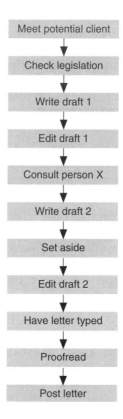

Figure 1.2 Flow chart of writing sub-tasks

Date	5/9	6/9	7/9	8/9	9/9	10/9	11/9	12/9	→
Meet potential client	■								
Check legislation		■	■						
Write draft 1				■	■				
Edit draft 1							■		
Consult person X							■		
Write draft 2								■	■
Set aside									→
Edit draft 2									→
Have letter typed									→
Proofread									→
Post letter									→

Figure 1.3 Gantt chart, showing writing sub-tasks and dates

The 'when' question can also be used to designate the document's time frame for its topic. Are you writing about an event in the past, present, or future? The time frame may dictate how much you need to include for your readers, or how your points should be ordered.

Why?

When writing business documents, one aim is usually to complete a task—we communicate information which helps others complete tasks. For example, we write to others to inform, inquire, request, motivate, and persuade. A survey of 265 professionals at twenty research and development organisations showed that 30 to 50 per cent thought that certain task-functions of writing were 'vitally important' to

- provide answers to specific questions
- keep others informed about major activities
- help plan and co-ordinate activities (individual and organisational)
- analyse the elements and interrelationships of a situation
- instruct others
- establish accountability.

(Anderson, 1985, p. 63)

When writing business documents our aim is also to develop a relationship. We use writing to establish a type of professional relationship with the reader. This relationship is dependent on the 'tone' of our documents.

For the investment advice letter, your tasks are to save yourself time and provide information. You can also develop your relationship with the potential client. For example, highlighting your knowledge of the legislation can help to persuade and reassure.

IMPROVING YOUR PROFESSIONAL WRITING

In the above example, we illustrated how to focus on the writing challenge, and use it to help you understand the writing choices available. A large part of improving your writing is becoming aware of these choices and systematically applying them to your writing tasks. It is also beneficial to work on specific problems or types of writing with a writing expert (for example, enrol in a short writing course). If this is not possible, you can still undertake activities which can help you become a better professional writer.

First, set a two-week period to become aware of your writing habits. During this time, analyse your writing: think about your writing process and evaluate the documents that you produce. This means that you are going off automatic pilot and no longer using your familiar, subconscious writing habits.

During this time, you can also practise being a meticulous writer. Give yourself more time than usual for your writing tasks, such as finding ideas (Chapter 3), evaluating them (Chapter 4), writing (Chapters 6 and 7), rewriting (Chapter 11), and setting out your work (Chapter 12). As you write and revise, spend extra time checking your spelling, word use, and punctuation. Keep standard reference books within reach. We recommend a large dictionary like *The Macquarie*, a general style manual like the *Style Manual* published by the Australian Government Publishing Service, and a good usage book like H.W. Fowler's *Modern English Usage*. Consult these books frequently to learn about language and become more confident about your writing.

Should you brush up on grammar? This is a difficult question. Research has shown that learning grammar alone does not necessarily improve writing. However, if you do not know language fundamentals, you may not be able to appreciate that some expressions are considered less acceptable. Some training in language structure gives you the necessary terminology to understand instructional books on writing and to discuss writing more specifically. Unfortunately, few grammar textbooks are adequate for the needs of organisational writers. Our chapter on sentences (Chapter 7) provides a guide to sentence-level problems.

As well as practice and study, there are other activities to help you improve your writing.

- Read!—Most good writers are people who read. It does not matter what, although it is helpful to read the works of people generally known to be good writers. Reading journals or magazines in your profession can show you different ways to approach and develop a familiar subject.
- Collect writing guides—Save examples of clear, uncluttered writing in the formats that you commonly use, for example, letters and reports. When you need to write in the same format, use these examples as guides to appropriate tone, language, length, type of development.
- Incubate—Learn to set aside your work, when possible, to give your brain a chance to incubate ideas. This time also allows you to return to your document with fresh eyes for picking up mistakes and inconsistencies.
- Write more—Jot notes to yourself, sketch plans, develop your ideas in writing. Keep a notebook with you for recording notes throughout the day.
- Write differently—It is sometimes helpful to get a new slant on your usual writing by trying something completely different. For example, try some experimental creative writing like simple 'word-picture' poems. Or keep a diary to challenge yourself to explain and describe each day. Enrol in a recreational writing class to learn to play with words and get feedback on your writing.
- Have someone edit your work—You can help someone be a good editor of your work by stipulating only one or two items to look for, for example, logical flow and clearly-stated purpose. However, be prepared for inappropriate criticism, particularly as you begin to communicate more efficiently. For example, a simply written document is sometimes still considered inappropriate organisational writing. If you think that some criticism is unwarranted, ask for more specific feedback. Requiring

your critics to put into words what seems wrong often indicates that the real problem rests not with the writer but with the reader ('You didn't mention the company's name enough'), or the organisation's actions (inadequate briefing or inappropriate use of the document).

• Find other writers—If others in your organisation are interested in writing, you may be able to persuade your staff development section to run writing courses. Join professional communication associations, as some sponsor regular communication lectures, workshops, and journals.

CONCLUSION

Effective business writers use their knowledge of an organisation's communication etiquette to develop successful documents. Each writing task involves a communication challenge, as the writer attempts to meet the needs of readers and answer questions ('How?' and 'Who?', 'What?', 'Where?', 'When?', 'Why?') concerning the purpose of the document. Professional writers can improve their writing by pursuing different opportunities, such as coursework, editing by others, involvement in professional communication associations, and staff development activities. Writing regularly can also improve writing.

References

Anderson, P. (1985). 'What survey research tells us about writing at work', in L. Odell and D. Goswami (eds), *Writing in nonacademic settings*, pp. 3–83, New York: The Guilford Press.

Faigley, L. (1985). 'Nonacademic writing: The social perspective', in Odell and Goswami (eds), pp. 231–248.

Paradis, J., Dobrin, D. and Miller, R. (1985). 'Writing at Exxon ITD: Notes on the writing environment of an R&D organization', in Odell and Goswami (eds), pp. 281–307.

CHAPTER 2

READING IN THE BUSINESS ENVIRONMENT

As a member of an organisation, you may be adept at reading and assessing documents. However, when you write, you forget that your readers read in the same way that you do. Writers who are aware of how people read know how to customise a document.

YOUR READERS AND WHAT THEY WANT

To determine the appropriate content and approach for your readers, you need to assess who they are and decide their needs. In other words, why do they want to read your document?

Who are your readers?

As an organisational writer, you often write for a potentially large and complex audience of readers within the organisation, all with different needs, expectations, levels of knowledge, and types of expertise. For example, you may write three memos to one person and each can address a different role, such as 'accountant', 'member of the special projects committee', and 'staff club treasurer'.

Organisational writers also contend with multiple readers within the organisation. For example, your report to your manager may be sent to others for comment or action, or your memo may be attached to agenda papers for discussion. The effective business writer is aware of this possibility and crafts documents to appeal not only to the primary reader, but the most likely secondary ones as well.

It may be helpful to think of your readers as forming two audiences: primary and secondary. In the primary audience are the decision-makers, that is, those who will act on your document. In the secondary audience are those who receive your document for noting or those who advise a decision-maker. An effective document meets the interests of both audiences.

Outside the organisation, the readers are even more varied. Documents are prepared for government bodies, consumer groups, and other agencies associated with your organisation. Some documents are designed for the general public, while others are targeted to special categories, such as people in a certain region, occupation, tax bracket, age, or other qualification.

With all these variables, what can and should you know about your readers? Business writing textbooks are often clogged with complicated graphs and questionnaires, which the authors suggest you use to discover more about your readers. For example, our own study of the leading textbooks found that they give an overwhelming number of reader characteristics for writers to consider, including

- educational level (general and specialised)
- experience
- skills
- questions they might ask
- preferences or interests
- tasks they will undertake as part of what they read
- roles within the organisation.

We suggest a simpler approach: KAN, for Knowledge, Attitude, and Needs. If you think about your readers, you will probably agree that it is important to know their level of knowledge, their attitude to both the subject and you, as well as their needs. By studying your readers in these ways before you write, you will find that you gain a much clearer idea of what to write and how to organise your ideas.

Knowledge

You help keep your readers interested in your document when you pitch your information to their level of knowledge. If you pitch your writing too 'high', your readers feel lost and possibly resentful. The result can be disastrous. A computer manual that is too technical may invite readers to ignore it and find their own, possibly less economical, method of solving a problem. On the other hand, pitching the information too low insults your readers.

There is no foolproof way to discover your readers' knowledge, but several strategies can help. Before you write, you may be able to talk to your intended reader and gauge the person's knowledge. This becomes the background level from which you build your document. What the reader already knows should stay in the background and not become part of the document. Alternatively, you may talk to others and find what seems to be commonly known about the subject. This too, makes up the background.

When writing for people outside the organisation, try to imagine what they do and do not know. Or try out your writing on others. A recent study of popular writers of scientific articles found that one secret of their success is that they usually have a non-expert friend or relative who checks their writing to ensure that it is understandable.

Attitude

Readers may approach a document in a neutral frame of mind, but as they read, they will usually develop an attitude both to the document's content and its writer.

Check your readers' attitudes by asking yourself these questions before you begin writing.

- How strong are my readers' beliefs, interests, or prejudices on the subject?
- How do readers view me? For example, as a decision maker, as authoritarian, as a concerned colleague?
- How do readers view themselves? For example, as a technical expert, as a benevolent manager?

By studying your readers beforehand, you gain some idea of their attitudes. This can help you select and organise information. For example, you can guess that a manager worried about the budget will react negatively to a request for travel funds. Knowing this reader's attitude toward the subject can help you decide what to include in the request and how to organise it to make the strongest argument.

Deciding what the reader thinks about you as the writer is more difficult. If you are aware of a reader's attitude, use this information. Otherwise, consider the impression you wish to make on your reader and ensure that your document reflects appropriate choices. For example, it seems reasonable to assume that job-seekers try to give the impression that they are responsible and dependable. It would be surprising, then, to find an application letter containing flippant remarks and disparaging comments about past jobs. The writer would not have thought about how the document will shape the reader's attitude as he or she reads.

Need

Why do your readers read? You can generalise that people in business read for a purpose: they look for essential information to make a decision, to get background information, to keep up with developments. If you know what motivates your readers, you will not lose sight of this as you write, but will shape your document to meet their needs. It is easy to become so involved in details of interest to you that you forget to check that your readers are interested as well.

Gather as much information as you can about your readers' needs. Either talk to your readers directly or consider possible questions from them. For example, people who telephone about a job advertisement before applying often gain helpful information. They can use this to tailor their application to meet the needs of their reader.

If it is not possible to talk to your readers, find their needs by asking yourself why readers need your document. What action are they going to take? Do they need to follow instructions, compare possible solutions, place orders, or file documents for reference? What information will readers need and what information do they want to enable them to undertake action?

These questions, by helping you to evaluate your writing task from your readers' perspective, can give you a better chance of making your documents complete, persuasive, and appropriate.

READING STRATEGIES OF ORGANISATIONAL READERS

Research in reading is well developed, but it tends to focus on children learning to read and less on adult readers. Less research has been done on adult reading because the number of variables affecting the reading process make it very difficult to study.

As a reader within an organisation, consider how your reading speed and degree of comprehension are affected by the following elements

- type of document (formal letter, memo, report)
- length of the document
- importance or relevance of the document
- document appearance (colour of paper, typeface)
- writing style
- physical environment (noise, lighting)
- emotional state.

One of the few studies about the reading strategies of corporate readers is striking. James W. Souther's study of a group of managers (Anderson, 1987, p. 135) shows that they read reports selectively, choosing to read only those parts of the report they believe are most important. This study highlights a common statement about readers, that is, that they see themselves as 'busy' readers. To cope with their reading workload and save time, they develop reading strategies. For example, most organisational readers probably use a style of quick reading called **skimming**, in which they glance over a document and try to take in only the main points. In a report, they pay particular attention to the headings, summary, and conclusion.

Table 2.1 Managers' frequency for reading different parts of a report, in a study by James W. Souther

Part of report	Reading frequency (per cent)
Summary	100
Introduction	60
Conclusion	50
Body	15
Appendix	10

However, readers may also move to reading slowly and carefully, closely studying the document. This type of reading strategy is used when the argument is complex, the action to be taken is extremely important or problematic, or the content is highly technical, for example, legal documents.

Effective readers change their reading strategies, depending on the type of document, its importance, and the reading time available. If you assess what reading strategy your readers will use, you can create a document that has more chance of being read. If your readers will more than likely skim your document, use headings to 'signpost' information, omit details and complex information, and set your important points in the summary, introduction, and conclusion. If you are sure that your readers will study the document closely, you can confidently develop a more complex writing style.

THINKING PATTERNS OF READERS

Investigation by cognitive psychologists into the thinking patterns of humans gives us more information about how readers think and read. We now know that readers understand what they read by using communication maxims, inferences, constructs, and mental templates.

Using communication maxims

Effective communication is a co-operative venture between the writer and reader. Readers expect that what they read will have meaning—they expect the document to communicate something to them. H. P. Grice, a linguist, suggests that the following maxims or conventions create the basis on which effective communication is built

- **quantity**—contribute neither less nor more information than is needed
- **quality**—communicate what is true and what you have evidence for
- **relation**—be relevant
- **manner**—be brief, orderly, clear, and unambiguous.

(Brown and Yule, 1983, p. 32)

Grice suggests that readers accept these maxims in general and assume, when they start to read a document, that the writer intends to communicate. Readers expect to find meaning, and will try to make sense, even of nonsense.

What does this suggest to the business writer? If readers expect you to communicate, they may accept even the worst gobbledygook (see Chapter 9) at the beginning, but they will become impatient if they cannot discover your meaning. For example, the writer who writes that a program is 'excessively consumptive of funds' rather than 'over budget' is violating the communication maxim of manner, and risks losing his or her readers as a result.

Using inferences

Readers are sometimes faced with information which, on the surface, seems to go against the maxims. For example, consider this extract from a memo

Our photocopier is broken. However, there is another one in Personnel.

Strictly speaking, the message violates the maxim of relevance. Why intro-duce one photocopier then 'jump' the discussion to another? Most readers, however, correctly infer that the two separate sentences are related and that the writer is implying that Personnel's photocopier can be used.

Writers count on readers making such inferences all the time; otherwise everything would need to be spelled out. In this humorous letter in the *Sydney Morning Herald* (5 April 1990), W. McKeown shows what can happen if a writer assumes that readers cannot make their own inferences.

> SIR: The plethora of parentheses [square brackets] in your publication is approaching plague proportions.
>
> Almost every line [in the paper] is littered with annoying explanations for those of us [readers] unable to comprehend simple sentences [without super-fluous clarifications or complications].
>
> Had your sub-editors been around in the days of [playwright William] Shakespeare they would doubtless have given us lines like:
>
> A horse! a horse! [I am willing to exchange] My kingdom for a horse.
>
> Or in [British wartime Prime Minister Winston Spencer] Churchill's era:
>
> Never [before] in the field of human conflict has so much [deep gratitude] been owed by so many [besieged British citizens] to so few [brave RAF fighter pilots].
>
> If things [these persistent parentheses] get much worse [than they are now], I [the writer] shall [be compelled to] stop reading your [the editor's] paper.
>
> Even my dog finds it [the paper] hard to digest. He [the dog] is choking on the brackets [[]]!

Effective writers consider their readers' knowledge to assess what they can be assumed to know and the contexts that they are familiar with.

Using constructs

Readers do not read in a mental vacuum. They are influenced by their personal mental constructs. These can include their experiences, expecta-tions, emotions, and attitudes toward the topic and the writer. Personal constructs that readers bring to the reading task will differ from reader to reader. This means that no reader will comprehend your document exactly as you do.

To help make your writing successful, you need to find those constructs that you have in common with your readers. The **common ground** that you and your readers share includes the wide context of culture, the context of organisations, and the brief context of particular situations. To illustrate these types, think of three concentric circles (see Figure 2.1).

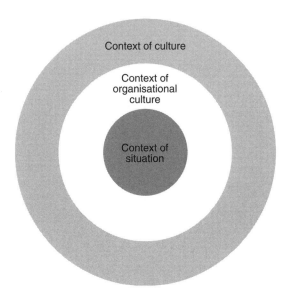

Figure 2.1 Different communication contexts for organisational readers

The outermost circle is the context of culture. Our culture gives us a common ground of experiences in education, sports, politics, arts, and possessions, as well as manners, interests, concerns, and teachings. Because of this shared cultural context, readers from our own culture usually understand our references, allusions, and vocabulary. For example, when Australian author Janet Turner Hospital used the term *gravel rash* in a recent work, the term called up a specific image to Australians—but meant nothing to her American editor.

The middle circle is the context of the organisation, that is, the corporate culture. As writers, we assume that we have shared experiences, expectations, and concerns with our co-workers. But different elements direct our sense of an organisational common ground. The organisational roles of readers 'map' the common ground by directing how organisational readers should react to different subjects. Readers may personally disagree with some issue but within their organisational role support it. For example, a manager may personally like a staff member, but as a supervisor reject the person's bid for promotion.

The context of the organisation is influenced by the organisation's climate, the general emotional atmosphere of a workplace. Climate is usually described as either supportive ('warm', 'open') or defensive ('cold', 'closed'). The climate of the organisation 'colours' the way a document is interpreted by suggesting which meanings are more probable. For example, when Michael submits a report about his recent fact-finding tour, the CEO replies in a memo, 'You certainly were busy during your tour'. How does Michael interpret this comment? If the communication climate of his workplace is positive, where writers communicate openly, he probably interprets the comment as praise. However, if the climate is defensive, supporting negative and 'hidden' messages, Michael may translate the comment as a reprimand that he tried to do too much, or as an ironic remark that he did not do enough. Consider the climate of an organisation when deciding how your readers will comprehend your own document.

The innermost circle in the diagram is the context of individual, short-term situations, each with its own context. For example, board meetings may seem similar, but each one provides a different context, based on the members who attend, their mood, the time of day, the venue, and the agenda. This level of the common ground of communication is difficult to predict. We usually become aware of it when there is a problem. For example, you may find that your memo to someone backfires. Why? Your particular reader may have negative associations attached to some of the words you have used, associations not shared by others in the culture. If the person is feeling unwell or in a bad mood, he or she can react negatively to your tone. It may even be that a previous, unsatisfactory interaction with this reader creates a residue of bad feeling which affects this new interaction. Any of these problems at the situational level effectively weakens or destroys the chance of having a common ground of communication.

Effective organisational writers are sensitive to the shared attributes of their culture and the organisations that they communicate within and to. They use their understanding of these contexts to create a common ground with their readers. Good writers also learn to 'read' the more fleeting contexts of situations to discover the cause of miscommunication.

Using mental templates

Research in cognitive psychology has shown that we generalise from our particular experiences to form broad, abstract mental patterns called **schemata**. Each schema is like a mental template into which we fit our communication and experiences. These mental templates are developed not only from the general context of our activities and communication, but also from our beliefs, opinions, attitudes, and ideologies (van Dijk, 1982).

How does this affect our readers? People understand new information more quickly or more comprehensively when it more closely mirrors the schema they have already created. If your reader already has a developed mental template for a situation or topic, the information relevant to this template slots in easily—it is more easily understood.

Think of how we use our mental template of restaurants to negotiate a dining experience. Through our past experience, we have developed expectations about what activities will take place (eating), their manner (being served by another), and the common types of communication strategies (reading the menu, giving an order, discussing only 'acceptable' dinner topics). If a customer tries to buy raw vegetables or begins talking to diners at the adjoining table, this behaviour will be construed as inappropriate—not fitting the schema.

In the same way, we have expectations about written documents. For example, when we read the phrase, 'Once upon a time', we expect a particular style of writing, pattern of development, and subjects to be discussed. Even the formats or types of documents (described in more detail in Chapter 5) suggest a mental template. For example, readers in the organisational setting have expectations about communication style, depending on whether the information is packaged as a memo, a letter, or a report. Or consider linguist Noam Chomsky's famous nonsense sentence: 'Colorless green ideas sleep furiously'. If we set it out as a poem and place it in a poetry book or on the arts page of a newspaper, readers would probably find it acceptable. Why? Because the sentence fits the mental slots of our poetry template by looking like a poem and being where we expect to see poetry.

Figure 2.2 Example of a 'poetic' format that provides a familiar context for a nonsense sentence

Writers can help readers comprehend a document by first imagining their readers' mental template. It is thought that readers with 'rich' mental templates have more developed expectations about what they will read (Sharkey, 1986, p. 50). Consider this example. Two managers are asked to read a finance proposal. The one with extensive finance experience has a rich template on this subject, which she draws upon to read the proposal. In contrast, the manager with less finance experience has a more impoverished template to use for the same reading task. Here are two people in the same organisational role, but with such differently developed templates that they are quite different readers.

If you think that you share with your readers similar mental templates about a particular subject, you can take writing shortcuts, confident that they can follow. But if the templates do not match, you need to take these differences into account as you write. For example, a set of poorly written instructions for operating technical equipment suggests a mismatched schema between the technical writer and the readers. An instruction such as 'set up the computer properly' suggests that the writer thinks readers have the same computing schema.

Testing Document 'Readability'

Is there a way to evaluate whether your document is readable? Understanding your organisational readers' thinking patterns and reading practices helps you decide what to write and how. Readers are complex, and choosing text elements—such as tone, vocabulary level, and degree of explanation—requires writers to think of the different influences on the reader.

Despite the complexity of writing for readers, simple readability formulas remain popular with some writers. Readability formulas are simplistic mathematical formulas that provide writers with a rough guideline to the 'reading level' of their document. Although discredited by writing researchers, these formulas have been given a new vogue by being included in some computer writing and style-check programs.

Most readability formulas comprise a mathematical equation based on two variables: word length and sentence length. By applying the equation to your document, you get a numerical rating which suggests how easy the document will be to read. For example, in one formula, the rating represents the number of years of formal schooling which readers supposedly need to comprehend the document.

The two most well-known formulas are Rudolph Flesch's Reading Ease Scale and Robert Gunning's Fog Index.

The Flesch Reading Ease Scale

The Flesch Reading Ease Scale uses this formula

$$206.835 - (0.846 \, SY + 1.015 \, SL)$$

SY = average number of syllables per 100-word sample.
SL = average sentence length

Steps

- If possible, take three to five samples of 100 words each. Pick these at random. Start each sample at the beginning of a paragraph. Count as a word everything that has a blank space on either side of it, for example, 'week-end', '1989'. Stop your count at the sentence which ends nearest to the 100-word total.
- Count the number of sentences in each 100-word sample. Total these and divide the total number of words by the total number of sentences to get the average length of sentences.
- Count the number of syllables in each sample, total, and divide by the number of samples to get the average number of syllables per 100 words.
- Multiply the average sentence length (SL) by 1.015.
- Multiply the average number of syllables per 100 words (SY) by 0.846.
- Add the two averages.
- Subtract this from 206.835.

The resulting number (between 0–100) is the 'reading ease score'.

A rough guideline of the reading ease is

very easy:	90–100
easy:	80–90
fairly easy:	70–80
standard:	60–70
fairly difficult:	50–60
difficult:	40–50
very difficult:	0–30

The Gunning Fog Index

The Gunning Fog Index is slightly easier to use than the Flesch scale. The formula is

$$0.4 \ (SL + \%WD)$$

SL = average sentence length
WD = 'hard' (polysyllabic) words.

Steps

- Find the number of sentences in samples of 100 words. Stop your count with the sentence which ends nearest to the 100-word total.
- Divide the total number of words by the number of sentences to get the average sentence length.
- Find the percentage of 'hard words' in the sample by counting the number of words that have three syllables or more. Do not count words that are proper names ('Reginald'), combinations of short, easy words ('bookkeeper'), or verb forms ('transmitting').
- Total the two numbers and multiply by 0.4.

The resulting number suggests the educational level that your readers will need to understand your document. For example

university education:	13–16
high school education:	11–12
school certificate:	10

What is wrong with readability formulas?

If readability formulas are so simple to use and provide a definite reading level for a document, what is wrong with them? The major problem, according to writing researcher Janice Redish, is simple: 'No one is quite sure what a readability formula measures'. (1980, p. 84).

The calculations of the formulas are far too simple and ignore important influences on the document. Most formulas are based on an equation using word length and sentence length, which suggests that these are the most critical elements in the document. However, there is little proof that these make a document harder or easier for the reader. In the readability formulas, the word 'elephant' is considered more problematic than the more difficult but shorter word 'tort'. Readability formulas also assume that shorter sentences are more acceptable, but writers know from their own experience that well-written and punctuated long sentences can still be clearly understood.

Recent research in cognitive psychology also suggests that readers' comprehension strategies depend less on a document's sentence and word length and more on its structure. If the topic and supporting ideas are easy for readers to follow, long words and sentences may not weaken comprehension. Other elements, such as punctuation, grammar, and syntax may affect the reader more.

Professional writers should also be aware that some readability formulas are based on specifications for only one type of text and are not applicable to other types. For example, formulas originally developed to assess children's textbooks or fiction writing cannot be realistically applied to business writing. Unfortunately, the basis from which the formulas have been developed is rarely explained to their users.

As well, most formulas assume that a document will be made up of sentences. Technical documents, however, often rely on lists, charts, and tables. They also use more jargon, assuming that their specialised readers are familiar with a technical vocabulary. Although readers do not find these elements and patterns a problem, readability formulas are unable to take into account these reading factors for specific types of documents.

These problems indicate that readability formulas are over-simplified prescriptions. If you wish, use them to provide a rough guideline of the general reading level of your document. But, if you find that the reading level of your document is too high, do not simply remove words and shorten sentences; think in more detail about your readers, and the context in which you are communicating. Then rewrite accordingly.

Conclusion

Although readability formulas are popular, they provide only a simple assessment of the document and can be misleading. To design a document for your readers, think about who your readers are, what they know, and their attitudes and needs. You can develop a common ground of communication with your readers by understanding what you share in terms of the context of the culture, the organisational culture, and the situation. And by understanding your readers' thinking and reading patterns, you are more likely to produce a readable document.

References

Anderson, P. (1987). *Technical writing: A reader-centered approach*, San Diego: Harcourt Brace Jovanovich.

Brown, G. and Yule, G. (1983). *Discourse analysis*, Cambridge: Cambridge University Press.

Redish, J. (April 1980). 'Issues in the study of readability', in D. Felker (ed.), *Document design: A review of the relevant research*, pp. 84–93, Washington DC: American Institutes for Research.

Sharkey, N. (1986). 'A model of knowledge-based expectations in text comprehension', in J. Galambos, R. Abelson, and J. Black (eds), *Knowledge structures*, pp. 49–70, Hillsdale NJ: Lawrence Erlbaum Associates.

Van Dijk, T. (1982). 'Opinions and attitudes in discourse comprehension', in J–P. LeNy and W. Kintsch (eds), *Language and comprehension*, Amsterdam: North-Holland.

CHAPTER 3

USING EXPERIMENTAL THINKING

Do you envy writers who can move their readers beyond the obvious to contemplate new problems or possibilities? Have you wondered how some of your colleagues can consistently produce far-sighted reports which cover more than the usual 'angles'? You can develop depth in your own writing by learning to play with ideas and explore the not-so-obvious points of your topic. Such mental play is called experimental, lateral, or creative thinking. This chapter gives you specific strategies for experimental thinking that can help you generate new ideas for your writing.

UNDERSTANDING YOUR THINKING AND WRITING STYLE

Thinking is not an isolated and specific activity reserved for the planning part of the writing process. Research now shows what most of us knew all along: thinking, writing, and editing are inseparable. How and when you will use experimental thinking depends on you, the type of writer you are, and the writing style you favour. By knowing how you normally operate in your thinking and writing, you can better evaluate the experimental thinking strategies given in this chapter and choose those that seem more suitable.

To consider your thinking and writing style, read the four questions listed below and select the answer that you think best suits you.

1 How do you begin planning a major document?
   A I construct a complete, detailed outline, showing both major and subordinate ideas.
   B I jot down any ideas as they come and wait to structure them after I start writing.
   C I establish the main points and leave the rest 'open'.

2 How do you write your first draft?
   A I write as if it were the final draft.
   B I write down everything possible and expect to make major changes in several subsequent drafts.
   C I develop some parts fully and sketch in others to 'flesh out' later.
3 When do you usually check spelling, punctuation, usage?
   A I check during writing the first draft.
   B I check only when writing the final draft.
   C I usually check after writing the first draft.
4 If you were giving a last draft to a typist to make a final copy, what would it look like?
   A Tidy, with only a few minor corrections.
   B Messy, with many major corrections.
   C Half and half, with a few major corrections and more minor ones.

The 'A' style writer

If you chose mainly 'A' answers, you are probably a methodical thinker who thoroughly develops your subject before starting to write. Such planning is economical, as you save writing time by ensuring that you are not charging up blind alleys and then having to rewrite. Writers who are often interrupted may train themselves to plan in the 'A' style way, as it is easier to start and stop. Team writing can benefit from the 'A' style writer's willingness to construct a clear and detailed outline, which ensures that everyone knows what is to be written.

The drawback in being an 'A' style writer is that sometimes you can over plan and get enmeshed in detail too early in the writing process. If you allow only the first (and often most pedestrian) ideas to develop and cut off new lines of thought, the result is unoriginal, 'canned' writing.

The 'B' style writer

If you selected mostly 'B' answers, you have what can be called an emergent approach to writing. You remain open to suggestions and new lines of thought throughout the writing process. You are comfortable with ambiguity. The main benefit of this style is that you allow new ideas to be developed as you write rather than confine them to the planning or pre-draft stage of your work.

The main disadvantage of this style is that it is time-consuming. It is not unusual, for example, for a 'B' style writer to make over five rough drafts before establishing a firm idea of his or her main ideas. If you are a 'B' style writer, you may be frustrated when you have a lot to write or are under time pressures. You can also frustrate others in a writing team, or your secretary, when your major rewrites seem never-ending.

The 'C' style writer

If you selected more 'C' answers, you probably alternate in your approach to writing tasks, being methodical for some and open-ended for others. You particularly may find team writing enjoyable, as you can accept that different people employ different writing styles.

This flexibility can be problematic, however, if you do not take advantage of it. You may get locked into the easiest style and ignore other ways to develop your writing. Also, there is no advantage in being able to alternate if you choose the style that is inappropriate to what needs to be done. Assess each writing task and decide which style is the most suitable.

Writing and creativity

Whatever your predominant writing style, your success as a writer depends on your ability to match your thinking and writing to the task at hand. One way to do this is to use the strategies of experimental thinking to help you explore a subject or problem creatively. Unfortunately, the term 'creative' in writing is sometimes wrongly narrowed to mean only those formally recognised as creative writers, for example, novelists, poets, advertising copywriters. Such a definition suggests that the rest of us, by default, are uncreative writers.

Untrue! Organisational writers are highly creative—they have to be. Their writing is based on making knowledgeable and sensitive choices about language and structure in order to address their readers effectively. Nearly all use some type of creative exploration as they write. They do not get their message across by merely 'filling in the blanks' of standard formats for letters, memos, reports, and other documents.

As a way of stimulating your own creativity when you are thinking of your topic, we suggest certain methods of experimental thinking called idea generators.

Idea Generators and How They Work

Idea generators are just that, ways to help you find ideas. They are also called **heuristics**, from the Greek word 'heuriskein' meaning 'to find' or 'to discover'. (The word *Eureka* is related.) They are not like sure-fire writing formulas that you may have read about in other writing books. Idea generators offer no guarantee: instead, they offer methods of exploration which may work or not, depending on the topic and on you, the writer.

Computerised idea generators or 'organiser' programs are also available. Are they any good? Gareth Powell, computer journalist for the *Sydney Morning Herald*, says that he has tested thirty or so and found none particularly useful, and we agree. It is usually simpler to jot ideas down on paper. However, some writers may find that having such a program reminds them to explore their ideas more often.

Most of the idea generators require you to jot down ideas freely, without evaluation. Like the character who was unable to write the great novel until the first sentence was perfect, many organisational writers expect too much too early in the writing process. Few ideas sound great until worked on, and writers may scrap potentially good ideas without sufficiently exploring them.

Writing educator Peter Elbow terms this free exploration of a topic our mental 'voyage out'. After exploring the topic, we make the voyage in, that is, we assess the material we have collected. Idea generators help you make the voyage out, and afterwards, when you have gathered your material, you can select and organise it to suit the subject, your particular readers, and your organisation.

Another writing educator, Ann Berthoff, calls this period of exploration the 'chaos' that a writer needs before imposing order. This term follows the scientific theories of chaos, in which the stability of the whole material world is questioned. A written article may seem so static or 'solid' that we forget it represents a collection of choices created by the writer from a range of possibilities. During creative chaos, the writer focuses on exploring ideas and only afterwards chooses what to make solid in the form of a report, letter, or memo.

Whether you think of yourself as making a voyage out or indulging in creative chaos, using the idea generators can help your thinking and writing in several important ways.

Discover more ideas

Successful writing is often based on getting enough ideas from which to choose the best. Idea generators can help you find more ideas by encouraging you to think more on the topic and recording more of what you think. The generators allow you to discover and play with new ideas. You can always discard unworkable ones later.

Consider this example. Jonathan, a computer expert, is writing a memo describing some of the problems that the introduction of a computing program has caused for the organisation. He expects this first draft to be the final one, as the problems seem straightforward. But as he writes, he starts thinking of solutions, and one in particular stands out. Half-way through his writing task, he realises that his purpose has changed; he now wants to write about this solution rather than just list problems. Thinking more experimentally first might have helped him to explore more ideas (and discover this one) earlier.

Discover new paths

The old saying that 'what comes first to your mind also comes first to everyone else's' is true. If your writing seems trite or predictable, you are not exploring enough. The generators can help give you a different slant on the topic because they push you beyond what you already know to explore what you do not know.

This new slant can benefit any but the most mundane professional writing. For example, some speeches and reports require you to develop possibilities and motivate your audience. These more speculative writing tasks require you to be imaginative and structured, two seemingly opposite characteristics. By using idea generators, you can explore your speculative side and then organise the best ideas that you come up with.

'Kick-start' your brain

Sometimes a writing task seems so problematic or boring that you do not start it until the deadline is upon you. This crisis-driven style of writing can usually be avoided when you use the generators to 'kick-start' your brain and bring the topic to your mental forefront.

Writers who use an idea generator frequently team it with a period of incubation, when they put aside the ideas generated and let their sub-conscious continue to work on them. For example, one writer uses the generators at the end of the day to 'program' her sub-conscious with ideas on the next day's writing tasks. The next morning, she usually finds that her ideas are so developed from this overnight incubation that her writing and editing time is reduced.

Prevent or dissolve writer's block

There are many kinds of writing fears that create writer's block. Like stage-fright, the fear of writing can be all-pervasive, or triggered by a particular audience or the importance of the writing task. It is not unusual to trace a person's fear or loathing of writing to a negative incident as far back as primary school.

If you suffer from writer's block, the tyranny of the blank page increases if you dwell on the amount or the quality that you must produce. The usual writing advice, to 'concentrate on just one paragraph at a time', is not always helpful. If you are unsure about what or how to write, constructing a single paragraph can be just as daunting as a twenty-page report.

The generators can dissolve writer's block by focusing your attention on smaller parts of the writing task and giving you ways to record your thoughts. For example, a trainer asks for help in writing a speech on a familiar topic, but for a different audience from the one she normally works with. This new element has caused writer's block for two months, and now her deadline is a week away. Using an idea generator, she focuses first on exploring her knowledge of her audience, and then uses this information to select her main points. This positive activity breaks the block. She develops an outline within half an hour, and has her speech ready to deliver two days later.

Generators also alleviate writer's block by demonstrating that writing is a process, with ideas fluid and subject to change. We do not need to get everything correct in the first draft. The information generated can be used as a first draft, and be used to elicit more feedback before being crafted into sentences and paragraphs.

Manage time more effectively

Part of the problem of managing time is knowing how much time different tasks take. Many business writers seriously under-estimate their thinking, writing, and editing time. The idea generators, by concentrating your mind on the 'big picture' of the writing task, can help you to judge more accurately the work and time for each sub-task. (As a side benefit, writers who are more aware of these specifics often become quite assertive about their time!)

How to Use Idea Generators

Each idea generator is described below. We suggest that you try each several times. Not all of the generators will seem equally suitable to you. However, do not decide too soon that one is not workable. What is new is usually uncomfortable because it takes you out of the worn groove of your writing habits. Cultivate a sense of adventure!

The idea generators are also not equally suited to all writing tasks. You may find some appropriate for minor, informal documents and others more suited to longer, complex ones. You also do not need to use the generators in the same way. In some writing tasks, use a generator to explore *what* you want to communicate; in others, use it to plan *how* to communicate. Use a generator at any stage of writing. At the beginning of your writing task, a generator can help you get ideas down on paper or screen. Later in the writing process, you might want to use a generator to motivate you to dig deeper into your topic.

One warning: Under no circumstances try out a new idea generator when you are writing under a tight deadline. Deadlines usually cause writers to go on automatic pilot, when they have neither the time nor the correct attitude for exploring new methods.

The brainstorming generator

Brainstorming is used to produce a large number of possible topics or ideas on a particular topic.

Brainstorming has two distinct stages: generating and evaluating. In the generating stage, you concentrate solely on recording your ideas for a set time period, for example, five to twenty minutes. Jot down ideas as they come to you. Usually, these will be words and phrases rather than complete sentences. Your goal is to get the most ideas on paper, so include everything, no matter how unrealistic. It is important not to criticise or evaluate your ideas at this stage. Whether you are working alone or in a group, allow *all* ideas to be written down. Prohibit evaluative questions (to yourself or others) such as, 'What do you mean by that?', negative comments such as 'That's not on the topic', 'That wouldn't work', or 'That's silly', or even positive comments such as 'That's a good idea'.

When you have reached the time limit, you enter stage two. Evaluate all of your ideas and discard those which seem inappropriate. Keep your mind open, however, as something that seems 'odd' can often end up being workable.

Figure 3.1 gives an example of both stages of Pat's brainstorming for a report on training for drug and alcohol workers. In stage one, Pat lists everything that comes to mind about the topic. In stage two, he arranges the ideas into categories or developmental paths as a preliminary to deciding which to develop and which to discard.

The freewriting generator

Freewriting is like connected brainstorming. You are still concentrating on getting your ideas down on paper, but in freewriting you write without

Stage one: Brainstorming

drug types
alcohol
working with alcoholics
why addiction
families, siblings
school children
interpersonal skills
family counselling
educational theories
psychology
types of people
Myers-Briggs test
feeling good about yourself
nuns who did Myers-Briggs test to learn to live harmoniously with each other
putting people into others' shoes
board game where people don't win
do they see addicted people as victims or free agents?
political nous
performance indicators
media presentation and speaking skills if this is important
more info first about them
their feelings about this
new drugs new users

Stage two: Evaluating

- personal skills to work with addicts and their families
- presentational skills for education role in community
- training about relevant political/governmental policies
- empathy about drug use and addiction
- performance indicators to link training and skills
- up-to-date information about drug use/abuse

Figure 3.1 Brainstorming for a report on training drug and alcohol workers

stopping. Freewriting is a good method when you are unsure how to start a topic, because the act of writing itself often clarifies what you want to communicate. It helps you to 'clear the decks' mentally and focus on what is significant about the topic.

To freewrite, have on hand several sheets of paper. If you are using a computer, turn the brightness down so that you are composing on a totally darkened screen. Set a timer for your writing time. Freewriting usually lasts at least ten minutes and sometimes up to thirty minutes.

As you write, follow these guidelines.

- Keep writing for the whole time; do not stop. You will find that your mind may go blank at first, but you will soon think of something. If you get stuck, write the word 'nothing' until something occurs to you.
- Write in complete sentences if you wish, but phrases are also suitable.
- Write at your own pace. You do not need to write quickly.
- Do not read your work during this time.

- Do not correct spelling or grammar. (Your ability to follow this rule will probably tell you a great deal about your past writing education!)

After you freewrite you can do several things with the result. Writing researcher Peter Elbow suggests that you underline the single most important thought in your freewriting and use this to begin a second freewriting session. This more specific freewriting can take you from the obvious ideas on the topic to the more 'meaty' issues which may interest your readers more. Or, you might highlight anything in your freewriting that you think could be developed further and construct an outline from these ideas. Some writers use this first act of writing only as a mental 'kick-start' and prefer to discard what they freewrite.

Figure 3.2 gives an example of freewriting for a job application letter. This was composed on a computer, with the screen brightness turned down. From this very short freewriting example, the writer can freewrite again to develop one major idea, extract important points to include in the letter, or start writing after using the freewriting as a mental 'kick-start' for ideas.

Stage one: Freewriting

I'd like to apply for position in the public service. Public service opportunities to advance. Consider the position, could develop skills in educational training, and research. Using the computer databases and stats packages. Need some computer training. Don't say that. Confidence. Put in more about latest job and the supervision role. Would be close to where I live nothing nothing nothing interpersonal skills, like working well with others, and being able to work by myself or with others to get things done on time and at a high standard.

Stage two: Evaluate

- Freewrite again to develop an idea
- Extract important points
- Begin writing task

Figure 3.2 Example of freewriting before writing a job application letter

The flow charting generator

In flow charting, you plan your main ideas by constructing a flow chart. It is not just another name for an outline. For many people, outlining is a static plan of the structure that they have already written or have decided on. To make a flow chart, however, you must think in terms of the flow of logic from one element of your topic to the next. Flow charting can be used effectively after brainstorming or freewriting to structure the ideas generated.

To make a flow chart (see Figure 3.3), record your first major point and draw a box around it. Below this, draw a second box for your second major point. Connect the first box to the second with a downward pointing arrow that shows the directional 'flow' of your information. Continue working downward, with boxes for all your major points and with arrows showing the flow.

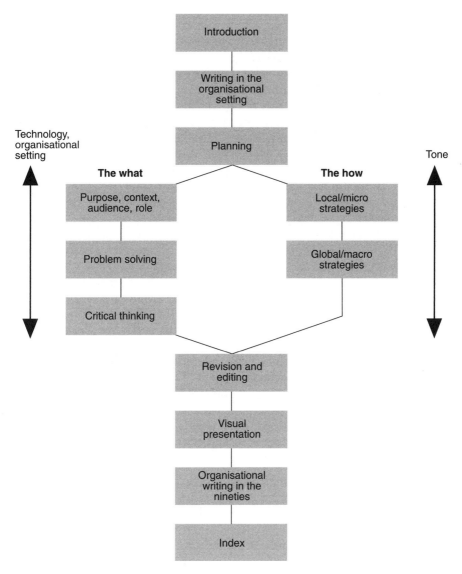

Figure 3.3 The first flow chart we used to begin planning this book

Some writers elaborate on this basic flow chart by

- adding 'side' boxes for subsidiary points
- adding details near the arrows to show how the move from one box to the other is to be accomplished—by planning these connections beforehand, writers ensure that they do not lose their readers
- drawing large vertical arrows the whole length of the flow chart to indicate main themes or considerations to remember, for example, audience, tone, secondary purpose.

The mapping generator

Mapping is the strongest generator for exploring your views of a topic. It relies on free association and can generate ideas, themes, and examples that you might not otherwise consider. The result of mapping is a record or 'map' of how your mind has worked on the topic.

To use mapping, write your topic in the centre of a page and box it. Remaining relaxed and non-judgemental, let your thoughts flow from your mind to the paper. Jot down any images, ideas, and phrases that come to mind and box each one. Connect each boxed item by a line to the idea that triggered it. Do not try to work too quickly, and do not mentally edit out whatever seems irrelevant. You can decide later what is appropriate and useful. The page will eventually look like a spider's web of ideas, associations, feelings, images.

Once you have finished mapping, look at the outer edges of the spider's web. Why? The first ideas recorded, towards the centre, are usually the most tentative, vague, generalised, or common. To get beyond the obvious approach to your topic, move outward along the web. Sometimes you can make interesting and useful connections and analogies by looking at the web and seeing if something 'clicks' for you as you view the information as a whole.

As an example of mapping, consider Chris's dilemma. She's been asked to give a speech on motivation. When faced with a task like this, writers too often cobble together something from different sources rather than develop what has not already been said on the subject. The result is often devoid of any real appeal for the audience because the writer has not become involved in the topic.

Chris decides to use mapping to explore what she associates with the word. Looking at her completed map or web (Figure 3.4), she decides that some ideas are worth further exploration

- motivation requires finding out what people are really interested in, such as time and freedom
- people should be given the freedom to be creative and to be evaluated on their productivity
- one can recreate the excitement of a sports team, with its training, goals, and drive
- people are desperate because businesses are not giving people more than a pay cheque
- reduced stress can make the environment more pleasant.

From these ideas, Chris is satisfied that she can move away from platitudes and develop a more thoughtful and perhaps inspiring speech.

The 'because' generator

The 'because' generator can help you consider your views or position concerning an issue. If you use a formal outline or just jot down ideas, you run the danger of including information which, although related, does not support

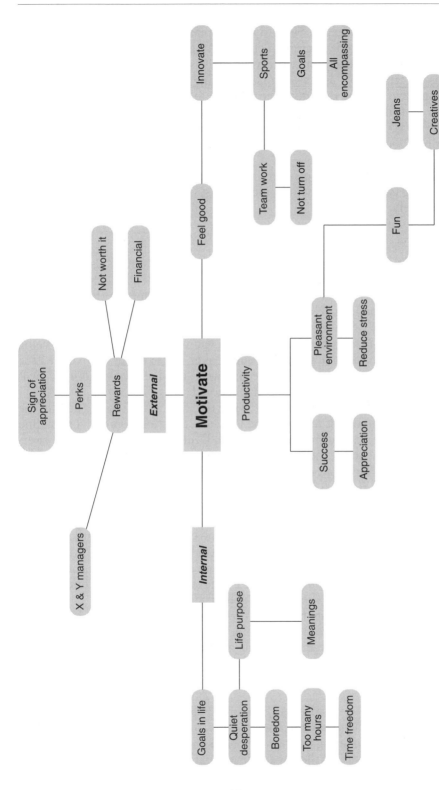

Figure 3.4 An example of mapping to develop the idea of motivation for a speech

the topic. Writing expert Sanford Kaye explains that the 'because' generator encourages you to tie your main points strongly to your topic.

To use this generator, write your main statement and then give your reasons and proofs as statements beginning with the word 'because'. For example, if you are drafting a memo to state your opposition to a proposed restructuring of your department, you can use the 'because' generator to develop your points. First, write your major message, 'I'm against the restructuring' (your main statement), and follow this with the word 'BECAUSE...' and list all your reasons.

Like the other idea generators, you can evaluate your list afterwards, deciding both what to include and the best order for presenting your views effectively.

The force-field generator

The force-field generator (see Figure 3.5) provides a quick, visual aid to an issue, particularly when you want to examine both sides. It is good in helping you focus on your goal (persuasion) rather than the format (for example, a memo or report). Writers too often ignore points that do not fit into their argument.

The force-field generator encourages you to consider the issue as being made up of forces, some stronger, some weaker. This visualisation of the issue can help you construct an effective argument, in which the opposing view is discussed and challenged rather than ignored.

To use the force-field generator, write the issue at the top of a page in the centre. It is often best to phrase the issue as a question. Draw a vertical line from the issue, so that the page is divided. Decide the two 'opposite' answers to the issue-question: these might be yes and no, for and against, or option A and option B. Write one of the answers at the top left of the page and the other one at the top right. You have now constructed the issue's 'field'.

The force-field generator has two stages. Stage one is brainstorming. Think of the issue as existing on that central, vertical line. What 'forces' will push the line (that is, the issue) toward one of the answers at either corner? Write on the appropriate side of the vertical line all the points that you can think of. It may help to imagine that the ones that you write on the left side can actually 'move' the line to the right-side answer and that the ones written on the right can move the line to the left-side answer.

In stage two, evaluate the forces that you have written down. Either rank each force according to its strength or importance, or indicate the relative importance of each force by drawing an arrow to the central line. Use the thickness or length of the arrows to show each force's power to 'move' the line. Consider which forces are the most powerful for your readers, and plan your argument.

Figure 3.5 gives an example of a force-field developed by George, a staff development officer asked to prepare a report for a major new staff development activity. Suffering from writer's block brought on by the importance of the report, George uses the force-field generator to focus on the issue. He first

No	Should the activity be supported?	Yes
Column A		**Column B**
Staff morale increased		Not essential
Cost effective		Outsiders more professional
Skills increased		Essential to get people out of office
Shows managerial concern		Low correlation between training and results
Short periods because in-house		
Can be individualised		Commercial ones cheaper in long-term
Would follow company ideas		Dept doesn't need local focus
Key staff interested		Not enough interested staff

Figure 3.5 An example of the force-field generator

writes the issue as a question: 'Should the activity be supported?' He writes the two opposites ('Yes' and 'No') and then brainstorms for forces to support these. The forces in Column A are those that can 'move' the line to the 'Yes' point, while the ones in Column B support the 'No' point. He then adds arrows to show which forces are the most important.

By using the force-field generator, George uncovers several important forces that he had not fully considered. More importantly, because he has a clear idea of the strength of the opposing views, he feels more confident about presenting his own argument.

The fishboning generator

Fishboning, like some of the other generators, helps you visualise your thinking and organising. Your ideas concerning the topic are placed in branching lines, which end up looking like a fish's spine.

To fishbone, draw a box at the left margin of your page and within it write your topic. From the box draw a horizontal line across the page. This line is the backbone. From the backbone, you will represent your thinking on the topic by drawing in lines or 'major bones' at 45 degree angles to represent sub-topics. You can branch out from these, adding more lines ('minor bones') to represent supporting details. If some detail affects two sub-topics, add it to both bones. Work on the fishbone chart quickly and feel free to jump from one level to another as you think of ideas, rather than trying to complete everything at one level before proceeding to the next. A completed fishbone chart is given in Figure 3.6.

After you have completed your fishbone, evaluate it. When you see the whole topic before you as a structure, you may think that some of the minor bones should be major ones and vice versa. Double-check that each minor bone's details tie in with the sub-topic and that each major bone develops an idea for the backbone. After making changes, 'cook' your fish by putting it aside (preferably overnight) and then review the whole structure once more.

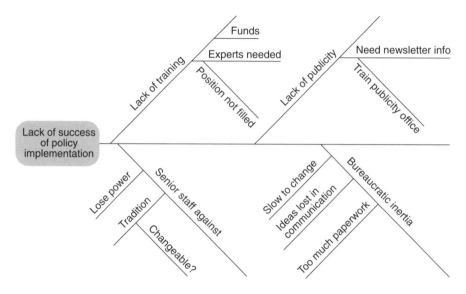

Figure 3.6 An example of 'fishboning' to plan a report

Other Ways to Promote Experimental Thinking

The idea generators are specific techniques for thinking about a topic. As well, there are other ways that you can train yourself to think experimentally and improve your writing.

Use notes as a writing 'kick-starter'

Jot down ideas immediately after or during a meeting or discussion. Do not rely on your memory. Notes written on a letter or agenda papers, for example, allow you to 'jump' immediately into detailed writing when you pick up the piece of paper again, instead of having to re-read the whole document or remember a discussion. As you make notes, focus on your reader and list important points to include.

Find your optimal writing time

Everyone has an optimal creative working time. Try to write during this time and, if possible, limit interruptions.

Those who find that their most productive time is outside normal working hours are sometimes able to count it as part of their work day, and some companies even supply computers for employees to use at home. If this is not feasible, try arriving at work early or working back to use the least interrupted part of the day as your writing time. If you are in an open office, perhaps ask people not to disturb you during a certain time. If you do have an office, close the door.

If long uninterrupted writing periods are impossible to get, spend your optimal production time using the idea generators to help you point out your direction, thus making it easier to write off and on during your work day.

Find your optimal method of incubation

Part of experimental thinking relies on having a period of incubation, during which your sub-conscious can work on ideas. The best method of 'switching off' varies. It may mean spending a lunch break in a museum or reading the latest 'sci-fi' magazine. Some writers find it beneficial to go for a long walk, undertake some type of exercise, listen to music, or have a quiet drink. Work into your writing schedule your optimal method of allowing ideas to incubate.

Record quotable items

Fiction writers often keep what they call casebooks or journals, small note-books in which they record conversations, descriptions, and musings that ultimately find their way into their published works. Do the same and be on the look-out for quotable material to record. Include anything that strikes you as interesting, for example, quotes, news items, conversations, or ideas. Get on paper whatever points seem striking or interesting at the time, as these are often infuriatingly only half-remembered when you need them days or weeks later.

Alternatively, use index cards for this purpose. When you listen to a talk, watch a program, or read an interesting article, put the main ideas onto large index cards. These are easy to flick through when you are looking for a specific fact, example, or quotation. Index cards can also reduce the mountain of papers it is necessary to keep for items that 'might come in handy some day'. If you are extracting information from an article, always record the author, title of article, source (for example, magazine, newspaper), page number, and date. This allows you to give credit when you use the information.

CONCLUSION

Most writers can be helped to think laterally or experimentally by using idea generators and other methods. These methods can make writing easier for you by helping you to come up with more interesting ideas. They also give you ways to organise your material early in the writing process.

References

Anon. (1970). 'The "fishbone" method of solving problems'. *Rydge's*, December, 129–130.

CHAPTER 4

CRITICAL THINKING

Critical thinking is the process of evaluating information. We are usually aware of applying critical thinking when reading persuasive documents, for example, advertisements or proposals. However, we are sometimes less attuned to evaluating our own writing according to its logic. This chapter provides guidelines for applying critical thinking to your writing.

WHAT DOES CRITICAL THINKING INVOLVE?

The following terms can help you understand what is involved in approaching a subject critically when you write.

The *topic* is the subject of your document. For it to have a purpose, you need to focus on an *issue*, that is, the central problem or concern about the topic. Critical thinking involves choices in how you 'package' information. One choice is your stance on the issue. We call this the *main message* of the document. A single issue can generate different main messages, depending on the viewpoint of the writer. The other choices that you use to develop and support your main message comprise the whole *argument* of your document.

To illustrate these terms, imagine that a manager asks her two division heads to respond to a memo from head office regarding computer developments. Using the terms above, the task can be described as

- **topic**—computer developments
- **issue**—what is important in considering computer developments
- **main message**—developments should be introduced gradually (division head one); some developments should not be introduced (division head two)
- **argument**—each division head's memo contains an argument which expands and explains the writer's main message.

By first deciding on the issue and your main message, you will find it easier to clarify the information and strategies needed to develop your ideas and avoid producing a document which seems misdirected or scattered. (Use the idea generators in Chapter 3 to explore ideas about your topic and issue.)

SELECTING INFORMATION

Evaluating information related to your topic is often an art in itself. After gathering information (both the pros and cons), evaluate to see what is relevant first to the issue and then to your main message. Do not ignore information which does not support your main message, as you need to consider the issue as a whole.

To have the necessary material to begin constructing a successful argument, assess your information to ensure that it is sufficient, relevant, accurate, up-to-date, and unbiased.

Is the information sufficient?

Collect enough information for your purpose. Writers who base their main message and supporting ideas on too little information weaken their document. Some writers go to the other extreme and gather too much information, confusing the amount of information with writing quality. Obviously, your information should be reasonably complete, but you can prevent yourself from getting bogged down by focusing on the most important information first, and then, if time permits, pursuing details.

Is the information relevant?

How relevant is the information to your main message? To your audience? Answering these questions can help you separate essential information from interesting but less relevant details.

Essential information is that which concerns the central topic. It is usually more highly regarded if it comes from a major source, for example, a senior person in the organisation, a respected publication, or a government agency. But its relevance depends on your readers. For a report on staffing possibilities within an organisation, the following information could be classed as relevant: the organisation's past reports on the subject; a review of actions from a rival company; and the CEO's last annual message, which addressed this issue. If the report was being prepared for a broader readership outside the organisation, information from relevant professional journals and people known to the audience could be relevant.

Is the information accurate?

Writing based on hearsay leaves you open to criticism. Clearly differentiate between facts and possibilities; ensure that your sources, both people and material, are reliable. Always double-check your information.

Is the information up-to-date?

Dated information can mislead readers into making unfortunate decisions. Drawing on old material can also make you look very much behind the times.

Check that your information, or the situation that it applies to, has not changed. Material in some fields dates rapidly. A quick search, especially using electronic databases, can often lead you to more recent information. If you have access to a specialist, such as a company librarian, use that person. Talk to others, both within and outside the organisation, formally and informally, to discover the latest thinking on your topic.

Is the information unbiased?

In a formal argument, the facts and viewpoints of the different 'sides' are aired. You may think that you weaken your message by including opposing information. However, not dealing with all the relevant information available can raise questions in your readers' minds and sometimes reduce your credibility.

DEVELOPING A GOAL-CENTRED MESSAGE

Knowing your writing goal helps you develop a strong main message. One of the biggest mistakes that writers make is addressing a topic but not developing a main message to guide readers. Occasionally you may withhold your main message deliberately, to create suspense or allow readers to consider the topic before explaining your particular viewpoint. It is more usual in factual writing, however, to present your viewpoint early in the document, as this gives your readers a focus as they read.

Is your main message appropriate? Consider your writing goal, as it will influence what and how you develop your main message. Do you plan primarily to give facts, suggest actions, or make values clear?

Give facts

You provide your readers with information, defining terms or actions and pointing out what you think is true and false. Examples of 'fact-centred' documents are minutes and memos or reports on past events.

Effective organisational writing is characterised by

- an immediately recognisable goal and significance
- information that is up-to-date, relevant, sufficient, accurate, and unbiased
- clear structure through signposting
- coherence
- a style that is concise, graceful, and compelling
- a tone that is appropriate
- professional presentation standards

Figure 4.1 The elements involved in creating effective writing

Suggest actions

You propose a course of action, usually from other possible choices, and argue why your choice is best (for example, most cost effective, easiest to initiate, most useful). Many reports about future developments are written with this goal.

Clarify values

You point out why a topic should be considered favourably or unfavourably and apprise or remind your readers of certain values, for example, those of the organisation, profession, or the community. Documents developed around a discussion of organisational values can include policy papers, annual speeches and reports, and staff appraisals.

Obviously, most documents combine these three goals, but a unified document has one dominant goal. For example, if asked to comment on an unsatisfactory employee, you could choose any one of the three goals and each would influence you to develop the document in a certain way. If proposing actions, you would have your document focus on the best actions to take to relieve the problem. If emphasising facts, you would present evidence that the employee's work is or is not satisfactory. If emphasising values, you could focus on the detrimental effect that the employee has on others or the need to be supportive because of extraordinary circumstances.

Writing which lacks a strong main message is often characterised by 'flabby' beginnings, as illustrated in these three examples.

Example 1: There are three methods that we can use.

Example 2: The computer change-over will take place in two months.

Example 3: The recent decision to cancel this contract is not without problems.

A stated main message firms these beginnings by providing readers with a framework to consider the document as an argument.

Example 1: Of the three methods that can be used, I favour the first.

By emphasising one method as the main message, the writer establishes the document's goal as 'action'. Readers can read with the expectation that the document will develop support for this idea. (If the main message is not presented at the beginning, the effect is less persuasive, as readers must digest information about all three methods before learning the writer's opinion.)

> Example 2: The computer change-over will take place in two months because of the necessary lead time to develop appropriate software.

If the goal is to 'give information', the writer must decide what is important and ensure that this is at the beginning of the document. Here the date is important because of the issue of software development.

> Example 3: The recent decision to cancel this contract is not without problems, primarily because of our advertised policy about customer service.

In the revised version, the reader is not just told about problems, but directed to evaluate them in the light of the company's values.

AVOIDING THE PITFALLS IN CRITICAL THINKING

Critical thinking, by providing you with information that is complete, accurate, and fair, helps you to write logically. Despite this, logical writing is sometimes difficult to achieve. Unwarranted assumptions may crop up in a document when the writer has not sufficiently considered the issue or the readers. An argument which sounds good may sway readers by emotion, misuse of the language, or faulty reasoning. Of course, illogical writing is sometimes used deliberately to evade issues or win support for certain ideas. Three problems can create pitfalls for the writer trying to develop a logical argument: false assumptions, fallacies, and insidious fallacies.

Avoiding false assumptions

One important part of critical thinking is understanding the assumptions we make as we write. When we construct an argument on assumptions that our readers may not share with us, our chances of convincing them are reduced.

As an example of this problem, consider the following story, which was used by a large insurance company to promote life insurance. Its highly emotional appeal could easily prevent readers from appraising a number of assumptions being made. We have listed the misleading assumptions at the end of each extract.

> Cheryl is six years old and she's bewildered. Her father died a few months ago, and the world hasn't been the same since.

Cheryl used to come running home from school, eager to tell her mother all the wonderful and exciting things that happened in class. Now she returns reluctantly to the elderly neighbour who keeps her until her mummy gets home from work.

- Assumes that children always are excited about school.
- Implies that elderly people cannot respond to a child's enthusiasm.
- Implies that children need their mothers to stay at home.

She used to have a new Christmas outfit every year. This year her mother has let the hem down on last year's dress. Cheryl used to go to her best friend's place every Saturday and afterwards her parents would pick her up and go to McDonalds or the Pizza Hut. Now she just stays at home.

- Suggests that the only choices are a new dress or altering last year's.
- Makes an illogical link between socialising with her friend, and going to a fast-food place—without food money, Cheryl also cannot go to her friend's place.

Cheryl used to go to ballet classes with all her other little friends. Now she listens wistfully when they talk about their costumes for the recital. She used to curl up on the sofa beside her mother every night for a bedtime story. Now her mother usually says, 'I'm sorry, darling, I'm too tired to read tonight'.

- States that all Cheryl's friends go to ballet class—this may or may not be true.
- Suggests that mothers who do not work outside the home are not too tired to read at night.

Cheryl used to talk her parents into picnic lunches in the park when the weather was nice. Now her mother says, 'I'm sorry dear, but I don't have the time'. So Cheryl has stopped asking. She used to laugh, and play and sing with a little girl's uncomplicated happiness in being alive. Now she's quiet and subdued. She can't understand why her life has changed so much. Cheryl is only 6 years old. She's paying for the life insurance her father never bought.

- Assumes that being a sole parent means no time ever for enjoyable events.
- Implies that Cheryl's changed personality is due to the lack of material wealth and lack of her mother's time.

Writers continually make assumptions about their topic and their readers (see Chapter 2). However, critical readers may question some of these. If a document raises too many questions in readers' minds, their trust in the writer is lost.

Avoiding fallacies

We are not suggesting that good writing omits all persuasive devices just because they may be illogical. For example, appeals to our emotions—humour, anger, or pity—can be powerful when used as a supplement to a reasoned argument. Persuasive devices become problematic only when they are used instead of reasoning.

Illogical writing results when writers make unwarranted claims or mistakes in their reasoning. These are called fallacies. Fallacies are most commonly found in highly persuasive documents, for example, advertisements and political speeches. Understanding fallacies can help you as a reader to evaluate documents and become more critical of writing that is long on emotion and short on logic. As a writer, you can then be more aware of using logic in constructing your own documents.

The most common fallacies are defined and described below. In order to illustrate the possible negative effect of the fallacies, we have listed after each the possible responses of critical readers.

Appeal to authority

The common appeal to authority figures to support claims becomes fallacious when the person cited is not an authority on the topic being discussed. This fallacy is illustrated by advertisements showing famous sporting heroes talking about non-sports products and by glowing work references written by people not in the position to comment on the job seeker's work.

> Lisa, our chief accountant, does not think that the staff development for the sales team is suitable.

If Lisa's objections are based on cost, then she is a suitable authority figure to quote. However, she probably does not have the expertise to comment as an authority on the program's aims or content.

Readers may discount the whole argument of a writer who has introduced a bogus authority to comment on the subject.

Appeal to force

The writer suggests that the viewpoint is correct because others in power agree.

> **Example 1: Senior management is behind me on this point.**

This assertion is certainly persuasive, as it shows that powerful organisational members support the writer. From the standpoint of logical reasoning, however, the statement is suspect, for senior management's support is not proof that the writer's views are accurate or well-founded.

Readers may be sceptical if they think that the writer's claim is not true or that management has not been given correct or full information. Some readers may not find claiming this type of support impressive.

A similar appeal asks readers to believe something because everyone else does.

> **Example 2: Everyone knows that the new office plan will prevent the type of efficiency we're used to.**

Readers who oppose this viewpoint may be put off by having their ideas ignored in this way.

Appeal to ignorance

This fallacy is based on the idea that if you cannot prove that something is false, then it is true—or vice versa.

> **As it cannot be proved that our new work policy in NSW caused the sharp increase in staff absenteeism, it should be implemented by the other states.**

There is insufficient evidence to evaluate the policy. However, the policy may still be part of the problem.

Readers may want more information and expect the writer to make only conditional judgements until this information is available.

Appeal to pity

In this fallacy, the reader is asked to make a judgement based solely on emotions rather than reason.

> Moving the head office to the western suburbs would create countless disruptions and destroy the fabric of family life for our employees.

Although the issue of family life may be strong, this emotional appeal needs to be backed up with 'hard' evidence, for example, increased travelling times for staff.

The appeal to pity often backfires when readers become suspicious of the writer's motives, feeling that they are being tricked in some way. Critical readers will ask themselves questions, such as 'Who is involved/affected?', 'What is the problem/concern?', 'How many are involved?', and 'What proof is there?'.

Appeal to tradition

The writer relies on tradition, not reason, to convince readers.

> I suggest that we buy Schuster computers, as we have been a loyal customer since they produced their first typewriter in 1932.

Although trade loyalty might be an important issue, readers could criticise the value of this criterion, especially because the product itself has changed.

Black and white

The black and white fallacy suggests that only two extreme views are possible.

> Example 1: Which type of manager are you: autocratic or caring?

Although this simplification is occasionally acceptable to illustrate a point, an ethical writer states that in reality these categories are not so closed.

A similar fallacy is the false dilemma, when the two extremes are given as a problem that must be solved.

> Example 2: We either convert completely and immediately to computers, or relegate our administrative staff to typewriters.

Obviously, there may be other choices, such as gradually converting the office to computers.

In both fallacies, critical readers will probably realise that other choices exist and discount the writer's argument.

False cause

In these two examples, a faulty cause-and-effect relationship is created.

> Example 1: Because I criticised the latest advertising campaign, I wasn't asked to join the task force set up by the CEO last week.
>
> Example 2: Because employees don't want to work overtime, we've had twenty resignations in the last year.

In both examples, the result (not being asked, the resignations) may have been for reasons other than those stated.

Readers who are sceptical of the cause–effect relationship suggested may feel that the other possible causes should have been mentioned.

Faulty analogy

An analogy is a developed comparison of similar points between two things. It is often used to explain the unfamiliar by comparing it to what readers find familiar. Carefully used, analogies add colour and support readers' understanding. But stretching or forcing the analogy, or trying to use too many points of comparison, leads to absurdity, as shown by the examples.

> Example 1: Like a criminal holding a knife at our jugular, the union forces us to be powerless victims, unable to do anything more than hand over our hard-earned money and pray that our lives be spared.

This analogy is colourful, but simplistic. An organisation is not similar to a criminal, a union disagreement is not really like a knife to the jugular, and legal negotiations ensure that one side is not completely powerless.

> Example 2: Our company is presently like an ocean cruiser, being pretty stable no matter what the weather and providing a pleasant trip for its passengers. But as our skilled financial navigators steer us past the shoals of higher exchange rates and the sandbars of union unrest, we must batten down our hatches for the typhoon of recession just glimpsed on the horizon. And although the storm may be fierce, using the safety anchor of our long-term contracts will keep us on the major shipping lanes of progress.

Readers may either groan or enjoy this extended analogy, but if it constitutes the backbone of the writer's argument, they might justifiably feel cheated in being entertained rather than informed.

Faulty generalisation

Faulty generalisations base claims on too few cases, or atypical cases.

> No further staff development activities will be held because of negative evaluations received.

If only four negative evaluations were received, this would probably be too few to base this judgement on. Four negative evaluations would be atypical if there were fifty positive evaluations in comparison. The judgement should be made on what is typical.

Critical readers would expect specific details which would answer their questions, for example, 'How many?', 'Over what period?', 'Under what circumstances?'.

Hasty generalisation

With a hasty generalisation, the writer makes a general assumption from a single case.

> My request for promotion was rejected last month. It's difficult working in a company that does not value its staff.

The particular case may be true, but jumping from this to a general condemnation of company treatment of all staff is fallacious, as there could be other reasons for the rejection.

Readers who spot a hasty generalisation may feel that a writer is trying to fool them by inflating the issue.

Personal attack

Instead of attacking the other person's main message or viewpoint, the writer attacks the person. Common types of personal attack are deriding the person for being inexperienced, foreign, unpopular, eccentric, or for not practising what is being advocated.

> Of course, those below management level do not have the vision to appreciate the need for this change.

Here the writer tries to expose as false an opposing opinion, not by refuting it with evidence but by attacking those who hold it as being inexperienced.

Readers may feel uncomfortable if they believe that they are being given an emotionally 'loaded' argument. They may find the criticism unjust unless the opinions of the criticised person or group are presented.

Pointing to another wrong

Here the writer does not answer a charge but merely brings up some misdeed of the opponent. Although often effective emotionally, the 'one wrong justifies another' view is illogical.

> Example 1: My department may be criticised for over spending, but at least it meets budget.
>
> Example 2: While I understand Ms Dunnett's criticism about the standard of my work, I wish to point out that, unlike others here, I'm undertaking special duties during the restructuring.

In both examples, the writer tries to deflect the criticism by bringing up a wrong that someone else has committed.

Readers who do not fall for this appeal would focus on the original issue.

Prejudging

A writer who prejudges tries to sway readers by using emotional, prejudicial language rather than evidence.

> Right-minded shareholders are against the takeover as it is obvious that such mining results in more disastrous problems than gains.

Rather than facts, prejudicial language, such as 'right-minded', 'obvious', and 'disastrous', is being used to encourage readers to be against the takeover.

Especially in longer documents, readers may be suspicious of not finding enough facts.

Slippery slope

The slippery slope appeal is based on the idea that accepting an undesirable proposal will set off a chain of undesirable consequences.

> If we cut back our staff now, we will not be able to bid for the new contract. Without this contract, we will lose the profits for next year, and this will mean that...

This appeal is sometimes difficult to counteract, especially as the scare tactics encourage readers to use emotion rather than reason. Critical readers would try to assess separately each part of this complex argument.

Avoiding insidious fallacies

Although all fallacies can be insidious, some particular fallacies not only severely damage an argument, but the writer seldom makes them ignorantly. Quite common in political writing, insidious fallacies may also find their way into organisational writing.

Barrage of objections

Instead of answering the issue at hand, the writer buries a simple action or proposal under irrelevant considerations. This tactic, used within a proposal, can be used to stall major decisions, as the proposal gets shifted from one committee or working party to the next.

Card stacking

Here the writer deliberately tampers with the evidence, omitting what does not support his or her view. Probably the most well-known examples of card stacking are the scientific reports in which test results are suppressed when these do not prove the researchers' hypothesis.

Engineered suspicions

Some people side-track an issue by creating misgivings or suspicions that have little to do with the issue itself. Particularly in a defensive organisational climate, staff may be more prey to this tactic, as they have learned to read 'between the lines' of organisational documents.

Inappropriate humour

Humour is sometimes valuable in organisational communication, particularly as a social lubricant. It can become inappropriate when it is used deliberately to encourage readers to laugh at or ridicule an issue that deserves serious attention. If directed at those holding the opposing view, this type of humour may reduce their chances of opinions being aired.

The red herring

Here the writer brings in irrelevant information that turns readers aside from the issue at hand. A skilful user of the red herring technique can get whole committees tied up in considering a topic completely outside their original brief.

Evaluating Critical Thinking in Your Writing

When reading your writing, evaluate your main message by asking these questions.

- Is my main message clear?
- Is it stated early enough in the document to direct readers?
- Have I given the opposing view and raised relevant questions?
- Have I chosen convincing reasons and main points?
- Have I provided evidence?
- Have I made realistic assumptions?

By asking these questions as you read your writing, you will locate where your argument is strong and where it needs to be more developed.

Conclusion

Critical thinking helps you strengthen your writing by clarifying your topic, developing a sound main message, and creating an effective argument. Critical thinking can lead to logical writing, that is, writing that is free from false assumptions and fallacies. Such illogical appeals may sway some readers, but alienate others.

CHAPTER 5

CHOOSING AN APPROPRIATE DOCUMENT FRAMEWORK

Writers provide structure at all levels of the document, for example, by choosing particular words and phrases and shaping sentences and paragraphs. In particular, structuring and sequencing at the macro-level, that is, the major sections, create a framework which helps to keep your readers with you. This chapter explains how a document framework assists both writers and readers and discusses the formats or frameworks most common in professional writing.

WHY CONSTRUCT A DOCUMENT FRAMEWORK?

Many writers in high-pressure jobs are given little time to research, develop ideas, edit, or even proofread their work. In some organisations, a poorly written report presented on time may be more acceptable than a well-written one presented late. However, time saved is often communication lost.

By concentrating on developing a clear framework for your document, you can save time and check that the document communicates. How? A framework created early in the writing task highlights your main message and makes you aware of the material needed to support it. By clarifying the framework, you should be able to write more quickly, have fewer substantial rewrites, and ensure that you keep your readers with you. It helps you to focus on your material, test the logical relationship between the different parts of your document, and allows you to continue writing despite the usual workday interruptions.

You can also use the framework as a blueprint when you discuss your document with others. In the same way that it is easier to remove a wall on a blueprint than an actual wall once a house is built, a framework allows you to incorporate others' suggestions more easily than if you have already finished the first draft.

Our view of structure is influenced by research in cognitive science and artificial intelligence, particularly the work being done with schema theory (refer to Chapter 2), which suggests that the brain stores information in mental 'slots' or schemata. How does this theory relate to business document frameworks?

Consider the schema of a letter. Through your past experience, you have expectations of what you will find when you open a sealed, rectangular envelope addressed to you. Finding a sandwich instead of a folded paper would violate your expectations. Your letter schema also provides you with expectations about the paper's appearance: you expect a series of short lines at the top of the page, then a line beginning with the word 'Dear' followed by your name. Your schema may also suggest what is acceptable content, subject matter, tone, timing, and vocabulary. You may experience a momentary mental jolt when you receive a letter which does not meet these expectations, for example, one which omits the salutation 'Dear' and just begins with your name.

Schema theory underlines the point that formats are not always logical or even universally accepted. Their value develops from the shared expectations of their readers. The communication etiquette of these expectations can change from one culture to another and even from one organisation to another.

USING BUSINESS FORMATS AS DOCUMENT FRAMEWORKS

Some writing books suggest that the common business formats are written either correctly or incorrectly according to rules, for example, the 'correct' way to write a complaint letter. The document's surface conventions are being confused with the wider framework or macro-structure of the document. Surface conventions (for example, spelling and punctuation) are usually considered as correct or incorrect. The idea of correctness is not as appropriate, however, when applied to the overall structure of information, for effective writers arrange material according to the way which seems most appropriate for the reader.

Writers rely on standard frameworks or formats for business documents such as memos, letters, and proposals. Such formats help communication by establishing conventions of content, appearance, and material for readers. The successful professional writer learns to use these formats to signal his or her understanding of what is common within the business community. As writing educator Paul Anderson states,

> ...[A] writer's ability to use conventional forms in the customary way shows that he or she is a bona fide member of the culture of the workplace; a person who cannot use these forms may appear to readers to be generally unqualified (1985, p. 12).

These conventions comprise the written communication etiquette among professional writers.

However, formats are merely accepted arrangements and are not inherently logical. Just following the formats unthinkingly is like painting by numbers: you may end up with something acceptable but you will not create a masterpiece. You need to be flexible and assess the particular writing situations. Sometimes what is needed is a deliberately fresh approach which results in an unconventional framework. For example, income tax forms in Sweden were designed to look like the Sunday comics to appeal to readers. A recent booklet about abuse, aimed at teenagers, uses a story format rather than the more usual, and didactic, question-and-answer pattern.

MAKING YOUR DOCUMENT READER-FRIENDLY

Within the accepted structure of business documents, the effective writer shapes information according to different influences within the organisation, but is particularly attuned to the dictates of the readers' needs. For example, the framework that you construct may be the result of assessing your readers against your knowledge about a subject, the strength of your views, the amount of research time available, or the sensitivity of the topic. All can affect your arrangement of material.

Whatever the variables, your aim is to reach your readers. You can use this aim to establish your document's structure and make it more reader-friendly. American writing researchers Linda Flower, John Hayes, and Heidi Swarts found that too often the reader is 'left out' of the information. The remedy that they have written about is what they call the 'scenario principle'. It relies on the writer viewing writing as communication *with* readers. A document is only complete or activated when someone reads it. The writer should encourage the reader to become involved in the document by establishing a scenario or situation which includes the reader. For example, consider this instruction.

> Switching the computer off is not to be completed until after the disk has been ejected.

Readers are not included in this situation. Being left out, they are forced to interpret the information on their own and work to comprehend what to do. In a sense, they are being expected to 'translate' the information into the actions they need to perform. A writer interested in making the instructions reader-friendly, and so saving them from this extra work, would revise the instructions to communicate directly with the readers. Following is an example of reader-friendly writing.

> Eject the disk before you switch off the computer.

This example illustrates how to change one instruction, but the document's macro-level itself can be revised to make it more accessible to readers. For example, when you plan your document's framework, anticipate your readers' questions and expectations. What do they want to know? What do they expect to know? How does this affect what they want to read first? What *will not* interest them? Use your views and knowledge of your readers to structure the whole document. Structuring your document around readers' needs helps you develop a discernible plan. If a document seems to have been merely thrown together, not only are readers forced to work harder to comprehend the message, they can as a result become confused, frustrated, or angry.

Examples of documents which seem to lack concern for their readers are the computer user manuals which scare users by beginning with highly technical instructions about installing the software. Truly reader-friendly ones move the installation section to the back, since it is usually referred to only once. Instead, the reader is invited to read something more interesting, such as an overview of how the program will benefit the reader.

You can make the framework of your document reader-friendly by using macro-signals to highlight the document's framework. The following guidelines explain how to provide macro-level signals.

Guideline one: Use headings and sub-headings

Headings and sub-headings are valuable macro-signals in memos and reports, as they focus your readers' attention immediately. By placing major points in headings and sub-headings, you provide a clear overview for readers who are used to skim reading.

Research has shown that readers retain information more easily when headings are used, as they provide a context for reading. For example, if this book had no headings or sub-headings, you would find it frustrating, even though an index is provided.

When you create headings, remember that the title is an important heading which directs readers to your subject. Because the title is important, engage your readers. Serious business documents usually have straightforward, factual titles. Use key words from your document. For example, if you are writing a grant submission for a project to install a new accounts system, these terms should be included in the title. Documents directed to the general public (for example, speeches, conference papers, and some publications) may have more creative titles.

You can help your readers even more if you repeat the pattern for headings and sub-headings which are at the same 'level'. For example, can you see what is wrong with these three consecutive headings of a report?

Secretarial staff's use of word processing
Financial modelling
Training clerical staff to use graphs

The structure of the headings does not match up, leaving readers to make the connections themselves. The relationship between the headings can be clarified simply by using the same pattern for all three.

> Computing requirements of secretarial staff
> Computing requirements of accounting staff
> Computing requirements of clerical staff

Engage your readers by addressing them directly in the headings. By using verbs, you include your readers in the action.

> Original: Consideration of Superannuation Bonds
> Improved: Consider Superannuation Bonds

The improved heading invites the reader to do something, and by establishing interaction also encourages the writer to continue including the reader.

You can also use implied interaction. The improved heading below sets up a theme, for the reader might mentally reply, 'Yes, I want to know if I'm eligible'.

> Original: Definitions of Eligibility
> Improved: How to Decide Whether You are Eligible

Question headings also establish a theme, but use them sparingly, as they can easily become boring or too directive and thus alienate readers.

> Are You Eligible?
> Are Superannuation Bonds a Good Investment?

Guideline two: Emphasise your main message

Translate your purpose into a single sentence. This main message should be placed at the beginning of your document as a signpost, helping readers predict its content. This seems like a simple writing hint, but it is surprising how many documents delay or ignore presenting a discernible main message to readers.

Without a clear main message, a 'mystery' document is created. The writer provides clues but leaves readers to piece together the central, unifying theme. Will readers continue to read until the main message is revealed? The answer is probably 'yes' for fiction pieces but 'no' for business documents. To prevent yourself from inadvertently writing a 'mystery' document, ensure that your main message is established early.

Consider this case study. Richard completes a report recommending computer purchases for the next year. He thinks he has covered the alternatives accurately and fairly, so he is surprised at the hostile reaction that his report causes.

What has gone wrong? The problem is not in the content but in how Richard has structured his report. He gives no main message, leaving his readers to interpret the information on their own. By clarifying a main message, Richard could have directed readers on *how* to consider his document. Two examples of a main message that he could have included are given below.

> Of the four alternatives discussed below, I support the first one as being most cost-effective.
>
> Four alternatives are discussed below for section members to decide upon.

In both, the main message ('I support' or 'members to decide upon') directs readers how to consider the information given.

Readers do expect the main message to guide them by indicating how the rest of the document will be developed. For example, consider this lead sentence in a memo.

> My business trip to Tokyo was fruitful.

Readers would expect the rest of the document to develop the idea of what was fruitful. If they read the following instead, they would be confused.

> My business trip to Tokyo was fruitful. What I'd planned to accomplish on this trip did not eventuate. My forced change of plans made me realise how often the unusual can happen and so should be taken into consideration. As it was, I discovered some exciting new developments in technology, which the company could profitably pursue.

The problem here is that the follow-on to 'fruitful' is 'exciting new developments', but seemingly contradictory messages intervene, such as 'did not eventuate' and 'forced change of plans'. Creating a main message often helps writers stay on track by clarifying the way the document needs to be developed to support the message.

Train yourself to incorporate your main message in your document by jotting it as a note at the top of page one of your first draft. As you redraft, your message will evolve into a polished final form. In the three examples below, the original main message first used by the writer changes to a final form which adequately signposts the content and structure of the whole document.

> Original: The position is an important one to us.
>
> Final: The position of Administrative Assistant should be filled now, before the company's busy period in July.
>
> Original: Employing fewer senior staff cuts personnel costs.
>
> Final: If personnel costs are to be reduced, we will need to employ fewer senior level staff next year.
>
> Original: My qualifications match the job.
>
> Final: My strong marketing qualifications would enable me to handle the responsibilities of the job.

Guideline three: Use a familiar pattern of development

Once you have pointed out the framework of your document in your headings and sub-headings, continue to give your readers a clear sense of order as they read. Think of each heading and sub-heading as introducing information which can be arranged into patterns that your readers will find familiar.

Why is this important? Without a pattern, you may write *around* your main ideas instead of developing them. Readers who feel that they are going in circles instead of moving forward become upset and lose the thread of your message. Familiar patterns present information in what seems to be a logical way to readers. The following are conventional organisational patterns of writing development in Western society

- the more familiar then the less familiar
- the more popular then the less popular
- the more acceptable then the less acceptable
- the closer then the less close
- the more recent then the less recent.

An effective writer considers the particular circumstances and chooses an appropriate pattern of writing development that best fits the subject, audience, and main message. For example, Sheila is writing a report about budget constraints for staffing, capital works, and marketing, to table at her department's next meeting. What pattern would be best? Considering her readers and her topic, she decides to lead with the least contentious issue, in order to have a point of agreement before introducing the issues more likely to be challenged or debated.

Guideline four: Arrange by function

Information within the document is also arranged by function, that is, the document is a response to your communication goal. To consider the most appropriate framework for a document, think of your goal, that is, what you want of your readers. Do you expect them to make a certain decision, take action, or just know something? Your answer will suggest the appropriate structure.

Table 5.1

Purpose	Structure
Suggest action (a decision)	Define/explain/argue problem Explain/request action or decision Suggest consequences Suggest limitations to action
Give facts and then details	Explain reason for giving information Sequence information, with overview
Clarify values	Explain reason for clarifying values Explain/define/illustrate Suggest consequences

Some functions are conventional in the business community, becoming another part of its communication etiquette. For example, so-called 'good news' and 'bad news' letters use formulas to suggest a conventional arrangement of information. However, such formulas are usually too simple to be effectively applied to real-life writing tasks. Formulas can lock writers into one supposedly correct pattern and make them less adaptable to the particular situation.

Consider, for example, how to reply to the complaint letter in Figure 5.1. The respondent's goal is complex: it should justify the action but probably apologise for the distress caused. The information to meet this goal could be structured by using the following conventional format for complaint letters

- acknowledge the complaint letter
- discuss the complaint and give facts to justify actions
- provide a decision, especially to a request for action
- express interest in the complainant.

By considering the function of each segment of your document (that is, your goal), you control both what to write and how. This approach is used in at least one insurance company to give writers guidelines on writing adjustment letters quickly and effectively by interpreting their writing task in regard to their reader.

CHECKING YOUR FRAMEWORK

Using major signposts and familiar patterns develops a specific framework or macro-structure. To ensure that the framework you have developed is evident to your readers, you can test it in several ways: by outlining, conducting the 'so what?' test, and reviewing your main points.

Construct an outline

Business communicators are becoming more aware of the importance of outlining. It provides a visual plan of a document's organisation. Just as architects plan a building before construction is started, writers can plan their framework, check the document's structure, and test its logic before starting to write. The outline shows up what information is still needed, gives you something definite at the planning stage for discussion with others, and provides a back-up when things go wrong (for example, computer failure, interruptions, or illness).

Your outline does not need to be formal, as jotting down only main ideas is usually sufficient. Some word processing programs have an outlining facility, to encourage writers to plan in this way. Focus on your main message and decide on an arrangement that seems the most logical or helpful in developing your topic for readers. For example, if you are writing about problems at three retail locations, you can arrange material by location, or by problem.

Make your outline a working planner by adding connections for your readers within it. Jot down information that would be beneficial to include as background or as transitions between main points. For example, you may want to remind yourself to explain why you are developing a topic, or to include a connecting phrase to clarify the link between one point and the next. This type of planning saves you time, as it is much easier to revise an outline than a whole document. Trying at the editing stage to 'fix up' a document with a muddled main message is not only time-consuming but also frustrating.

Try the 'so what?' test

The 'so what?' test is a simple means of checking that you are staying on track within your document. After writing your major points, consider each one separately and ask yourself, 'so what?'. Does the point promote your main message? Does it develop the framework of your document? Writers may ignore their macro-structure and choose instead to include less relevant information which sounds good. The 'so what?' test clarifies what is important and what is not. Use the 'so what?' test again after you have written the document to remove 'dead wood' that may lose or bore your readers.

Review the main points

After writing, check that your headings and sub-headings contribute to your main message. Are they geared to your readers? As you write, your thinking on a subject often evolves, and what you write at the beginning of a long document may not 'connect' with what comes later. If this happens, do not feel tied to your original arrangement. Major changes later in the writing process, if thought through, can clarify and strengthen the document.

RE-ORGANISING YOUR FRAMEWORK

An example

Figure 5.1 is a complaint letter from a client to an organisation. It can be used as an example of how re-organising the framework along the guidelines stated in this chapter can help a writer more clearly express his or her writing goal and main message. We do not negate the content, or trivialise the writer's distress; we are merely pointing out how better organisation can increase the letter's chances of communicating the writer's concerns and eliciting reader action. Consider how a stronger framework is created by applying the following guidelines.

Address a reader

A particular reader, specifically a decision maker, should be identified, especially if the writer wants action to be taken. By selecting one reader, the writer would have found it easier to select relevant points and omit the more general and confusing slurs and complaints.

Develop a main message

The expressed main message is that staff should not have made the request, but another important message is that the organisation should take some

---

To Whom It May Concern

Your request for further information has left me dumbfounded and angry, not the least because this message was relayed quite by accident when I just happened to be in head office.

How you can ask for this request in this instance is quite beyond me. I can only assume that as human beings you have forgotten (or perhaps never knew) what thinking of others means. It is an act of humanness and does not require an application form to be filled in.

As you are well aware this incident was painful for me and I can do without your weak offer of support, which is no support at all. I feel sad that you are so out of touch that you could even consider a request, even one given at second hand, such as you asked of me.

Yours in disgust

Figure 5.1 Original complaint letter from a client to an organisation

action. The original main message is fuzzy enough to confuse readers. We suggest that the writer create a clear main message (for example, 'I wish to complain about...') in the first sentence to provide a context for reading.

Develop a pattern

The writer could use the general to specific pattern, following up the complaint with specific facts, and then follow the convention of requesting action or recompense.

Add a heading

In this short letter, one heading at the beginning is sufficient.

Using these four recommendations, we have rewritten the letter (see Figure 5.2). We have left poorly worded phrases, to make the point that even with these surface problems, the document is still much more understandable because of its clearer framework or macro-structure.

Mr X
Department Head
Organisation X

Accident claim: 7 May 19..

I wish to complain both about your request for further information about the accident claim that I sent you on 15 February, and the way that the request was made.

Your request has left me dumbfounded and angry. How you can ask for more information before you support my claim is quite beyond me. The claim is documented and was sent to you over two months ago. Asking me to submit more paperwork is ridiculous. I wanted help, but I can certainly do without your so-called support.

I am also distressed that I was not informed about the request officially but by accident. A staff member told me when I just happened to be in head office. If I had not been in, I believe that I would have never heard of this request.

I am angry that you could even consider making this request, even at second hand. As you are well aware, the incident has been painful for me. Caring for others in distress is an act of humanness and does not usually require a form to be filled in.

Yours in disgust

Figure 5.2 The complaint letter slightly rewritten to make information more accessible to the reader

COMMUNICATION ETIQUETTE AND COMMON FORMATS

Writing formats are accepted arrangements of information. Common formats are used in business documents such as advertisements, brochures, handbooks, instructions, journals, lessons, letters, manuals, magazines, memos, pamphlets, proposals, reports of various kinds, research papers, speeches, specifications, and surveys. Some formats are common to the business world; others are developed within a particular organisation. All help to constitute the communication etiquette explained in Chapter 1. The effective writer uses the communication etiquette expected for each format, but 'breaks the rules' in special circumstances.

In the description of common writing formats given below, we suggest the communication etiquette that surrounds each and gives it a certain accepted format or arrangement, and we suggest how to develop the document in a way deemed acceptable or 'proper' in the business world. Obviously, differences and contradictions exist.

Articles

Producing a professional article is a skill which increases the more you write and study other articles. What makes some stand out while others have a high 'snooze' potential? To find out, dissect articles that catch your eye in magazines, newspapers, or professional journals and newsletters. The answer can usually be traced to the writer's interest in the subject and his or her desire to communicate with readers. Organisational writers commonly confine their writing to articles for publications within the organisation or a professional association. The article usually features something new or interesting.

Your first concern is to limit the scope of the chosen topic. For example, if you are asked to contribute an article because you are known as a computer expert, you need to limit this topic still further by using the following categories.

Table 5.2

Limit the subject	To give a possible topic
Specific kind	New Macintoshes
Specific time	Last two years
Specific place	Design department
Specific number	Five networked computers
Specific person	Computer adviser's role
Specific type	Mainframe
Specific aspect	Artwork and computing
Specific example	Creating a logo on the Mac
Specific experience	Attending electronics exhibit

Limiting the topic in this way forces you to delve more deeply into material and provide more interesting information, giving your readers the benefit of your expert knowledge or interest.

Some professional journals expect you to start your article in a formal, straightforward way, for example, 'Managers may not realise the value that editors can add to a document'. If you have the chance, however, create interest in your article from the very beginning by writing a short but enticing introduction in one of the following ways.

- Pose a question significant to readers.

> Can managers really change sexist attitudes in the workplace?

- Establish a claim.

> The new Zydec computer does everything that a professional writer would kill for.

- Provide an interesting description.

> Suspense filled the air as the editorial team awaited management's reaction to the new format of the annual report.

- Cite an interesting or startling statistic or fact.

> Over 70 per cent of managers have had no formal writing training since their post-secondary education.

- Provide a short example or story.

> Like many managers, Ralph did not know what his role should be in implementing the new training levy. He decided to...

- Create a relevant analogy.

> A poorly-run business meeting, like a poorly-managed classroom, brings out the worst in the participants and achieves little. Just as classroom bullies can dominate, certain negative types can dominate meetings and create problems. Major types are...

- Give a relevant, striking quotation.

'I just dropped into this career by mistake', says Ms Jane Sonoski, after becoming the first female president of Dycon company.

Once you have appealed to your readers in the introduction, keep them with you. Consider the appropriate language level, number and kinds of examples and analogies, the addition of specific facts and figures, the use of graphics, and the appropriate tone to adopt. See what is acceptable by studying several issues of the publication.

Instructions

Instructions involve directions about processes, that is, how to do something, how something works, or how something happens. Writing about a process often requires you to be precise and accurate, in order to reduce confusion or incorrect actions (and subsequent injury).

There are a few simple principles for writing instructions. First, instructions should follow chronological order, as your readers often try to carry out each instruction as they read. A poor example is the set of instructions for assembling a desk, which had as its final direction to the reader: 'Remember to glue all pieces as you assemble them'!

Second, use the conditional pattern 'if...then' when writing instructions. Do not give the action first.

Push red button, but only if procedure A has failed.

The chances are that the reader will push the button and then read on. Instead, give the condition first.

If procedure A fails, push red button.

The conditional is used to highlight warnings, as it asks the reader first to consider whether the condition applies before carrying out the action.

Original: Wear a face mask if you use this solution in a enclosed space.

Revised: If you use this solution in an enclosed space, wear a face mask.

Third, instructions may have each step numbered or highlighted in some way to help readers follow more easily. Readers differ in their knowledge of the topic, and if you try to provide enough information to meet all needs, you may lose the clear sequence of steps. An effective solution is to use only essential information for the steps, but inform the reader of additional information elsewhere in the document that they can refer to.

What about adding personal observations and experiences? This is a difficult question. If you are writing instructions as a tutorial to replace face-to-face instruction, you might want to include this information. However, if you are writing straightforward operating instructions, you will probably find that readers do not want this extra information. Research has shown that many readers of computing manuals seldom use written information until they come to a problem (and even then they seek only the specific solution).

Page design is a specialised topic that is worth pursuing if much of your writing involves instructions. Research has shown that an effective page design can promote readers' understanding and reduce mistakes.

Letters

The organisation often dictates a corporate style for letters, for example, the arrangement of text on the page, degree of punctuation, and type of salutation and closing. The most common format is the full-block form, in which the main parts of a letter begin on the left-hand margin. However, in a case where management desires a different corporate image from that achieved by full block—for reasons of conservatism or aesthetics—other formats may be preferred. The usual arrangement of material is indicated below.

- **Writer's address and date**—With letterhead stationery, the address is omitted. Some writers include their direct telephone number or a reference number for the correspondence.
- **Addressee's name, position, company, and address**.
- **Salutation**—If the person's name is known, use it. If not, write 'Dear Sir or Madam', use the person's title (for example 'To the Chief Accountant'), or ring the company to find the name.
- **Heading** (subject line)—A heading is often used to direct the reader. It comes after the salutation, or in some cases can replace it.
- **Body**—The body of the letter is developed effectively by constructing each paragraph around a specific point. It is conventional for the last paragraph to be a courteous expression of appreciation, regard, or willingness to provide more information or undertake an action.
- **Close**—The close of the letter is usually the phrase 'Yours sincerely', 'Sincerely', or even 'Regards'. The term 'Yours faithfully' is less popular now.
- **Signature**—The writer may elect to sign with only his or her first name, if the addressee is a friend.
- **Name and title**—The writer's full name and title is typed immediately under the signature.

- **Enclosures**—The reader is referred to enclosures by the term 'Enc.' typed below the title.
- **Copies**—Use 'cc' to indicate that copies of the letter have been sent to other people.

It is part of the convention of good business letters that major ideas are stated early rather than late. Readers process information as they go along, so requests or complaints suddenly developed at the end of the letter can be confusing. For example, Simon writes to request money for a special project, but begins with a detailed description of the project. A reader's reaction is predictable: 'Why is he informing me about this?'

However, delaying tactics are sometimes acceptable when the writer is making unsolicited funding requests, such as a charity appeal, or presenting bad news. The delay allows neutral or pleasant information to 'sink in' first with the readers before negative or less acceptable information is given. For example, someone writing to an unsuccessful applicant usually first thanks the person for applying before revealing the negative information.

Ensure that the major message that you lead with is followed and developed by clear supporting points. A letter which begins with a request for funds and then follows with two long paragraphs about the growth of the company sets up a large inference 'leap' that not all readers will make.

Job application letters often have this problem, as the writer may assume that readers will make the necessary connections. The applicant who writes, 'My frequent trips to Asian countries have been productive and satisfying' assumes that readers will interpret this as 'valuable business contacts'. More effective might be the direct approach, with the writer giving the major point, 'I would bring to the position valuable business contacts', and following this with supporting information: 'In my frequent business trips to Asian countries, I have demonstrated that I can work productively and sensitively in different commercial environments'.

Memos

Because memos are in-house documents, writing effective ones usually relies on shaping your message according to your knowledge of the specific reader and organisational context. However, some guidelines apply in general.

In-house documents should be as carefully planned as those going outside your organisation. It is easy to make the mistake of assuming that because your readers are in the same organisation, they will share your view and understanding of the topic and its context. One research study indicates that writers can miscalculate even the specific language shared by others in an organisation and use jargon which their readers cannot understand.

Memos as organisational communication are prone to two common problems. First, people can write too many memos. By burying others in paper, they reduce the chances of their readers taking their communication seriously. Reserve memos for times that face-to-face communication is impossible or when the information needs to be formally documented. The second problem is that memos are often regarded as general correspondence, so it is not unusual for someone to find his or her supposedly confidential memo up on a notice board or attached to a meeting agenda.

If in doubt, consider your information, the context, and your readers. You may want to handle important subjects by discussing them more informally first and then writing a memo. The discussion creates its own context for the memo and directs your readers. If asked to write a memo, find out if it is to be formal: you do not want a handwritten scrawl reproduced for everyone at a board meeting. If in doubt, evaluate your topic, the context, your readers, and the level of formality.

A memo can usually have a headline or title to establish the main point for your readers. You also direct readers by referring to their particular organisational role, for example, member of a committee. If you do not do this, your readers do not know which role to be 'in'. How you address your reader also signals the memo's level of formality. For example, even if Cecily Warner is a close colleague, addressing your memo to 'Ms Warner' rather than 'Cecily' signals that it has a serious, formal nature.

Proposals

According to writing researchers Richard Freed and David Roberts, professional writers often have trouble differentiating between a proposal and a report. They suggest that a proposal 'analyzes a problem and then proposes an approach for solving it', whereas the report is the document produced after a study of the problem is completed (1989, p. 323).

No matter what the content (for example, personnel, services, products, finance), proposals often use the following format (Freed and Roberts, 1989, p. 329)

- situation/background/rationale
- objectives
- methods/procedures/approach
- qualifications
- costs
- benefits/significance/justification.

This format obviously will differ according to the demands of the organisation. For example, funding organisations usually stipulate a particular order, length, and level of specificity for grant proposals.

Besides the format, how are proposals constructed? According to writing educator Thomas Sawyer (1987), proposal writers should think of their document as an argument. He suggests these guidelines. First, consider the proposition. Ask, 'What action is being proposed?' and ensure that only one action is being proposed. (We also suggest that you ensure that the proposition is logical: see Chapter 4.) Second, if you are supporting the affirmative side of the proposition, you must give proof and answer certain questions. Prove that there is a need for a change and then argue that your proposal provides benefits, for example

- it solves the need
- it is a practical solution
- it is a fair solution
- it is the best plan.

Third, if you support the negative side of the proposition, you must remind your readers that the 'other' side needs to prove the points above. You can argue that the evidence presented is insufficient, is not trustworthy or is invalid, or that the inferences drawn are not logical. You can propose a better plan.

Reports

Reports fall into different categories, for example, progress reports, feasibility reports, and annual reports. Whatever the type, a report usually follows the format below.

- **Cover**—This usually gives the name of the organisation and suggests the 'image' of the report.
- **Title page**—The title page provides the context for readers and contains the report title, author's name, name of the organisation, date, report number (if applicable), and sometimes the name of the intended reader. The title should 'point' readers to information by being informative, straightforward, and specific.
- **Summary**—The summary encapsulates the report's major ideas, conclusion, and recommendations in one to three paragraphs. It is usually on a separate page or placed on the title page.
- **Table of contents**—The table shows the report's content and arrangement, providing an overview.
- **List of figures**—This list is useful for readers who only scan the report, as it allows them to find the relevant references quickly.
- **Glossary**—A glossary of terms can be useful when presenting technical material to general readers.
- **Introduction**—The introduction identifies the purpose and scope of the report as well as introducing the main message. At the end of the introduction, the reader should know the subject and your attitude. Some writers believe that they should be strictly neutral, but your business reports are usually better received if you develop your views. For example, if you want to persuade your readers, you may use the introduction to establish a definition or measure as a basis for the ideas developed in the report.

  It is conventional for the introduction to have a straightforward lead-in: 'This report describes the activities of... and suggests that...' However, other types of lead-ins may be acceptable (see Articles, page 71), depending on the type of report, audience, and organisation.

  A special type of introduction is called the 'funnel' (see Figure 5.3), because information is more specific in each succeeding sentence until the main message is given. The funnel is used with controversial topics,

General
(broad statement)

- To say that 'there is no new thing under the sun' would be ridiculous today.
- Technological growth has drastically changed our world, making life much simpler, and more convenient.
- Telephone, televisions, and radios, allow us to communicate directly with all parts of the earth; mass transportation enables us to travel faster and further than ever before.
- At the same time, technology has been destructive.
- The results of technology—pollution, urbanisation, and nuclear weapons expansion—are well-known threats to our quality of life.
- Yet, there is a much less recognised by-product of technology that has become one of the biggest threats to our lives: processed food.
- Through chemical and mechanical processing, many foods are stripped of their nutritional value and actually become potential health hazards.
- The magnitude of the dangers involved in the consumption of processed foods has yet to be realised by most people.
- Unless the public is informed and educated about these existing dangers, life as we know it today may be in jeopardy.

Specific
(main message)

Figure 5.3 Example of a funnel introduction for a report or speech

as it encourages readers to agree on certain general points before they read the main message. It can also be effective in speeches, as it gives listeners a chance to settle themselves before hearing the main message.
- **Body**—The body of the report develops the main message, as the writer provides evidence; explains; gives details and examples; defines terms and ideas; explores reasons, causes, effects; and points out similarities and differences.
- **Conclusion**—A conclusion, if included, is developed when you give your own opinions, interpreting the results or summarising the report. Conclusions are usually considered weak if totally new or irrelevant ideas are introduced; a sudden reversal negates all previous information; impossible claims or promises are made; or the report ends on an apology or complaint.

To write a powerful conclusion, end with a significant, relevant idea, for example, the greatest consequence or implication of the report's information. Some writers repeat a key term used in the introduction to tie together the whole report.

- **Recommendations**—Recommendations may be developed separately to assist those who will not read the whole document. This section is usually placed at the beginning of the report or after the conclusion.
- **Bibliography**—The bibliography is a list of all references used for the report. Sometimes writers include references to material that they believe their readers would find useful. References include books, articles, government reports, brochures, letters, talks, television and radio programs, and interviews. The bibliography is always in alphabetical order and should follow a standard arrangement (for an example, see the *Style Manual*, AGPS).
- **Appendices**—The appendices are reserved for information that is too extensive or unimportant to fit comfortably in the body of the report without interrupting the flow. For example, the results of a survey would be presented in the body, but interested readers should be able to read the survey itself and the details in the appendices. Readers should be alerted to the existence of an appendix by a reference to it as they read, for example, '(see Appendix B)'.

Problematic reports

Following the report format guarantees only that your information is set out in the expected way. Other problems commonly crop up for writers.

The report can be too long. The trend is for concise reports. This means more material is consigned to the appendices while the body of the report is divided more, with sub-headings to signal the different sub-topics to readers. Padding a report impresses only the least discerning readers. If you are concerned that your readers will not read the whole report, refer them to other sections rather than repeat information in different sections.

The report may contain inaccurate or conflicting data. Even one inaccuracy or data problem can weaken your credibility with readers. Always double-check facts and figures.

The report may be laden with jargon. Reports filled with jargon are acceptable when the readers are specialists in the particular subject matter. However, if the report is to be distributed to a wide range of readers, too much jargon destroys its power to communicate. If you must use jargon, try to keep at least the summary as simple and clear as possible.

The report may be hastily written. Some employers and clients have little idea of how much time is involved in writing a well-documented, succinct report. Many badly written reports can be traced to writers not being given the time to do a good job.

Résumés

The résumé is a difficult piece of writing: you must be succinct but thorough, persuasive but not boastful, present yourself well without unduly falsifying information, and suggest a steady accretion of relevant skills.

The résumé must be more than a fact sheet. It should reflect you, not only as an inventory of your qualifications and experience, but interpret these for the reader. The format of the résumé is usually as indicated below (see Figure 5.4 for a sample entry).

- **Personal information**—Give your name, address, telephone number. (Many applicants now do not state on their résumé their marital status, family details, ethnic background, or age.)
- **Education**—Record each educational institution that you have a degree or certificate from, and give both the degree/certificate awarded and the date of graduation. New graduates often include a summary of their subjects and results. Include all professional and on-the-job training, for example, staff development.
- **Work experience**—Give the most recent job first and develop it more. Include your job title, company, duration of employment, and your most important responsibilities and duties. Early jobs can be dispensed with or only briefly referred to.
- **Referees**—Provide names, titles, addresses, and telephone numbers. This information can also be placed instead in the application letter.
- **Additional information**—You may want to include your career objective, special activities or achievements (in work, the community), or personal interests.

| March 19..–April 19.. | Widget Production Pty Ltd |
| | Head of Accounting Department |

Achievements
- used the prototyping systems technique to implement a new accounts receivable system on schedule and 5 per cent below the projected costs
- developed an in-house invoicing system, managing a special team of departmental employees and consultants.

Other responsibilities included
- ensuring accuracy of a billing system for 10 000 customers or $3M monthly
- supervising ten staff
- dealing with all non-routine problems

Figure 5.4 A sample résumé entry, illustrating action and specifiying results. This entry could also have been developed in paragraph form

To develop a successful résumé, use the following tips.

Use action verbs

Activate your résumé by using action verbs like restructured, achieved, implemented, created.

> Original: I made the department more efficient by changing people's duties.
>
> Revised: I re-organised the department to...

Use 'boss' words

When applicable, use words that indicate management—'boss' words—such as managed, initiated, co-ordinated, chaired (see Figure 5.5). Steer away from 'helper' words, like assisted in, helped, took part in.

> Original: Was working in the record section as the manager.
>
> Revised: Managed staff of twelve in the records section.

Give specific results

Highlight your achievements, such as problems that you have solved and above-average gains that you have made. If possible, give specific outcomes.

administered	decided	expanded	introduced	presented
advanced	designed	extended	led	produced
analysed	determined	guided	managed	regulated
approved	developed	handled	negotiated	resolved
assigned	directed	headed	operated	revised
began	employed	implemented	ordered	scheduled
conducted	enlarged	improved	organised	served
controlled	established	inaugurated	oversaw	steered
co-ordinated	evaluated	increased	planned	supervised
created	executed	initiated	prepared	trained

Figure 5.5 Enliven your résumé by using some of these 'boss' words and action words

Original: Restructured department last year.

Revised: By restructuring the department last year, I reduced absenteeism by 10 per cent and reduced manufacturing costs by 8 per cent.

Apply the 'so what?' test

Asking 'so what?' questions ensures that only relevant information is included and suggests how material may need to be made more significant for readers to understand. For example, the 'so what?' test may encourage you to list only those personal interests which are valued in the work environment.

Follow the standard appearance

The standard résumé is typed. Of course there should be no typographical or spelling errors. Some people suggest that a résumé should be no longer than two pages; others prefer a more detailed résumé. A good rule is to reduce your information as much as possible, but opt for more pages and white space rather than make your résumé cramped and difficult to read.

A résumé is usually printed on neutral-coloured paper (white, tan, or grey). If you want your résumé to stand out, you can of course print it on different coloured paper or use a different colour of ink. Choose carefully: one applicant presented a résumé with brown type on very bright yellow paper, which looked great but was impossible to read. You can also try a different format. We have seen résumés made up like a PR release, a 'wanted' poster, and a brochure. Remember your readers and the type of job you are applying for. What may work well in some fields may not be acceptable in others.

Avoid 'form' résumés

You need to tailor your résumé for each application. Do not rely on a form résumé. We do not recommend your getting one professionally printed (with your photograph on it) that you use for job after job.

Write a persuasive application letter

Gone are the days when an applicant would write an application letter that said only, 'Enclosed is my résumé. I look forward to talking to you'. The application letter is now seen as a chance to 'sell' your key attributes. Because of this purpose, the following information is often included.

In the introduction, refer to the position (and position number if applicable) and the source, for example, the name of the newspaper carrying the advertisement. Remember also to state that you are applying for the position.

In the body, you can develop an argument that you are the best candidate by using some of the following guidelines

- give evidence of your interest in the position and the organisation
- state your career goal and shorter-term objectives
- highlight your most important qualification
- state what makes you an asset for this job, this organisation
- consider how you can significantly contribute to the organisation
- make sure that you address the specific, advertised selection criteria.

In the conclusion, you can

- refer to your résumé being enclosed (or just have 'Enc.' below your name)
- request an interview at a time convenient to the reader
- if necessary, state how and when you can be contacted
- invite the reader to contact your referees
- state details of your availability.

What should *not* be included in the letter? Readers usually respond negatively to applicants who mention salary or work conditions, such as holidays; complain about their present position; or argue that the position be given to them on compassionate grounds (for example, because of their age, family problems, or other difficulties).

Prime your referees

Referees vouch that you have the experience, personal qualities, and work habits needed by the organisation. Help yourself by choosing your referees carefully. Select people who are senior to you and who have some standing in your organisation or profession. It also helps if they can write well.

Help them support you. If you leave a job, ask for a reference immediately. If you wait too long, your referee will forget the details of what you did and how you handled the work.

In many cases, general written references are ignored, as companies prefer to ask your referee to comment on your suitability for a specific position. You can help your referees handle this by informing them that you are applying for a position and then sending them the advertisement and a copy of the résumé that you have used for the specific job application.

Develop a work portfolio

In some professions such as photography and architecture, potential employers expect to see an applicant's portfolio. Organisational writers can be invited to include written work samples, descriptions of achievements and responsibilities for projects, and testimonials (thank you letters, evaluations).

Summary

The summary or synopsis is an accurate, condensed version of a document, talk, or meeting. If part of a report, the summary is usually presented on a separate page at the front or included on the title page. A summary of a book or article includes bibliographical details on the same page.

Use the following steps to make it easier for you to write a useful summary.

- Read the document through to establish the main message and tone.
- Then, taking one paragraph or section at a time, locate key points (find important words or phrases) and important relationships between main ideas (for example, cause and effect). Ignore whatever seems repetitive, trivial, or incidental. It may help to photocopy the document then use a highlighter pen to mark the key points.
- Summarise the document, using your own words and not looking at the original document. This is usually written as a sentence outline or a paragraph.
- Check your version against the document to ensure that you have covered the main message and key points.
- Condense and re-arrange what you have written. Replace a phrase with a word, a sentence with a phrase. Re-arrange the sequence if this will help your readers.

A summary is a condensation of the writer's words. In a sense you replace the original writer and summarise as that person. Imagine an article, written by Smith, about a peer review system. You must write for Smith

Not: Smith wants to establish a peer review system.
But: A peer review system should be established.

You cannot interpret or comment within the summary itself. Such comments belong in a separate paragraph, in which you clearly move from summarising to evaluating. Imagine that the original document states: 'The mission statement is important to any organisation as it brings together the diverse elements and provides a unifying force for planning what the organisation will achieve'. How would you summarise rather than evaluate?

Not: I thought the comment on the mission statement was good.
But: The mission statement unifies the organisation.

CONCLUSION

Formats are part of the communication etiquette surrounding professional writing. The etiquette is made up of expectations about what is written, when, how, and why. To be an effective writer, you not only need to know these general expectations for the different types of writing, but be confident of when they can be ignored to improve the communication for a specific audience or situation. When this etiquette hardens into strict writing formulas, writers lose the flexibility which business situations usually require. Writers can meet their readers' needs by clarifying the function of their document: 'What do I want the reader to do?' They can then establish a framework or macro-structure which clearly identifies how the main message will be developed.

References

Anderson, P. (1985). 'What survey research tells us about writing at work',
    in L. Odell and D. Goswami (eds), *Writing in nonacademic settings*, pp. 3–83,
    New York: The Guilford Press.
Freed, R. and Roberts, D. (1989). 'The nature, classification, and generic structure
    of proposals'. *Journal of Technical Writing and Communication*, 4, pp. 317–351.
Sawyer, T. (1987). 'Commentary: argument'. *Journal of Technical Writing and
    Communication*, 17, 3, pp. 253–263.

CHAPTER 6

STRUCTURING PARAGRAPHS

Clearly-structured paragraphs help your readers understand the development of your main message. Research suggests that certain ways of structuring a paragraph can increase the amount of information your readers comprehend.

WHAT IS A PARAGRAPH?

When people define paragraphs, they may think first of appearance. A paragraph is sometimes thought of as merely a visual unit, that is, a way to 'clump' information to make a document more attractive. They may consider the paragraph's length, as this has changed over the years, from ones over a page long in nineteenth-century fiction to the present practice of shorter paragraphs. Certainly we can pick out paragraphs by their appearance.

The important point, however, is that effective writers create paragraphs not on a visual basis but on the basis of function. They structure information to meet the needs of their readers by signalling the topic and its development.

A paragraph, then, identifies to the reader what the writer believes is related material. In medieval manuscripts, scribes placed a mark (¶) in the margin to show a change in topic. This mark evolved into the indentation used today. Writers use this method of arranging material to signal differences in these informational 'clumps'. For example, one paragraph may introduce new ideas, while another develops previously stated ideas or presents a shift in time, space, or direction.

A paragraph which successfully communicates information to readers exhibits three important qualities

- **it is complete**—it provides as much information as the reader needs
- **it is unified**—it is built around a central idea and has a consistent tone and point of view

- **it is ordered**—it is coherent; it provides a pattern that makes sense to the reader.

These three qualities indicate how information can be effectively developed within paragraphs.

MAKE PARAGRAPHS COMPLETE

Effective paragraphs are complete, that is, they provide as much information as the reader needs or expects. A common writing problem is that of leaving readers with an immediate question in their minds at the end of a paragraph without answering it in the next. This problem suggests that the writer is not sensitive to the readers' level of knowledge or the connections that they are trying to make as they read. Research on reading and mental processes helps to explain how readers read and comprehend.

What is your opinion of this paragraph?

> Basically human beings organise in order to get things done. Corporate executives try to build a strong culture for two reasons. Dale Carnegie was the first to link communication skill with managerial effectiveness. The presence of these linkages reveals patterns of horizontal communication between different groups. Some experts reject the claim that electronic information-processing technology leads to recentralisation of authority. (?)

The paragraph above *looks* like a paragraph but it lacks logic. It was deliberately developed so that it lacks coherence (it was concocted by taking five sentences at random from a book on organisational communication). Yet you probably tried to make sense of it and perhaps even re-read it in attempting to comprehend its main message. Why?

The answer lies with *schema theory* (see Chapter 2). We interpret new experiences and information by comparing them with already familiar experiences and information. Readers do this as they read, using their expectations of what paragraphs look like and how information should be developed. If information is set up to look like a paragraph, readers will try to process the information accordingly. Readers also interpret information according to its context and to their knowledge.

By imagining what readers know and understanding how they process information, writers can more confidently decide the content and structure of paragraphs. For example, consider this memo Andrew wrote to remind staff to use the dot matrix printer for drafts instead of the more expensive laser printer.

> Warning: Use the dot matrix printer for drafts. The laser printer costs much more, and this is all charged to the department. Some people are even using the laser printer for multiple copies, like a photocopier!

A week later, everyone is still using the laser printer. What has gone wrong? If Andrew had considered how little the staff know about computing, he would have realised they probably do not know that the printing costs differ or that they can choose which printer to print from. Their poor computing schema suggests that Andrew must also educate them if his communication is to be successful. Including more information helps these particular readers.

> When you are printing a draft or an in-house document, use the dot matrix printer instead of the laser printer. It gives good quality print-outs and is much cheaper to run.
>
> To use the dot matrix printer, follow these steps.
> First...
> Second...
> Third...
>
> A laser-printed copy is also much more expensive than a photocopy. For multiple copies, always use the photocopier, not the laser printer.

CREATE UNIFIED PARAGRAPHS

A paragraph is unified if it keeps to the same topic, tone, and point of view. Violating one of these aspects of the paragraph can create problems, especially if the reader must re-read the paragraph to make sense of it.

Keep the same topic

Consider this paragraph.

> The last shipment of goods has not yet showed up. My company needs to know the shipments, so this is a problem. My father, who founded the company, always said that it's best to be honest to customers and expect them to be the same to you. This is a trait that is too often missing these days. Notification of shipping dates would be helpful, as it would help us schedule our workers more effectively.

Instead of providing straightforward information, the writer lets the topic of the paragraph veer from a shipment problem to honesty. The writer could help the reader comprehend by settling on one main topic and ensuring that the rest of the paragraph supports it.

> The last shipment has not yet showed up. Planning around shipments is important to our company, as staff workloads can be flexible. Consequently, I would appreciate knowing the actual shipping dates of goods being sent to us.

This paragraph could still be improved, but with its focus made clear, readers do not need to re-read to comprehend.

Keep the same tone

Changing tone within a paragraph can be jarring to readers. Consider this example.

> I have great pleasure in informing you that your job application has been successful. Please reply within one week regarding your acceptance. You will be expected to take up duties within the month, and re-location expenses will be paid if the necessary receipts are presented to finance division. And if you aren't too flaked out after your move, drop in for a chinwag before taking up your duties.

This example is extreme, to illustrate how changing the tone from formal to highly informal within a single paragraph can confuse readers. Other examples of tonal patterns are impersonal–personal, enthusiastic–doubtful, friendly–hostile, serious–humorous, authoritative–modest. A move from one to the other may be plausible within a document, but not within a paragraph.

Keep the same point of view

Changing the point of view is a common fault that can usually be picked up during revision.

> You will need to fill out the Authority to Travel form before you leave. Then take it to your supervisor for a recommendation. Once this has been signed by the supervisor, the employee may proceed with travel arrangements.

The writer has moved from addressing the reader in second person (you, [you] take, your) to third person (the employee). This change may be acceptable within a longer document but can disturb the unity when made within a single paragraph.

Make Paragraphs Ordered

An ordered paragraph uses a familiar pattern to help readers understand the logical connections between ideas. A pattern ensures that sentences are not completely independent. Each sentence has a function, that is, a reason for being there. Think of each sentence growing out of the sentence preceding it.

Functions of a sentence include

- compare
- concede
- conclude
- contrast
- define
- describe
- evaluate

- elaborate
- exemplify
- identify cause/result
- narrate
- particularise
- prove

- qualify
- refute
- rephrase
- state
- summarise
- support.

These functions can fit into larger paragraph patterns. Writers may use *conventional patterns*, *top–down processing*, and *thematic development* to establish an order for readers.

Use conventional patterns

Readers are used to certain patterns of information, so effective writers use these patterns to help readers follow the development of their ideas. Common patterns developed within paragraphs are analogy, cause and effect, classification, comparison and contrast, definition, description, process, example or illustration, partition, problem and solution, and question and answer.

Analogy

The analogy clarifies or explains an unfamiliar idea by comparing it with what is familiar to readers.

> Example 1: Tokyo Station (unfamiliar) during peak hour/a disturbed ant-hill (familiar).
>
> Example 2: Learning to use a computer (unfamiliar)/learning to use a sewing machine (familiar).

> Example 3: The departmental review (unfamiliar)/employee appraisal (familiar).

Cause and effect

This pattern is developed in two ways. Either by explaining a cause and then the effect, or by giving the effect first and then its cause. Depending on your audience's level of knowledge, you can explain the causes and effects or merely list them.

> Example 1: Poor working conditions (cause)/high absenteeism (effect).
>
> Example 2: Funds shortage (effect)/lower sales figures (cause).

Classification

Classification means grouping according to common characteristics. Consider what groupings are most relevant to your readers. For example, a report on equipment orders that has information classified by prices or distributors may be unsatisfactory to managers wanting information classified by functions or needs. Make the basis of your classification clear to your readers and stick to it.

> Staff development programs could be classified by costs, popularity, subject matter, or target group.

Comparison and contrast

Comparisons present at least two possible options. Decide the most relevant points of comparison and the order in which they should be presented. Two patterns are common

- develop the points for Subject A and then the points for Subject B
- develop point 1 for Subjects A then B, then point 2, and so on.

> Example 1:
> Site A: parking, office space, rental costs
> Site B: parking, office space, rental costs.

Example 2:
Parking: Site A and Site B
Office space: Site A and Site B
Rental costs: Site A and Site B.

Definition

Definition is not often used to develop a whole paragraph, except in legal documents and policy reports. However, it is a valuable way to develop information. You can use a formal definition when dealing with technical information that your readers may not understand.

Some writers find it helpful to write a formal definition by creating three distinct parts: the term itself, its general class, and the characteristics that differentiate it from others in this class. This short definition can then be expanded within the paragraph.

Diffusion of innovation
is a theory of communication
that suggests a predictable acceptance pattern for new products and services.

You can also use other techniques to define

- representative example, anecdote, or incident
- comparison or contrast
- description (distinct or typical features, parts, qualities)
- example
- partition
- classification
- origin (history, background)
- effect or result
- use or application
- negation (distinguishing terms from related ones), for example, 'when we talk about... we don't mean...'

Description

Description helps readers visualise an object, event, or process. There are some points to remember about writing descriptions.

Decide how 'colourful' your description can be, by considering your readers and the context. For example, what is suited to advertising differs from what is acceptable in scientific writing.

Choose a logical method of progression, for example left to right, outside to inside, up to down.

If you are describing something that is abstract ('maturity'), evaluative ('a good employee'), or qualitative ('perceptions of management'), you should also define your terms. Giving your terms of reference helps to prevent misunderstanding. For example, readers could have extremely different views of what constitutes a good employee.

Process

The process pattern is used primarily for instructional material, as it involves the steps or processes of making or doing something. The steps are given chronologically, that is, in the sequence that readers are expected to follow.

Example or illustration

A developed example or illustration can help readers understand an abstraction or generalisation. The writer can also give an example and then move to the relevant generalisation. This shifting from the abstract to the concrete provides the variety and depth necessary for effective writing. Writing completely at an abstract level quickly loses readers, while writing completely at a concrete level ignores the necessary connections and inferences that readers need to make.

Partition

Partition is the term used for describing the parts of an entity. For example, if you are describing the new departments of a restructured company, you are using the partition pattern. The writer must select a reasonable basis for separating something into parts; for the above example, you could focus on function (what the departments do) or organisational location (where they will exist in the hierarchy).

Problem and solution

In a sense, the problem and solution pattern is like cause and effect. A problem is developed or stated and the solution given and explained. The link between the problem and its solution needs to be made. It is not enough to write the following.

> The workload is too great at year's end. We need to hire a temporary accountant.

Your reader would expect a line of argument, with proof or reasons, linking the problem to the proposed solution. Consider how the problem–solution pattern of the example is strengthened by adding an argument.

> The workload is too great at year's end. All four members of the accounting department had to work back consistently for six months this year. Instead of expecting them to do this next year, we could hire a temporary accountant.

Question and answer

A variant of the problem–solution pattern is the question and answer. Ensure that the question you pose is worthy of your reader's consideration.

Use top–down order

Research has shown that writers have a better chance of communicating effectively if their readers can immediately place what they read in a context. Readers commonly use a mental process called the top–down method to process and organise information. They use the first idea that they read to develop a context for the information which follows. Research into top–down reading suggests that writers should develop the first sentence of the paragraph carefully as it does operate as a signal to readers. A writer unaware of this may inadvertently miscue the reader. For example, consider this beginning for a paragraph.

> The demands placed on some of the electronic withdrawal methods, particularly those requiring the involvement of different financial institutions, caused difficulties for some members.

What does the reader expect next? As the organising cues are the terms electronic withdrawal methods and difficulties, readers would probably expect to read more details about the electronic withdrawal methods and ways that the difficulties were solved. After setting up this immediate context, however, the writer does not follow through.

> The demands placed on some of the electronic withdrawal methods, particularly those requiring the involvement of different financial institutions, caused difficulties for some members. A great deal of analysis and refinement is being undertaken to reduce the instances of 'failed' transactions and members are assured that every effort is being made to improve the service. While our Representatives and member cheque book holders were asked to participate in a trial of the bank's point-of-sale network, that trial has not yet been completed. It is hoped to make

> the bank link available to the broad membership during the new financial year.

The second sentence seems to progress logically from the first, but the last two relate only vaguely. To provide a clearer top–down development for readers, the writer could have started with a more encompassing sentence.

> Research and changes in the electronic transaction service will make it easier and more convenient for members.

A clearer line of reasoning can then be developed if the second sentence concerns the research of the point-of-sale network, followed by information about changes to prevent failed transactions.

Use thematic order

Reading is a progressive activity, as readers develop meaning from one word, phrase, and sentence to the next. A writer can control the pattern of emphasis by deciding what comes first in a sentence. This front part of the sentence is called the **thematic slot**. Linguists suggest that writers can govern how a theme or main message develops within the paragraph by deciding what to place in the thematic slot.

For example, consider how the effect of the same message changes depending on how the first sentence begins in the four variations below.

> Example 1: The company cannot continue its high level of employment because of budget constraints. We see no alternative but to dissolve your position.
>
> Example 2: The high level of employment that this company has offered is no longer possible, because of budget constraints. We see no alternative but to dissolve your position.
>
> Example 3: Unfortunately, the company cannot continue its high level of employment because of budget constraints. We see no alternative but to dissolve your position.
>
> Example 4: Because of budget constraints, the company cannot continue its high level of employment. We see no alternative but to dissolve your position.

In a longer paragraph, the progression of information at the front of each sentence can create a definite pattern and make the information easier to comprehend. Consider the poor use of the thematic slots in this somewhat wooden paragraph.

> *Budget constraints* have lifted and the company can redevelop its research branch. *We* see as the first priority that the three unfilled positions in your department be advertised immediately. *Discussion of* this as soon as possible would be appreciated. *Perhaps* some thought should be given to revising one position so that we have specialist staff for our new sales campaign.

The thematic pattern of—budget constraints/we/discussion/perhaps—seems confusing, whereas slight changes could highlight the 'solution' theme or pattern.

> *Redevelopment* of the research branch is now possible, as budget constraints have been lifted. *The first priority* is to advertise immediately the three unfilled positions in your department. *As well, revising* one position would provide a specialist staff member for our new sales campaign. *Could* we discuss this as soon as possible?

Here a clear thematic order is prominent, with readers progressing from the main idea, redevelopment, to details (the first priority and as well), and then to an action (could) being requested.

SIGNAL RELATIONSHIPS IN PARAGRAPHS

Words and phrases within the paragraph provide the links which signal to readers the relationships of ideas. Used appropriately, these links are the 'invisible glue' holding the paragraph together; used poorly, they can mislead readers.

The most common ways to link information within the paragraph are to repeat words and phrases, and to use synonyms, parallel structures, pronouns, and connectors.

Repeat words and phrases

Repeating key words or phrases provides a common thread that unifies the paragraph. In factual writing, such repetition is more acceptable than using elegant variations which can confuse readers. Consider how effectively key words are repeated in the following example.

> Costs of paper supplies have increased dramatically this year, and as a result, staff have been asked to *restrict* their *photocopying*. *Photocopying* is now *restricted* to the most important documents and personal *copying* is being discouraged. Staff have so far complied with these *restrictions*.

Use synonyms

Synonyms are sometimes appropriate, especially if repetition makes a document read like a primary school text. In the previous example, there are three variants of the word restricted; one could be replaced by the word curtailed.

Use parallel structure

Parallel structure (refer to Chapter 7) means that an identical pattern is set up, for example, noun with noun, phrase with phrase, clause with clause. Structures which are not parallel can be jarring to readers and force them to re-read to get the sense of the sentences.

> The company is interested in higher sales, lower overheads, and wants to help staff reach their potential.

The three equal components of this sentence become parallel when the same structure is used.

> The company is interested in making higher sales, lowering overheads, and helping staff reach their potential.

Use pronouns

You can create strong links by using pronouns which refer to previous information. Pronouns include

- this, that, these, those
- who, whom
- he, she, it, we, they
- his, her, its, our, their
- few, several, some, many, most.

The link becomes a problem when a pronoun does not connect to a preceding noun.

> The department will hold its Christmas party next Friday. Drinks will be provided. They will also have a champagne raffle.

Here the pronoun 'they' has nothing to connect to. It refers to the people in the department, but only the department itself is mentioned. It would be better to change the sentence to, 'A champagne raffle will also be held'.

Use connectors

Connectors are words and phrases that clarify relationships between ideas. For example, the term 'in contrast' lets readers know that the following information will be the opposite of what came before. Connectors which signal relationships within and between paragraphs include

- to add or extend an idea—and, too, also, in addition, next, moreover, finally, furthermore, or, again, in fact, indeed, besides; first, second, third; for one thing
- to show similarity—as, likewise, similarly, once again, in like manner, in the same way
- to show the expected or true—to be sure, of course, as a matter of fact, naturally, surely, it follows that
- to indicate an exception, reservation, contrast, alternative—however, even so, yet, still, nevertheless, but, although, on the other hand; on the contrary, notwithstanding, surely, whereas, conversely
- to indicate qualification—frequently, especially, usually, occasionally, specifically; in particular, in general
- to indicate concession—of course, no doubt, doubtless, granted that, certainly
- to repeat or intensify—in other words, indeed, to repeat, to put it another way, for one thing, as noted earlier, in any case
- to indicate a result or consequence—because, therefore, consequently, so, accordingly, hence, thus, finally, as a result, as a consequence, for this reason, and that is why
- to give a reason—because, since, for
- to summarise—therefore, in summary, to conclude, in brief, in a word, all in all, on the whole, then, what we have then, what this all adds up to, in short
- to illustrate or give an example—thus, for instance, for example, that is, namely, to illustrate
- to show a time relationship—presently, meanwhile, soon, shortly, later, thereafter, before, immediately, afterwards, when I returned, in the meantime, thereupon, at last following this, from then on
- to show a spatial relationship—between the two locations, in the next room, at the front of the building, beyond this point; across the way.

Writing problems develop when a writer uses a connector that miscues readers. For example, sometimes writers use words like 'therefore' and 'however' because they sound right, but they do not consider the relationship being signalled. The word 'therefore' should logically be followed by a conclusion or result, and 'however' should be followed by a contrasting statement.

CONCLUSION

Writing well-developed paragraphs takes practice and thought. It is important to consider how information is being developed from sentence to sentence and how effectively the paragraph communicates as a whole. A few simple rules can help prevent problem paragraphs.

Do not take your readers' knowledge for granted. Explain fully and provide definitions and examples.

Do not have missing links. Keep your readers with you by repeating words and using parallel structure, synonyms, connectors, and pronouns.

Do not leave questions unanswered. Consider questions that readers could still ask at the end of a paragraph and check where the answers are located in your document. If they are too far away, rewrite.

Keep a consistent topic, tone, and point of view. Switching these unnecessarily makes the paragraph difficult to read.

Ensure that paragraphs are not bloated. Be wary of what one writer calls 'intellectually empty kilojoules' in your writing. Bloated paragraphs stretch the patience of your readers by making your line of thought difficult to follow.

CHAPTER 7

SHAPING SENTENCES

WRITING SIMPLY AND CLEARLY

In this chapter we discuss ways to write sentences that are clearly structured and grammatically correct by examining the most common pitfalls in sentence construction. Having this knowledge will not guarantee that every sentence you write will be perfect on the first draft, but it will help you streamline your sentence-editing process and increase your chances of producing clearly-written sentences for your reader.

In our experience, high-school English does not prepare writers for creating the kind of clear, informative, focused, concise, and dynamic prose that professional readers require. Many business writers, both novice and experienced, think that the best writing style is characterised by big words and impressive-sounding sentences. They are unaware that impenetrable prose alienates their readers because they lack the wisdom of George Bernard Shaw, who said he was pleased that everyone knew he was a well-educated man, because that meant he could write simply and not have to impress anyone with a 'grand' style.

What is the best way to learn to write simply and clearly? As we pointed out in our Preface, you cannot learn to write by relying on the large body of what passes for scholarship in business communication. Too often the practical advice in business writing text books consists of empty commonplaces and unfounded precepts that are not particularly helpful to writers faced with complex stylistic decisions.

One of the most popular examples of this sort of advice can be found in handbooks for business letter-writing, in which authors recommend that writers use the seemingly-sensible 'Cs' mnemonic—clarity, conciseness, correctness, courtesy, credibility, concreteness, coherence, comprehensiveness, confidence, character, conversational tone, and the content of the correspondent's communication.

We do not dispute the fact that these qualities are desirable in letters, but lists like this constitute empty advice if they are not accompanied by specific training for writers in how to incorporate such qualities into their documents.

A more reliable way to improve your writing is to increase your knowledge of sentence structure and sentence-level problems. By doing this, you are better equipped to avoid the usage problems at the sentence level that may disorient readers and lessen your credibility as a competent writer. When readers are bothered by usage errors, their reaction may go beyond your document to your company's products and services.

COMMON SENTENCE-LEVEL PROBLEMS

A study reported in the Spring 1990 issue of *The Journal of Business Communication* (27:2, p. 146) revealed the most distracting usage errors recorded by 400 members of the American Association for Business Communication and 400 company vice-presidents. These are exemplified in the following sentences.

> Example 1: He focused all his energies on his personal goals he never wavered from his chosen path.
>
> Example 2: Small companies suffer in a tight labour market. One of their problems being that they can't compete for qualified personnel.
>
> Example 3: Employee pilferage though it can jeopardise a company's survival is often ignored by management.
>
> Example 4: Looking very tired and worn, a decision was finally reached by the committee.
>
> Example 5: Most people he encounters are impressed by his calm manner, meticulous attire, and being ambitious.
>
> Example 6: The vice-president directed my associate and I to submit reports to the executive committee.

Can you identify the problems in these sentences? Can you also rewrite each sentence, if necessary, to eliminate the problem and make the sentence even more effective? We have removed the obvious error in each sentence in our answers below and noted the page in this book where we discuss the problem, but further rewriting would make these sentences even more effective.

> Example 1: He focused all his energies on his personal goals; he never wavered from his chosen path. (See The fused or run-on sentence, page 106.)

Example 2: Small companies suffer in a tight labour market, one of their problems being that they can't compete for qualified personnel. (See The sentence fragment, page 107.)

Example 3: Employee pilferage, though it can jeopardise a company's survival, is often ignored by management. (See Chapter 10, page 165; commas are used to set off an 'aside'.)

Example 4: The committee, looking very tired and worn, finally reached a decision. (See The unattached or dangling 'modifier', page 108.)

Example 5: Most people he encounters are impressed by his calm manner, meticulous attire, and ambitiousness. (See Lack of parallel structure, page 110.)

Example 6: The vice-president directed my associate and me to submit reports to the executive committee. (Objective pronoun after a verb, see Pronoun problems, page 118.)

If you had difficulty identifying and correcting the errors, this chapter should be very useful to you in improving your writing. Most executives regard grammatically-correct and structurally-clear writing as essential to a positive image.

Before dealing in detail with the errors, however, we need to examine the most common sentence patterns that occur in English, because we believe that to write clearly you need to understand basic English sentence structure (syntax) as well as grammar (conventional rules).

Standard Sentence Patterns

First things first. How do we define the term 'sentence'?

A sentence expresses a complete thought, which can be in the form of a statement, a command, a question, an exclamation, or a condition.

Statement: This book examines principles for effective professional writing.

Command: Make sure that you practise these principles.

Question: Do you expect your writing to improve?

Exclamation: What far-reaching changes have taken place in the management of information in organisations since the advent of computers!

Condition: If all professional writers were supplied with PCs, organisations would cut costs considerably.

In a straightforward statement such as the first example, a sentence usually has a subject (This book) and a verb (examines) which tells us something about the subject. Verbs express action (examines) or state of being (is, seem).

Being familiar with the six basic sentence patterns that are listed below can help you to construct sentences which can be expanded or inverted.

> Pattern 1: Subject + verb
> Writers   write.

The subject 'writers' tells who or what is doing an action or being described. The verb 'write' tells what the action is.

> Pattern 2: Subject + verb + direct object
> Writers   write   documents.

The direct object 'documents' tells who or what is receiving the action.

> Pattern 3: Subject + verb + direct object + indirect object
> Writers   write   documents   for the organisation.

The indirect object 'organisation' is the object of the preposition 'for'. Prepositions (for example, by, with, for, to, of, and from) relate (in time or space) the nouns or pronouns that follow them to another part of the sentence.

> Pattern 4: Subject + verb + modifier
> Writers   write   clearly.

The modifier 'clearly' gives more information about the verb.

> Pattern 5: Subject + linking verb + subjective complement
> Writers   are   useful.

'Are' is a linking verb and 'useful' complements (rounds off) the subject.

Pattern 6: Expletive construction
There are many writers in organisations.

An expletive construction such as 'There are' or 'It is' displaces the subject of a sentence. Expletives have no meaning. They simply take the subject's place. Over-using expletives will weaken your sentences, as you can see from examples 1 and 2 below.

Example 1: It is necessary for organisational writers to write reader-friendly documents.

Example 2: There is a need for organisational writers to write reader-friendly documents.

Pattern 5 also produces a weak sentence.

Example 3: Reader-friendly documents are a necessity for organisational writers to write.

Pattern 4 produces a sentence that is preferable to the others.

Example 4: Organisational writers need to write reader-friendly documents.

By not using an expletive construction or the weak verb 'is', it is more direct, it is clearer, and it is more concise—qualities that Aristotle considered to be the chief virtues of good writing style 2500 years ago. Nothing has changed.

The above sentence patterns are examples of simple sentences—sentences that have only one verb. There are two other sentence types within this classification: compound sentences and complex sentences. They are illustrated in the examples below.

Sentence type 1: Simple sentence

The proposal was complete.

Sentence type 2: Compound sentence—two complete thoughts in co-ordination

The proposal was complete and was ready to send out.

Sentence type 3: Complex sentence—two complete thoughts, one in subordination to the other

The proposal was complete when I read it.

You can start off with any of these three kinds of sentence and build up your sentence further by adding or 'embedding' more information. We discuss this further in the next section.

INEFFECTIVE SENTENCES

An effective sentence is one which can be easily and unambiguously understood on a first reading. The most commonly-voiced complaint about sentences is that a reader needs to re-read them because they are too long and rambling and/or unclear. This problem usually occurs

- because a writer tacks 'extra bits' onto a sentence by using the conjunction 'and', or
- embeds 'extra bits' into a sentence, separating parts of a sentence that should be reasonably close to each other.

The following sentence is an example of one which rambles. It needs to be broken up into more than one sentence.

Original: The members present spanned many years reflecting the wide interest in the Association and it is to be hoped that this interest will continue with a strong turnout for the Annual General Meeting.

Improved: The members present spanned many years. We hope that this wide interest in the Association will continue with a strong turnout for the Annual General Meeting.

Resist the temptation to fit as much into a sentence as you can. Break up longwinded sentences such as the following.

Original: The distribution of this document commences the 'Live Operation' of this department and remember we are here to HELP.

Improved: The distribution of this document commences the 'Live Operation' of this department. Remember, we are here to help.

Original: The project has enhancing learning as its central focus and it will aim to assist trainers to critically reflect on their training practices.

Improved: The central focus of this project is to enhance learning. Its aim is to assist trainers to critically reflect on their training practices.

The following sentence is difficult for a reader to process because the writer has included an explanation which interferes with the main message of the sentence.

Original: Whoever borrowed the office copy which is the only copy of the manual at the beginning of the year, could you please return it to us as soon as possible.

Improved: The office copy of the computer manual, which was borrowed at the beginning of the year, has not been returned. We need the manual for reference. Please return it urgently.

You can see the possibilities for embedding information in a sentence. There is nothing intrinsically wrong with an embedded construction; try to make sure, however, that you do not strain your reader's short-term memory.

Which of the following sentences do you prefer?

Example 1: Because a proposal needs to be persuasive, Janet checked every aspect of its presentation.

Example 2: Janet, because a proposal needs to be persuasive, checked every aspect of its presentation.

Example 3: Janet checked every aspect of the presentation of her proposal because a proposal needs to be persuasive.

Most readers would probably find the third version easiest to follow.

However, being able to construct sentences based on standard patterns is not enough. Professional writers also need to be familiar with the other subtleties of syntax and grammar that we identify in the following common sentence-level problems.

Although we are reluctant to prescribe 'rules', here are sixteen sentence-level problems that you should try to avoid. These problems are, in general, structural ones, and can cause difficulties for your readers.

SPECIFIC SENTENCE-LEVEL PROBLEMS

The fused or run-on sentence

This occurs when two complete sentences run together with no separating punctuation. The reader gets to the end of the sentence then usually has to re-read, supplying the missing punctuation so the sentence can make sense.

> Original: The final figures were in the sitting member was re-elected.

Make the fused sentence into two sentences, or, if the two statements are closely related, use a semicolon.

> Improved: The final figures were in. The sitting member was re-elected.
>
> Or: The final figures were in; the sitting member was re-elected.

The comma splice

This is similar to the previous problem, except that a comma is used to join together (splice) two separate sentences—a job that it was not designed to do. Punctuate the two thoughts as two sentences.

> Original: The trams did not run, people were late for work.
>
> Improved: The trams did not run. People were late for work.

Here are some further examples of the comma splice:

> Example 1: If the duty programmer is not available phone the next available programmer, if there is still no response continue down the list until a response is received.

Improve the sentence by starting a new sentence after 'available programmer'.

> Example 2: This information is required urgently, please have your lists returned to the Exchange before Thursday.

Start a new sentence after 'urgently'.

> Example 3: Journalists spend many of their formative years seeking good stories, suddenly they have to turn around and direct a newsroom.

Start a new sentence after 'stories'.

The sentence fragment

A sentence fragment is a non-sentence. It is a string of words which is punctuated as a sentence but fails to make sense on its own because it lacks an independent subject and a verb.

> Original 1: Because the computer 'crashed'.
>
> Original 2: Even though they are unaware of this fact.

For sentence fragments to 'make sense', add a subject or verb, or join them to another sentence. When you are editing, check connecting words like although, whenever, because, since, and if to make sure they are integrated into the sentence by being linked to another thought.

> Improved 1: We couldn't process the results because the computer 'crashed'.
>
> Improved 2: Even though they are unaware of this fact, many people are eligible for this payment.

Some writers regard sentence fragments as acceptable when they follow a complete sentence and supplement, qualify, or contradict it. Sentence fragments are commonly used for emphasis in advertising copy and journalistic writing. For example, here is an extract from an advertisement (the two sentence fragments are in italics).

> One thing we couldn't refine any further was our concierge. He knows many of our guests by their first name. *And their precise needs. Like the best seats in the house at the theatre, the opera, or the cinema.*

Sentence fragments such as the last two sentences are not common in business writing because they can be distracting for a reader in the longer, more developed text that is characteristic. Avoid sentence fragments unless they are there for a calculated effect.

The unattached or dangling modifier

A modifier is a part of a sentence that describes, limits, or gives more detail about some other part of the sentence. A modifier can be a word (fine, expertly), a phrase (in good time), or a clause (although the report was finished). Make sure that your modifiers are unambiguously related to the words that they modify. A modifier 'dangles' when its position in the sentence encourages a reader to relate it to the wrong element. Consider the following sentence.

> Walking into the building the lifts could be seen.

The modifier 'walking into the building' has only the 'lifts' to connect with. What is missing is the genuine 'agent', that is, the one who is doing the walking.

Clearer versions of the sentence include the following.

> Walking into the building, I saw the lifts.
>
> When you walk into the building, you will see the lifts.

Because the reader of your sentence will make connections between the elements of a sentence that are the closest to each other, amusing juxtapositions such as the following can occur.

> I have discussed the question of stocking the proposed poultry plant with my colleagues. (Gowers, p. 305)

A particular problem occurs when placing the modifier *only*. Consider how readers could interpret the following sentences.

> I'll only ask you to work with me. I won't beg.
>
> I'll ask only you to work with me. I won't ask anyone else.
>
> I'll ask you to work only with me. Don't you work with anyone else.
>
> I'll ask you to work with me only. Don't you work with anyone else.

> Only I will ask you to work with me. Nobody else will ask you to work with them.
>
> I'll ask you only to work with me. Don't you work with anyone else. OR
>
> I won't ask anyone but you to work with me. OR
>
> I'll ask you to work with me, not to do anything else.

In the final example above, 'only' is regarded as a 'squinting' modifier. The reader cannot be sure which way the modifier is 'squinting' because it is placed ambiguously.

Consider the squinting modifier 'completely' in the following sentence.

> The job that he hoped would satisfy him completely frustrated him.

Which way is the modifying word 'completely' squinting? Towards 'satisfy' or 'frustrated'? There is no way of knowing.
Here is a further example of a 'squinting' modifier.

> Original: Consulting these books frequently teaches you about language and makes you more confident about your writing.

Will your reader understand you to mean that frequently consulting these books will help you or that consulting these books will frequently help you?

> Improved: If you consult these books frequently, you will learn about language and become a more confident writer.

You can improve your writing by making sure that all your modifiers are placed as closely as possible to the elements they modify. The writer of a sentence such as the following has ignored this advice.

> Please let us know what you think about our office improvements in a memo.

To clarify this sentence, shift 'in a memo' to after 'know'.

It is generally acknowledged that only rarely do we succeed in placing our intended meaning into our readers' brains. That being the case, we should aim to write clearly so that we reduce the possibility of being misunderstood.

Lack of parallel structure

You can help your reader comprehend two or more equivalent ideas or listed items by constructing sentences using parallel patterns.
Consider this sentence.

> Original: Most people he encounters are impressed by his calm manner, meticulous attire, and being ambitious.

The writer of this sentence ignored what is called parallelism, the use of identical constructions to help readers make connections between parallel elements. The sentence above reads much more smoothly if it is changed.

> Improved: Most people he encounters are impressed by his calm manner, meticulous attire, and ambitiousness.

By changing the three ideas to the same structural elements (nouns), parallelism has been respected.
Keep parallel structure in mind when you are creating lists, headings, and sections of documents. The following list from a letter sent by an insurance company ignores parallel structure.

> To enable further assessment of your son's claim, the following information is required:
>
> 1 Precise details of the theft or burglary
>
> 2 What were the security arrangements at the time of the event?
>
> 3 Make and model of camera.

If you change item 2 to 'security arrangements at the time of the event', the items in the extract become parallel.

> The purpose of this memo is two-fold: firstly, to remind staff to fill in their requisitions for furniture;...

If you write 'firstly' your readers will expect to find a 'secondly, to...'
You can feel the disorienting effect on readers in the following example.

> The proposal needs to address two distinct kinds of reader.
>
> The first is the specialist who requested the proposal.
>
> Executives who make the decision are the second kind of reader.

It would be much better to make the second sentence parallel with the first.

> The second is the executive who makes the decision.

The mixed sentence or shifted construction

This occurs when a writer changes course midway through a sentence, and the result is a mismatch between the beginning and end of the sentence.
Consider the following sentence.

> In all his efforts to please others got him into trouble.

The writer has started out the sentence intending to say 'In all his efforts to please others, he got himself into trouble'. However, somehow the structure has been altered to the structure of 'all his efforts to please others got him into trouble'. Instead of this mixed construction being corrected in the editing stage, the sentence has remained distorted.

The same process has occurred in the following sentence. Rewriting it can improve it.

> Original: The work involved in directing the use of resources is the definition of management.
>
> Improved: We can define management as the work involved in directing the use of resources.

Mixed sentences often occur because of muddled thinking or lack of time. Straightening out ambiguities like this in your writing may well help you to eliminate muddled thinking. Mixed sentences can also occur if you edit with your word processor and do not check the print-out carefully for continuity.

Over-reliance on passive verbs

Verbs have been traditionally defined as 'doing' words. A more contemporary definition of a verb is that it is 'the only word in a sentence whose form may change to express time change'. You can greatly improve your writing by remembering two simple strategies in using verbs

- express action
- identify your agent (actor).

Action is a general term covering many notions: movement, feeling, process, change, activity, condition—physical or mental. If you identify your agent in the subject of your sentence and your agent carries out an action, you will be using what, in the English language, is called the 'active voice'. Voice is a grammatical category that indicates the relation of the subject and verb in a sentence. English verbs have two 'voices'—active and passive.

In the 'active' voice, the subject of the sentence performs the action stated by the verb. For example, 'We used a computer', 'The secretary typed the report'. In both of these examples the use of the active voice emphasises the subject.

In the 'passive' voice, the subject of the sentence is acted upon. For example, 'A computer was used by us', 'The report was typed by the secretary'. The passive voice emphasises the object or receiver of the action.

A message can be constructed in the active or passive voice.

> Active voice: We used a computer to write this book.
>
> Passive voice: A computer was used by us to write this book.

Readers would say that both sentences have the same meaning, but the passive version is slightly more difficult for a reader to comprehend because it is wordier, and, by running counter to the usual word order of a sentence, forces the reader to restructure the sentence to process its meaning.

Although most contemporary discussions of writing style advise writers to avoid the passive voice, examples of the passive are pervasive in business writing. Do you prefer the active or passive versions of the following sentences?

> Passive: The annual report had been read by most of the stockholders.
>
> Active: Most of the stockholders had read the annual report.
>
> Passive: Computers can be used by analysts to chart financial data.
>
> Active: Analysts can use computers to chart financial data.

> Passive: The procedures are to be followed in all normal work, but in certain circumstances some variation in method may be permitted.
>
> Active: Follow these procedures in all normal work, but you may vary the method in certain circumstances.
>
> Passive: It was brought to our attention by the manager that we had not sent the invoice.
>
> Active: The manager told us that we had not sent the invoice.
>
> Passive: Your co-operation and assistance are appreciated.
>
> Active: We appreciate your co-operation and assistance.

Check your sentences to see whether the person, thing, or organisation doing the action is actually doing, has done, or will do the action stated by the verb. If it is, then the sentence is in the active voice. If it is not, then your sentence is in the passive. Very often, the agent or doer of the action does not even appear in the sentence. Work out who or what the agent is and rework your sentence. For example, check the sentences we have used below to illustrate the double passive (page 114). In all cases of the double passive, because there is no agent in the original sentence, we needed to supply an agent in our improved version of the sentence.

When is it acceptable to use the passive?

There are several situations when it is acceptable, and even preferable, to use the passive.

- When you want to shift the reader's attention away from the agent to certain other information. For example, the passive, 'Your proposal has been accepted' is more forceful for the reader than the active 'We have accepted your proposal' because it moves the most important information to the key part of the sentence, the opening.
  Telstra prefers to tell its customers that 'Detailed call-by-call information will be provided automatically as a standard service at no charge' rather than 'We have provided etc...' because Telstra wants to stress the service they provide. In a sentence such as 'The documents were delivered before 4 p.m.', the agent is irrelevant; what is important is that the documents arrived before 4 p.m.
- When you want to soften an unpleasant message by concealing the identity of the person responsible for the decision. For example, 'It is felt that your case doesn't warrant reconsideration', 'The inconvenience caused is regretted'.
- When the agent is unknown. For example, 'Complaints were put into the suggestion box', 'The computer was damaged at the conference'.

- When the agent is less important than the receiver. For example, 'The Prime Minister was greeted by the voters'.

Avoid 'old-fashioned' passives such as 'Receipt of your letter is acknowledged'. Using expressions like this creates an indefinite, impersonal tone, and can confuse your reader. A reader will understand your message much more easily and quickly if you write, 'We have received your letter'.

Also be careful to avoid the 'double passive', which creates a convoluted style.

Original: The contract is proposed to be cancelled.

Improved: The company proposes to cancel the contract.

Original: The grant is threatened to be withdrawn.

Improved: The governing body is threatening to withdraw the grant.

Original: A form may be required to be completed.

Improved: We may require you to fill out a form.

To sum up, use the active voice in preference to the passive to suggest immediacy and increase how efficiently your readers comprehend your sentences. Use the passive when it is a conscious decision, that is, only when you believe it is appropriate, useful, effective, or even necessary for reasons of tact or emphasis.

Overuse of 'heavy' nouns (nominalisation)

A nominalisation, which is itself a nominalisation, is a noun derived from a (usually Latin-based) verb or adjective. A nominal style is often accompanied by a passive construction because nouns rather than verbs are used to express action. For example, consider the following sentence.

An indication should have been given to you that your request was receiving our attention.

An active version of this sentence would eliminate the two nominalisations, 'indication' and 'attention'. We would then have, 'Someone should have told you that we were attending to your request'.

Nominal style is indirect, requiring more words to present the same ideas, and, most importantly, hiding action in nouns rather than expressing it in verbs. Weak 'to be' verbs are often left to carry the weight: 'We are in agreement with you' instead of 'We agree with you'. When we express actions as nouns we get sluggish, imprecise prose that requires the reader to work harder to extract the meaning because it is difficult to process. Research has shown that readers recall active structures better and faster than nominal ones. So, eliminate nominalisations that weigh down your prose.

Original: The committee made a negative recommendation with regard to the implementation of the scheme.

Improved: The committee recommended that the scheme not be implemented.

The noun string (sometimes called the 'stacked adjective')

Noun strings are noun 'collections', in which some nouns are used as adjectives to create phrases.

Original: Industry development policy; industry policy implications; public sector debt; off-site solid waste disposal facility; axle spindle fatigue fracture initiation site.

When you have unwieldy or ambiguous noun strings, unstring them. It would be better to rewrite these noun strings as follows to make them easier for the reader to process.

Improved: Policy for industry development; implications for industry policy; an off-site facility for disposal of solid waste; the fatigue fracture initiation site of the axle spindle.

The expletive construction

In an expletive construction, expressions such as 'There are' and 'It is' are used at the beginning of a sentence to delay the subject.

Original: There will be a variety of procedures adopted to disseminate the results of the traffic study.

Original: There is a need for more funds for development.

Original: It is required for all personnel to report to the office.

The verb 'to be' is considered to be a weak link that does not say much on its own. If 'is' verbs dominate your writing, this can be a symptom that you are using too many nouns and adjectives, which the verb 'is' connects. 'Is-writing' lacks the force and liveliness of writing that relies on verbs to communicate specific action. The examples above could be improved by re-writing.

> Improved: We will adopt a variety of procedures to disseminate the results of the traffic study.
>
> Improved: We need more funds for development.
>
> Improved: All personnel should report to the office.

Incorrect use of tenses

The tense of the verb indicates the time at which the action described in the sentence takes place. The six main tenses used in English are listed below.

- **Present tense** expresses action that is happening now or happens regularly.

> We write daily.

- **Future tense** expresses action that will take place in the future.

> We will write tomorrow.

- **Past tense** expresses action completed at a particular time in the past.

> We wrote a proposal last week.

- **Present perfect tense** expresses action which began in the past but is still going on or is completed in the present.

> We have been writing that report for months.

- **Past perfect tense** expresses action that was begun and completed in the past.

> We had finished that chapter last month.

- **Future perfect tense** expresses action that will begin in the future and be completed at a specific time in the future.

> We will have completed our tax returns by the end of this month.

Writers do not usually have any trouble with tenses, but they may occasionally have problems keeping tenses consistent. Competent writers would avoid the problem in tense in the following sentence.

> Since last week she was unpopular with her boss.

The past tense used here is incorrect because the action is still going on. The writer should have used the present perfect tense.

> She has been unpopular with her boss since last week.

Lack of grammatical agreement

Between subject and verb

Writers sometimes forget to ensure that their verbs agree in number with their subjects.

A singular subject needs a singular verb. A plural subject needs a plural verb. Below are three examples of lack of agreement between subject and verb.

> Example 1: Each of the organisations were represented.

In this example, the singular subject 'Each' needs to be followed by the singular verb 'was'. The best way to avoid problems with agreement is to simplify the sentence by isolating the subject and verb. In this case, you would have 'Each, was'.

Using this technique would have avoided the lack of agreement between subject and verb in the following sentence.

> Example 2: Servo motors have been especially developed for use in positional control and is one of the few motors which can be controlled through software.

It should be 'Servo motors... are...'

> Example 3: Australia, as well as a number of other countries, have legislated an accelerated phase-out by the year 1997.

'Have' should, of course, be 'has'.

The following words, each, either, neither, everybody, anybody, nobody, no one, are still regarded as singular by most writers. Although there are moves to loosen this requirement, in some cases because of problems with nonsexist writing, not everyone agrees about this. *The Oxford Dictionary* now accepts what has come to be called 'the singular they' because of the necessity to avoid sexist language. (See Chapter 8, page 135.)

What about nouns that can be used in a singular or plural sense—nouns such as 'government' and 'committee' that are commonly called 'collective nouns'? Be guided by the sense in which they are used. If plural, use a plural verb. If singular, use a singular verb.

Correlative connectives

With correlative connectives such as either...or, neither...nor, both...and, and not only...but also, the verb should agree with the part of the subject closest to it. For example, 'Neither the architects nor the builder is responsible for the delay'. The singular verb 'is' agrees with the singular noun 'builder'.

Between pronoun and antecedent

In the sentence, 'The stockholders were impressed by its dividends this year', the pronoun 'its' should be changed to 'their' to agree with its antecedent 'stockholders'.

In the sentence, 'If someone calls, they should ask for me', the pronoun 'they' should agree with its antecedent 'someone'. However, as we pointed out in the previous section, 'they' can be treated as singular to avoid the rather awkward construction 'If someone calls, he or she should ask for me'. Using the 'singular they' is becoming far more common in written communication.

Pronoun problems

There is a growing reluctance to use the pronoun 'me'. For example, in 'Between you and I, the director thinks we will get this contract', fear of 'me' has led the writer to the incorrect 'between you and I'. The preposition 'between' signals that the pronouns that follow it must be in what is called the objective case, that is, me, her, him, them, us.

A technique for checking your writing is to reverse the order of the pronouns. Would anyone write 'Between I and you'? No. Another technique is to leave out the extra noun or pronoun. Would anyone write 'Please contact I when you can'? No. Nevertheless, 'Between you and I' is so widely used in spoken communication that some people believe it is now an acceptable idiom in writing.

Another common problem with pronouns is the misuse of 'myself' (again more common in spoken communication, but also used in writing). Uncertainty about using 'me' leads to the incorrect 'They gave it to John and myself'. It should be 'They gave it to John and me'.

'Myself' is most properly used emphatically or reflexively.

Emphatically: I myself often have trouble.

Reflexively: I have nominated myself for the position.

A further potential source of ambiguity lies in omitting relevant pronouns in sentences such as the following.

Original: The director wants the report written by the department.

Does the director want the report which the department has already written, or does the director want the department to write the report? By including expressions such as Wh(ich)...is (was, are etc.), you clarify your meaning.

Improved: The director wants the report that was written by the department.

A final example in this section is the problem that occurs in the following sentence.

Original: Alice told Kate's secretary that she must contact her.

How many possible meanings can you extract from this sentence? At least six! (Kate must contact Alice. Kate must contact her secretary. Alice must contact Kate's secretary. Kate's secretary must contact Alice. Alice must contact Kate. Kate's secretary must contact Kate.)

The least awkward way to avoid ambiguity in this case is to use direct speech.

> Improved: Alice said to Kate's secretary, 'Please tell Kate to contact me'.
>
> Alternatively: Alice said to Kate's secretary, 'Please contact me'.

Inconsistent use of person

Consider this sentence.

> Original: I knew it was one of those lessons that you must learn.

In this sentence the writer has changed from the first person 'I' to the second person 'you'. The sentence would be better if the writer had consistently used 'I'.

> Improved: I knew it was one of those lessons that I must learn.

Possessive with the verbal noun (gerund)

A verbal noun is part verb and part noun; it is formed from a verb and is used as a noun. A verbal noun always ends in 'ing', for example, 'Marketing was my field'.

Consider this sentence, in which the verbal noun plus the possessive is marked.

> We look forward to *your joining* us in Sydney.

In the past, the practice has been to write 'your' because it is 'your joining' that we are looking forward to. 'Your' is the possessive case of the pronoun 'you'. However, its use is diminishing in some circles, and many people would write, 'We look forward to you joining us in Sydney'. Which do you prefer?

Newspaper editors still use it, as you can see from the following examples.

> The lawyers gave the Attorney-General a submission detailing claims they say should lead to the *case's being* reopened.

> The collector said he bought the painting because he could not stand the thought of *its being* sold to overseas interests.

The construction without the possessive is now prevalent in everyday speech and very widespread in writing.

> Example 1: The office manager disapproves of *Susan using* the laser printer so much. (No possessive)
>
> Example 2: The office manager disapproves of *Susan's using* the laser printer so much. (Possessive)

As a general guide, if it sounds awkward or affected, do not use it.

Problems with prepositions

A preposition is a word that establishes a relationship of time, place etc. in a sentence with the noun or pronoun which follows it. Prepositions include between, after, at, before, by, from, in, of, over, through, with.

The most common problem with prepositions occurs when they are used unidiomatically, as in 'If you wish to avail yourself with this service, please fill in the form'. Change 'with' to 'of'. 'An affinity between/with' not 'to/for'. 'Identical to' not 'with'. 'To prefer something to' not 'than'.

See page 123 for discussion of the 'rule' about not using a preposition to end a sentence.

Strings of prepositional phrases such as 'failure of notice of change of address' can be awkward. One way to pick up problems such as these is to 'listen' to the rhythm of your sentences. Although most readers generally do not read aloud, 75–85 per cent say that they hear in their inner ear what they are reading—and that would include the awkwardness of expressions such as the above.

CONTESTED ELEMENTS OF USAGE

Obviously, writers and readers differ in how seriously they ferret out and condemn errors. At one end of the spectrum are pedants who are proud to be so; at the other end are writers and readers who do not even notice errors. As a writer, you need to know the spectrum to decide on your standards of correctness. As writing educator, Joseph Williams, points out, 'not all rules have equal standing with all writers of English, even all careful writers of English' (1989, p. 176). We often receive telephone calls asking us to arbitrate on specific questions of usage—usually to solve office arguments.

About forty Grammar Hotlines exist in the USA and Canada, mostly connected with college and university writing centres, to handle telephone calls from people wanting help on grammatical points. An article in the March 1989 issue of *Simply Stated*, the newsletter of the Document Design Center, Washington DC, describes how a reporter rang a random selection of hotlines with the sample sentence, 'If I was director of this project, I would seek federal grants'. All but one of the hotlines suggested that the sentence was ungrammatical and that the verb 'was' should be changed to the subjunctive verb-form 'were', which is used when the statement is contrary to the situation—in this case the speaker is not the director of the project. If this survey had been conducted in Australia, it is doubtful whether it would have had the same result, because language experts in Australia are predicting the demise of the subjunctive mood of the verb. This example illustrates how usage differs from grammatical correctness.

As a guideline, the most important errors you need to eliminate in sentences are those which confuse and disorient your readers and lead to ambiguity and misunderstanding. The super correctness achieved by pedantic nitpicking is more suited to scholarly editors than to business writers. Be particularly aware of the danger of what is called 'hyper-correction'—changing a construction that is already correct into a form that is incorrect. Examples of this phenomenon abound in ungrammatical letters to newspaper editors complaining about other people's supposedly poor grammar.

WRITING RULES

In his book on writing, *Style: Ten lessons in clarity and grace*, Joseph Williams includes a useful discussion about rules. He identifies four kinds—Real rules, Nonrules, Optional rules, and Bêtes noires—with the aim of demystifying what many writers see as the overwhelming complexity of, and scope for error in, the English language.

Real rules

Real rules are the ones that competent writers never break; real rules are violated in this sentence.

> They done well in their staff review.

Any writer producing a sentence such as this lacks competence in using basic English verbs. No one would suggest that this sentence is acceptable in any business communication context because it breaks an inviolable rule of verb form and results in what we would regard as 'non-standard English'.

Nonrules

Nonrules are not rules, and they never were. Be that as it may, generations of school teachers have got it into their heads (and into the heads of their hapless students) that sentences should never begin with 'and' or 'but'. It is possible that nonrules such as this arose to simplify advice for beginning writers, because these rules are not based on linguistic principles or necessity. Many writers try to remain loyal to the 'rules' they were taught at school in the mistaken belief that they are exhibiting their knowledge of 'good' writing. Rigorously sticking to such outdated rules does just the opposite; it interferes with their ability to communicate effectively.

Optional rules

Two examples of optional rules that Williams gives are 'Don't end a sentence with a preposition' and 'Don't split infinitives'. It is surprising how many writing workshop participants beg to have the split infinitive explained, probably because it is often mentioned in discussions about grammar. One of us wrote an article for a business magazine in which this sentence occurred: 'The best way to improve employees' writing is for executives to actively participate in the training programs'. More than one reader felt compelled to complain about splitting the infinitive 'to participate'.

These rules are optional, and, if strictly enforced, can result in ridiculously contorted sentences such as Winston Churchill's famous outburst against the 'rule' about not ending a sentence with a preposition: 'This is the kind of bloody nonsense up with which I will not put'. Often, ending a sentence with a preposition is the *preferred* option.

'This is the report that I was telling you about' is far less awkward than 'This is the report about which I was telling you'. These rules are largely idiosyncratic and perhaps arose in a respectful but misguided attempt to mimic Latin grammar. In Latin, the infinitive verb cannot be split because it is a single word, for example, *monere* (to advise). In Latin it is *impossible* to end a sentence with a preposition.

Bêtes noires

These rules, according to Williams, are personal 'objects of special reverence' or what some writers would call 'pet peeves'.

Here is an example of one of Williams's bêtes noires. Never use 'like' for 'as' or 'as if'. He recommends avoiding constructions such as the following.

> Original: These operations failed like the earlier ones did.
>
> Original: It looks like we require further data on this matter.

He suggests rewriting.

> Improved: These operations failed as the earlier ones did.
>
> Improved: It looks as if we require further data on this matter.

Many writers cringe when they see the phrase 'different to' because they believe 'different from' is the only correct version because it suggests divergence and separation. However, this rule is optional. We checked it in several sources, and found that, although purists would never accept it, some authorities regard 'different to' as acceptable.

CONCLUSION

If you would like further help with sentence-level problems, we suggest that you investigate Joseph Williams's book further. Williams concentrates on sentence structure, word choice, and punctuation, providing sound advice and many excellent examples for writers to work through.

References

Gowers, E. (1979). *The complete plain words*, London: Penguin.
Corbett, E. (1987). *The little English handbook*, 5th edn, Glenview, Il.: Scott Foresman.
Leonard, D. J. and Gilsdorf, J. W. (1990). 'Language in change: Academics' and executives perceptions of usage errors'. *The Journal of Business Communication*, Vol. 27(2), 137–158.
Williams, J. (1989). *Style: Ten lessons in clarity and grace*, 3rd edn, Glenview, Il.: Scott Foresman.

CHAPTER 8

CONSIDERING LANGUAGE

WORDS AS TOOLS

Whether you are a professional writer by choice or by chance, words are your tools. The more proficient you are with words, the greater your writing skills. The greater your writing skills, the more opportunities you have to enhance your company's profile and your own career path, because writing competence raises your self-esteem as well as your value to your organisation.

This chapter and Chapter 9, Choosing the Right Word, will guide you to a greater understanding of how words work by outlining some useful principles for language use in professional writing.

BECOMING LANGUAGE SENSITIVE

To learn to use words well you need to appreciate their critical importance to you as a writer. Be verbally aware. When you read a piece of writing that works for you, keep a copy of it. Become attuned to the subtleties of language. For example, do you understand the nuances of 'style', 'élan', 'panache', and 'cachet'? Be respectful of language. Be curious about words. Be fascinated by new words. Enjoy words.

Becoming more verbally sophisticated does not give you a licence to use big words, however. You are writing to communicate. Use words that most people can understand, and make every word count, so that your readers can absorb your message as efficiently and accurately as possible. Your vocabulary should not distract your reader's attention from what you are saying to how you are saying it. This can happen just as easily when you have a poor vocabulary as when you sound as if you have 'swallowed the dictionary'.

How do you expand a limited vocabulary? Read widely; write constantly; get feedback on your writing from writing experts and from colleagues whose writing you respect. Use dictionaries, both general ones like *The Macquarie* and specialised ones like *The Hamlyn Dictionary of Business Terms*. Find out who is creating exemplary business documents in Australia. For example, the results of business writing awards such as the *Australian Business* Annual Reports Awards and the Serif Awards awarded by the Society of Business Communicators and the Australian Institute of Professional Communicators will give you an idea of the sort of writing that is respected in the corporate sphere.

How Words Work

We need to use words to name things. However, for most words there is no connection between how the word looks and what it stands for. Any meaning that a word has is based on agreement among the people who use it. Convention and usage construct potential meanings that readers attach to words when they see or hear them in context. Dictionaries are neither repositories nor arbiters of 'true' meanings; all they do is record how a word has been used in the past. They *describe* how language has been used, rather than *prescribe* how language should be used. The dynamic, fluid character of language is evident in its constant change.

'The word is not the thing', claim linguists, in the same way that 'the map is not the territory'. The word 'book' bears no resemblance to what you are presently reading. To be precise, you should really say, 'English speakers call this a book'.

Even when you use a familiar word, there is no guarantee that readers will get your message, because you cannot safely predict what meanings they will attach to your words. Readers are not dry sponges waiting to soak up your intended message. They construct their own meaning out of your written document.

Readers remember not what writers tell them, but what they tell themselves.

To test this, what points have you picked up so far from this chapter?

As a business writer, what aspects of language do you need to be conscious of? We believe that you need a knowledge of the following concepts: abstract and concrete words, denotation and connotation, tone, and non-discriminatory language—which we cover in this chapter. In the next chapter we discuss jargon, clichés, coinages and vogue words, archaisms, acronyms, verbosity, redundancy, superfluity, doublespeak, equivocation and weasel words, confusable words, foreign phrases, and commonly misspelt words.

Abstract words versus concrete words

Concrete words name objects or events that can be seen, touched, experienced, or felt. For example, 'computer' is a concrete word. When people write, they tend to use a lower proportion of concrete words than when they speak. They tend to overuse abstract words. Abstract words name qualities, ideas, concepts, relationships, emotions—things which usually cannot be perceived directly by our senses. Abstract words like ethics, integrity, efficiency, and feasibility enable us to extend the level of our thoughts and speech beyond the everyday, concrete world.

However, vague, abstract words like item, increment, facility, procedure, instrumentation, factor, and system in sentences such as 'We have decided to introduce a new facility into the system' can cause problems for readers because they are too abstract to give the reader a mental picture. The analogy of a ladder is often used to show levels of abstraction. In Figure 8.1, the most abstract word is at the top of the ladder and the most concrete expression is at the bottom.

Competent writers know exactly what part of the abstraction ladder to take their words from for each particular audience. Using words that are too high on the abstraction ladder may lead to ambiguity; using words that are too low on the abstraction ladder may lead to a condescending tone. In this case we might decide that 'laser printer' is on the appropriate rung of the ladder for a staff memo. For an equipment check later on we would use the words and serial number at the bottom of the ladder.

A rather extreme example of the use of an abstract word was reported when at one time the White House had a toll-free number that you could call

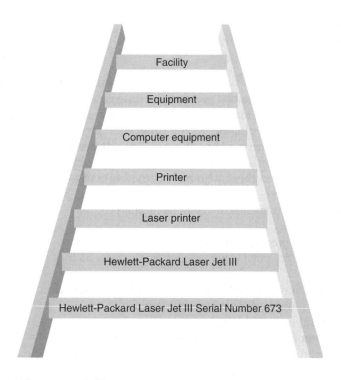

Facility

Equipment

Computer equipment

Printer

Laser printer

Hewlett-Packard Laser Jet III

Hewlett-Packard Laser Jet III Serial Number 673

Figure 8.1 Abstraction ladder

to get the latest important news. If you happened to dial when the answering machine was connected, a voice announced

> You have reached the White House Press Office Actualities Line. We have no actuality at this time. Thank you for calling, and please call again.

(Reported in The New York Times, 9 January 1989, p. 29.)

Denotation and connotation

Denotation is the literal or dictionary meaning of a word (remember 'D' for dictionary); connotation is the emotional association that a specific word has for readers. It might seem that connotations are more of a problem for writers and readers because everyone has different emotional associations for words such as 'business', 'takeover', or 'communication'. However, denotations can also cause problems.

The 500 most common words in English have around 14 000 denotations—an average of thirty each. Some of our commonest words have an extraordinary number of denotative meanings

- *around* has over thirty
- *back* and *low* have over fifty
- *draw* has over sixty
- *pass* has over eighty
- *hard* has over ninety
- *run* has over 170.

(Margulis, 1975, p. 65)

If such seemingly simple words have so many meanings, trying to write so that you cannot be misunderstood presents a strong challenge.

The problem of denotation is highlighted by a recent reaction to the phrase 'sustainable development', at a time when protection of the environment is such a sensitive political issue. In a letter to *The Australian* in December 1989, the then Federal Minister for the Environment, Graham Richardson, answered those who had accused him of a 'radical definition of sustainable development' by asserting that there were 'several dozen definitions' that the term 'means or could be applied to'

- protection of greatly increased areas
- making industry pay proper prices for resources such as timber and minerals
- further restricting population growth and/or immigration
- far more equitable distribution of income
- not farming marginal lands
- reduced per capita energy consumption
- shift to non-polluting sources and technologies, and not closing off future options in this regard
- and, according to the Brundtland Report, a drop in military spending.

Richardson's detailed explanation was doubtless appreciated as much for its uniqueness as for its thoroughness. Politicians do not usually go to such lengths to elaborate on their word use!

The lesson for professional writers is to be sensitive to the denotations and potential connotations of the words used. But do not overdo it like the writer of the following extract, who went to great lengths trying to explain the connotations of the title of a conference (the faulty punctuation and usage is in the original).

> As we begin a new decade, this conference seeks to help us clarify the issues and themes particularly relevant to the 1990's. The title 'INFORM' is offered with three main connotations:
>
> Firstly, is the concept of information, and the need there is to keep each other informed of new methods and research.
>
> The second, connotation intended is the notion of the art form of Drama, and a focus on how we choose the particular forms we use for the material we wish to teach.
>
> A third connotation is intended: that in 1990 Drama is no longer self-doubting, and, like a well-prepared athlete, Drama has struck form.

In attempting to remove any doubts a reader might have about the meaning of the conference title by explaining it at such length, the writer has generated even greater doubt about the intellectual quality of a conference which would produce such a poorly-written and punctuated blurb, with such an over-earnest tone. Tone relates to the response of your readers to the connotations of the words you use as well as your use of specific strategies such as 'hedging' questions and apologies.

Tone

Tone is the impression you create on your reader. Tone usually stems from your attitude as a writer to your subject and to your reader. Consider how concessional-fare passengers would react to these 'travel tips', contained in a brochure distributed by an Australian airline.

> Drinking to excess, unkempt appearance, loose language, and loud talk (especially to full fare passengers about your privileged position to 'fly anywhere for only a few dollars') could cause embarrassment to you and to [the airline]...

We do not know how long the airline distributed this version, nor how many concessional-fare passengers communicated their outrage to the airline management. We have noted that the same company changed 'loose language' to 'bad-taste language' and 'loud talk' to 'loose talk' in a later version of the brochure. Hardly an improved tone!

An even more notorious example of inappropriate tone is the reply that an industrial relations manager sent to Mining Unions in Western Australia who complained when a number of shop stewards were retrenched (faults are in the original).

Contrary to the belief of some unions, shop stewards are not members of Gods chosen race and therefore have no specific immunity when retrenchments are decided.

The proposal is novel and original but stupid.

If you find this reply unclear please advise and we will reduce it to two words one of which will have sexual overtones.

Despite the arrogant tone of this telex (to say nothing of the disregard for punctuation), we should applaud the writer's concern that the message be clearly understood.

To establish and preserve a suitable tone, you need language sensitivity and skill. Effective communicators know that how you write, as well as what you write, can establish your credibility as an honest and intelligent communicator.

So, do not make outrageous claims, do not be illogical, and do not violate the values of your reader. Curb your desire to be sarcastic. Do not reply to an unconvincing proposal written by a subordinate with 'I found your argument to be less than compelling'. Most people react adversely to this kind of tone.

As we explained earlier, tone is the impression that you create on your reader. Consider the impression created by the tone in this follow-up letter from a seminar organiser who has obviously had little or no response to a brochure and is attempting to entice readers to sign up (we have added the italics).

> Recently you received a brochure from us inviting you to a series of seminars. The feedback *from this effort* indicates there is a need to restate the objectives of these seminars and the benefits of attending.

Removing the colloquial phrase 'from this effort' considerably improves the tone of the letter by making the letter more formal.

The following examples show how a word or a phrase can create an adverse impression by creating an undesirable tone. Eager-to-please job-seekers have much to learn about the power of words to create tone if these examples of unintended and undesirable effects on readers are representative.

> Example 1: Please contact any/all of the referees I have included in my résumé.

The problem here is with the 'take-it-or-leave-it' effect of 'any/all of'. Deleting this phrase makes the tone of the sentence more acceptable.

> Example 2: I am available at any time should you require an interview.

The unintended message here is that this candidate may not need to be nor deserve to be interviewed. The original can be improved with a change to 'I am available for an interview at any time suitable to you'.

> **Example 3:** After seeing my qualifications, I hope you find it worthwhile to make an appointment with me.

The tone here is self-deprecating. 'I hope you regard my qualifications as being relevant for the job' creates a more suitable tone.

> **Example 4:** I would savour an opportunity to work with you. This would give you the opportunity to exploit the enthusiasm and imagination of a young communicator.

The negative connotations evoked by 'savour' and 'exploit' need to be eliminated because they create a most inappropriate tone. 'Savour' could be replaced with 'appreciate'; 'exploit' could be replaced with 'experience'.

> **Example 5:** I wish to inquire as to whether there are any openings in your news department for a cadet reporter. Presently I have no commitments and am willing to work under adverse terms and conditions.

The employer who received this example was considerate enough to point out to the applicant that, although the intention was obviously to convey an extreme willingness to work, to offer to work under 'adverse terms and conditions' was going to extremes.

> **Example 6:** I trust you will do me the courtesy of an interview.

Understandably, no potential employer likes to receive applications that are as presumptuous as this one. Instead of 'When may I come to see you?', try 'Would you be willing to see me at a time convenient for you?' Or, 'I'd appreciate your seeing me. Can we arrange a time that suits both of us?'

Problems in tone can occur when the reader and writer have different attitudes and make different assumptions, but we suspect that they frequently occur because many writers are insensitive to the effects of their words on readers. The following list includes negative words readers have used to describe unacceptable tone in corporate documents they have received:

bureaucratic, pompous, sarcastic, moralistic, accusatory, tactless, aggressive, argumentative, tentative, presumptuous, impersonal, patronising, smart-aleck, glib.

Check over letters that you have written to test whether any of them convey a negative tone. Could any of the above adjectives apply to your documents? For example, would any of your readers describe your letters as impersonal because you still use the archaic and arcane language fashionable in the nineteenth century? Expressions such as 'Pursuant to our recent conversation...' are no longer acceptable to readers because of their pompous tone. A good test is to ask whether, if you delivered your message orally, you would use such impersonal language? Why not substitute 'As we discussed last week...'? A friendly natural tone is much more acceptable to readers.

The following strategies can be useful in achieving a politely persuasive tone in documents such as memos and letters.

- Asking a 'hedging' question: 'Can you find the time to fill this form in and return it to me?'
- Minimising opposition: 'I would appreciate a small favour. Could you fill this form in and return it to me?'
- Giving deference: 'Could you give me the benefit of your experience in these matters by filling in this form?'
- Apologising: 'I'm sorry to bother you, but I'd like you to fill in this form and return it to me.'
- Nominalising: 'Your co-operation in filling in this form will be greatly appreciated.'
- Incurring a debt: 'I would appreciate your helping us to clarify your situation by filling in this form.'
- Stating a general rule: 'Everyone in your category needs to fill in and return this form to us.'

(Zhang, 1990)

It would be possible to be even more effective by using more than one of the above strategies in a single sentence.

Tone in public notices

It is difficult to achieve an appropriate tone in public notices because they have a very wide spectrum of potential readers. The anti-smoking campaign of recent years has challenged the ability of writers who have had to generate a set of polite messages such as the following example in an effort to discourage smokers from upsetting non-smokers.

For the comfort of all guests it would be appreciated if you would try to refrain from smoking in the dining room.

A growing trend in public documents is to personalise the tone as much as possible. Take this extract from a Telstra leaflet.

Hello.
You might like to know what's been happening at Telstra lately.
In a word, lots.
Firstly, we've developed some fresh, new approaches to service.
You see in our eyes you, the customer, comes first.

Telstra has gone to some lengths to use a tone that is very 'reader-friendly' by using 'Hello' and 'lots'. However, some readers may feel that this can easily be degraded to seem too colloquial, chatty, or slangy.

NON-DISCRIMINATORY LANGUAGE

A type of unacceptable writing behaviour that worries many readers is the use of sexist language—especially out of openly-acknowledged chauvinism. One Queensland ex-parliamentarian hit the headlines in 1989 when he refused to allow letters to leave his office addressed to 'Ms' anybody, thereby flouting the Sex Discrimination Act which the Federal Government passed in 1984.

In Australia over the past few years many organisations have followed what has become common practice overseas (particularly in the USA) and adopted what are called 'nonsexist', 'gender-inclusive', 'gender-neutral', or 'genderless' language guidelines.

After the Australian Government Publishing Service published the fourth edition of its *Style Manual for authors, editors and printers* in 1988, and included an extended section on nonsexist language, the reaction in the press was huge. Letters to the editor of *The Australian* ranged from the sane and sensible to the absurd and irrational.

Sane and sensible: 21 October 1988

As a practising Public Service lawyer I endeavour to write in a way which is not gender specific except when the subject of my text is definitely male or female. In my view, common courtesy to those men and women who are offended by sexist terminology is reason enough to adopt nonsexist writing style; the discriminatory and exclusionary implications of sexist writing is another excellent reason.

Absurd: 24 October 1988

The latest bit of temporary insanity to be inflicted on us is the attempt by frustrated feminists to change our English language.

Irrational: 28 October 1988

Women should understand that you cannot legislate or compel respect; you must earn it. If women want to prove equality with men let them give us composers to name with Beethoven, Handel, Mozart; painters to hang with Rembrandt, Turner, Van Gogh...

The vociferous debate which ensued invariably continues whenever and wherever anyone brings up the issue.

The controversy revolves around the absence, in English, of an effective, genderless, singular pronoun to refer to people in general the way 'it' refers to things. It is argued that, when the sex does not need to be nor cannot be specified, using he/him/his to stand for both sexes ignores the equal status of women. Linguistic research has revealed that language is so central to a person's thinking that it actually constructs the boundaries of a person's world. If children are taught to use he/him/his, they think of males as of primary significance and of females as playing a secondary role. When reading about he, him, his, women need to juggle the possibility that the material may or may not refer to them. Men do not have this problem because when females are the focus of the discussion, the writer uses 'her'.

Alternatives to sexist language

In the absence of acceptable substitutes for he/him/his, and because 'he' does not evoke 'he' or 'she' as the anti-feminists claim, there are ways to get around the problem.

How can a sexist sentence such as 'The long-term employee is anxious about his future prospects' be changed?

- Drop the 'his' altogether and use an impersonal construction.

  Future prospects are a worry for the long-term employee.

- Use the plural instead of the singular.

  Long-term employees are worried about their future prospects.

- Substitute first person (I, we) or second person (you) for the third person (he).

  We long-term employees are worried about our future prospects.

- Use 'one', but be careful. When one starts to use 'one', one needs to keep doing so and one can find oneself wondering how to extricate oneself.

  As a long-term employee, one wonders about one's future prospects.

- Use 'he or she', 'his or her', or 's/he' if you have no alternative.

> The long-term employee is worried about his or her future prospects.

Many readers and writers feel that this usage is awkward because it draws attention to itself.

- Increasingly, many writers feel that it is more acceptable to be ungrammatical than to be sexist.

> Everyone who is a long-term employee wonders about their future prospects.

'Everyone' is singular, and traditionally has been followed by a singular pronoun such as 'his' or 'her' rather than the ungrammatical 'their'. While this is the direction in which our language is evolving (and, indeed, where it came from—there are many examples of the 'singular they' in eighteenth and nineteenth century literature), this alternative is not yet widely practised in professional writing. We predict that it will become acceptable.

Most of the Australian business community has accepted that sexist writing is no longer respectable. Unfortunately, this has not extended to the Australian advertising community, because we still see sexist advertisements such as the following for a hotel chain.

Wouldn't it be lovely if there was just one hotel that treated each business-woman like a lady?

The *Style Manual* provides an excellent guide to nonsexist writing for the Australian context. If you wish to consult other material, *The Handbook of Nonsexist Writing* by Casey Miller and Kate Swift is the classic text.

Other discriminatory language

Racist references do not generally receive as much publicity as sexist ones, and are more likely to occur in spoken form. When microphones picked up the Prime Minister, Mr Hawke's under-the-breath 'silly old bugger' reaction to old-age pensioner Bob Bell during the 1989 election campaign, there was a public outcry about his ageist remark. Job advertisements can no longer specify gender, but they can still specify age. This is not comforting for those over forty.

General guidelines

Many people have very strong views on the subject of discriminatory language. Be sensitive to differing views, no matter how far they deviate from your own. Do not emphasise the fact that you may have gone to some trouble to avoid nonsexist language in your writing. Nonsexist writing can be achieved quite subtly.

Even if your organisation does not yet have a non-discriminatory language policy in place, it is part of government policy, and as an ethical writer, you need to avoid discriminatory expressions in your writing. The *Style Manual*, which changed its chapter title in the fifth edition from 'nonsexist' to 'non-discriminatory' language to cover ageism and racism as well, is very helpful for writers wanting to avoid sexist language as it gives alternatives to sexist words and expressions.

References

Australian Government Publishing Service (1994). *Style Manual for authors, editors and printers*, 5th edn Canberra: AGPS.

Margulis, J. B. (1975). *An awareness of language*, Cambridge, Mass: Winthrop Publishers.

Miller, C. and Swift, K. (1981). *The handbook of nonsexist writing*, New York: Barnes & Noble.

Zhang, J. (1990). 'Ranking of indirectness in professional writing'. *Journal of Technical Writing and Communication*, Vol.20(3), 291–305.

CHAPTER 9

CHOOSING THE RIGHT WORD

In this chapter we deal with jargon in its various forms, clichés, colloquialisms, coinages, wordiness, equivocation, foreign words and phrases, confusable words, and commonly misspelt words—essential aspects of language use within the business context.

WHAT IS JARGON?

When visitors looking for the monkeys at a zoo are confronted with a sign which says 'To the Arboreal Primates', we see jargon at work. Jargon, a type of specialised vocabulary used in various fields and professions, is a constant target of criticism from readers of business documents, who complain that documents like letters and insurance policies are difficult to understand because they are full of jargon. It is unfortunate that jargon has accumulated these negative connotations, because eliminating jargon completely would deprive business writers of valuable shortcuts. For example, it is doubtful whether reporting of stock market activities could function as efficiently without terms such as the 'All Ordinaries Index', 'weighted averages', 'blue-chip stocks', 'bull-and-bear markets', and the 'P/E ratio'.

Jargon is often justifiable and sometimes indispensable. However, you should use it carefully. To use it for its own sake, or to obscure or confuse, will probably alienate your readers. Buzz Kennedy (*Weekend Australian*, 29 April 1989), laments that 'today's specialists crouch complacently behind their jargon barriers and... Look with pity on those of us who have no inspeak'. General readers often have great problems with the jargon in certain fields. For example, it has been suggested that jargon used in the investment and superannuation fields 'frightens' potential investors. Apparently, many ordinary investors fail to earn dividend income which is tax-free because they do not understand the term 'dividend imputation' and thus remain ignorant of its benefits. Even a phrase so seemingly simple as 'on maturity' may cause problems for novice readers of insurance policies.

We now need to be able to comprehend complex jargon like reversionary benefits, highest average salary, reasonable benefit limits, unfunded funds, and annuity trap. Advisers in financial institutions are spending enormous amounts of time and money trying to explain the intricacies of the legislation to their clients. More than one cynic has suggested that the complexity of the superannuation jargon is having beneficial effects on employment by providing jobs for investment advisers. One company's sensitivity to the problem of jargon is evident in their superb leaflet which defines the terms people are likely to come across in that field.

Using familiar jargon should not create problems. If jargon is necessary and your readers are not familiar with it, define and explain your terms either in the text or in a glossary.

Overcoming Misuse of Jargon

The Australian Federal Government has recognised problems associated with the unnecessary use of jargon, and has taken the following steps.

- In 1990 the Australian Taxation Office went to great lengths and great expense 'to demystify tax time' with their *Tax Pack*. However, some sources reported an increase in the number of people using tax agents. This was not surprising. Not only was the document full of distracting advertisements, but it contained examples of jargon such as accruing, domicile, and abode.
- To overcome the confusion which many migrants have with Australian social security terminology, Professor Colin Yallop, Director of the Dictionary Research Centre at Macquarie University, is developing a computerised dictionary of terms used in the health and welfare fields. This dictionary will provide distinctions between apparent synonyms like stood down, dismissed, laid off, and sacked—essential information for social security claimants.
- The Social Security Act is currently being rewritten in plain English to give easier access to information to those who need it most.
- Because the success or failure of Award Restructuring may well rest on the extent of literacy in the workplace, an increasing number of literacy kits and workplace training courses in communication are now available.
- In 1990, the Australian Government commissioned plain English expert Professor Robert Eagleson to write a book to help public servants write more clearly.

All of these initiatives are new, and their effectiveness is yet to be ascertained.

Gobbledygook

Gobbledygook (a term coined by Maury Maverick, a Texan congressman) and sometimes spelt in Australia as 'gobbledegook', is used to describe pompous and unintelligible language. Ironically, writers who produce gobble-dygook often consider themselves to be sophisticated users of the language because it is usually characterised by words of Latin origin such as circular (rather than round), locality (rather than place), sufficient (rather than enough), and initiate (rather than begin). Gobbledygook usually sounds very official and important, but the importance of the message is often in inverse proportion to its inflation in gobbledygook.

Gobbledygook has been satirised in television programs like *Yes Minister* and in writing-kits called 'buzz-phrase generators'. Buzz-phrase generators surfaced in the USA around 1970 with the 'EMPTI Guide to Swollen Prose' created by social psychologists Peter Madden and Lloyd Engdahl—EMPTI being an acronym for the Engdahl-Madden Psychological Terms Inventory. The EMPTI provided three columns of words. A writer could randomly select a word from each column to produce a phrase which sounded impressive but was meaningless: for example, 'undifferentiated synergistic integration' or 'extrinsic developmental equilibrium'. (See Figure 9.1 for some other words.)

0	integrated	0	management	0	options
1	total	1	organisation	1	flexibility
2	systematised	2	monitored	2	capability
3	parallel	3	reciprocal	3	mobility
4	functional	4	digital	4	programming
5	responsive	5	logistical	5	concept
6	optimal	6	transitional	6	time-phase
7	synchronised	7	incremental	7	projection
8	compatible	8	third-generation	8	hardware
9	balanced	9	policy	9	contingency

Figure 9.1 Example of a buzz-phrase generator

Gobbledygook can include jargon terms, but whereas jargon is acceptable in technical documents, gobbledygook is never acceptable because nearly all readers have problems translating it. The computer industry and the legal profession are two areas renowned for their use of gobbledygook.

Computerese

Trained computer operators might have no trouble with the following sentence because the jargon is familiar to them. Lay people would find it difficult to understand.

> The ict purges the ict directory every five days, so a cron job copied all the files in the /usr/spool/ict directory into the ict save directory under /usr/spool to allow a seven-day purge.

Whereas the jargon of some fields consists of words that are specially coined, what is unique about much so-called computerese is that it has developed from commonplace words: bug, mouse, file, boot (hot, warm, and cold), save, memory, menu, branch, string, crash, bit, card, track, dump, and virus. This does not make it any easier for new computer users to handle the jargon, as they must learn new definitions for familiar terms. *The Random House Dictionary* estimates that computers have added 1200 words to our language.

LEGALESE

The Australian Law Reform Commission recently announced that the writing style of much Australian legislation is barely comprehensible and has recommended its total overhaul. The Commission is to be applauded for recognising deficiencies in the expression of the laws and making an effort to solve the problems. Legal academics throughout Australia are currently engaged in translating legalese into 'plain, precise, non-ambiguous, and gender-free English' that lay people can understand in a series of publications to be titled *The Laws of Australia.*

New South Wales, Victoria, and Queensland are currently rewriting their defamation laws, and the Law Reform Commission of Victoria has an active commitment to translate as much legalese as possible into plain English. Since mid-1990 all wills issued by the Public Trustee in Queensland have been written in plain English.

BUZZWORDS

Is the jargon of a specialised profession always unnecessarily pretentious? In an article in *The Australian Way* (December 1989) Colin Windsor, discussing 'buzzwords', which he calls 'expressive shorthand', says that in many cases people need to feel secure behind a protective wall of words which few others understand. Windsor lists jargon terms that are used in the corporate sector: unique scenario, ultimate situation, high profile, ultimate achiever, and level-playing field—to which we could add parameters, ballpark figure, game plan, frontline interface, fiscal drag, bracket creep, high profile, bottom line, meaningful dialogue, acid test, task force, spin-off, up-market, burnout, hot issue, worst-case scenario, and many more.

Some of these still have the status of vogue words and phrases—fashionable expressions which everyone seems to start using at about the same time. It has not taken very long for the term 'level playing-field' to reach the status of cliché. The expression irritates at least one corporate executive, BHP Steel's chief, John Prescott, who was quoted in *The Australian* (5 September 1990, p. 31): 'No one has believed in a level playing field since Christopher Columbus proved the world is round. And that's 500 years ago'.

CLICHÉS

A cliché is a phrase that, when first used, was vivid and fresh, but is now dated. Clichés are usually metaphors—comparisons that are not meant to be taken literally. Take, for instance, the expression 'glass ceiling', used in relation to women whose career paths seem to be clear through to the top. They do not see 'the glass ceiling' until they hit their heads on it. Will this new metaphor become a cliché with repeated use?

Deprived of clichés, writers would be in trouble. Because clichés are so familiar to writers, they come easily, automatically often, to a writer who is grasping for words to express an idea. We are not advocating that you abandon vogue words and clichés: we would merely like to suggest that, if you can think of a fresher or more vivid word or expression, use it in preference to a trite or jaded one.

Although clichés can exemplify writing at its most threadbare, they can be comforting because of their familiarity, and they are sometimes consciously included. They do have their place in professional writing. If sentences loaded with clichés are what is expected in your profession or organisation, it would show a lack of understanding on your part if you did not comply with that expectation. Of course, you could also try to change the kind of writing that is expected if you feel that a change is desirable. Figure 9.2 is a further sampling of common clichés. Which ones are essential to your vocabulary?

Ask yourself whether the cliché is effective and consider how relevant it is to the context in which it occurs. Many clichés used in the corporate context have their origins in military and sporting imagery: talk to the troops,

jobs for the boys	flat denial	gender gap
grave responsibility	blissful ignorance	life in the fast lane
bitter truth	the object of the exercise	viable alternative
face facts	the writing on the wall	conservative estimate
irresistible demands	to have an edge	ongoing dialogue
tolerable proportions	office Romeo	thrust of your report
inevitable delay	young Turk	circumstances beyond my
permanent fixture	fact-finding mission	control
manifest an interest	give the green light to	going down the gurgler
engage in activities	fine-tuning the plans	raising the ante
the too-hard basket	ample opportunity	quick and dirty
eye-opener	bite the bullet	number crunching
curtain-raiser	back to the drawing board	head hunting

Figure 9.2 Common clichés

let's run it up the flagpole and see who salutes, take the ball and run with it, front runner, and good team player.

Ration clichés, using only the most vivid.

Clichés that 'retain their currency' usually have a vividness that readers respond to, often without being aware that they are imports from another field: for example, grass roots, knee-jerk reaction, born-again, and pump-priming finance.

Always be the first to drop a vogue word or expression that is on its way out, having failed to make it as an 'in' cliché. When 'state of the art' started to produce groans, it was varied with 'cutting edge' and 'leading edge'. Journalists, conscious of the need to avoid tedium, have developed a useful set of variations for one of their most commonly-used words, 'sources': inform-ants, usually reliable sources, informed sources, authoritative sources, sources in high places, unimpeachable sources.

Metaphors

Metaphors express images that cannot be taken literally. The English lan-guage is very metaphoric, as you can see from the examples of clichés in this chapter so far. This is one of the reasons why English is so difficult to learn as a second language. Our writing and our conversation are 'riddled' with metaphors; they make our language vivid. However, some metaphors have become so over used that they have been pronounced 'dead'. Avoid 'dead' metaphors like 'Achilles' heel'. Also be careful of mixing metaphors. Do not 'gather the covered wagons in a circle', 'put on the war paint', and proceed to 'have a summit around the campfire'. Or write about researchers who 'mine data' to 'tease out' results to get to the 'bottom line'.

Euphemisms

Euphemisms are words and phrases that soften harsh expressions and create an aura of politeness.

There is a story about a dismembered female corpse being found in a suitcase in a London railway station in 1930. Despite the fact that the victim's arms and legs were severed from her body, the corpse was described as 'not having been interfered with'—a telling example of the lengths to which the authorities in times past went to protect the public from explicit details of sexual crimes.

For a long time after the AIDS epidemic surfaced in Australia there was a squeamish lack of detail about the ways in which the virus spread. It took columnist Phillip Adams to sweep away the 'exchange-of-bodily-fluids' eu-phemism. Because of the stigma attached to many AIDS–related deaths, a new style of euphemistic obituary is being written, containing euphemisms such as 'death was caused by a neurological disorder'.

Another area in which euphemisms are becoming more common is in terminology used to refer to older people in the community. The 'old people's home' has 'progressed' through 'retirement community' to become 'a senior congregate living community for the chronologically gifted' (*The Quarterly Review of Doublespeak*, April 1990, p. 2).

Different professions have a stock of useful euphemisms. Politicians have a favourite face-saving euphemism: 'My judgement was incorrect' instead of 'I was wrong'. When a journalist uses the phrase 'with respect' instead of 'I think you overstate your case', the euphemism usually indicates that the questions to follow will be anything but respectful.

In 1990 the Sydney Rail Authority announced that a ticket inspector would now be called a 'revenue protection officer'. Management's intention in replacing the term 'ticket inspector' (with its negative connotations of inspecting the customer), with the term 'revenue protection officer' (with its positive connotations of protecting the Sydney Rail Authority's financial interests) was commendable, but probably not achieved, because the new term sounds rather pompous, if not silly.

There is a long tradition in the USA of absurd job titles that raise the status of particular occupations: cashiers are 'customer-service representatives', grocery baggers are 'packaging agents', a person who presses clothes is a 'fabric-care technician', dishwashers are 'senior warewashers', people who fill orders in a mail order company are called 'fulfillment associates', and the weather announcers at a San Fransisco television station are called 'The Naturalists' (*The Quarterly Review of Doublespeak*, April 1990, p. 2).

A letter rejecting an academic request for industry support for a project relied almost totally on euphemisms.

> Unfortunately with the current downturn in our profession and the 'soft' insurance impacting our financial surplus for the year ending 1990, the company will be unable to respond in a positive financial manner.

The sector which has been the most prolific in providing new euphemisms has been the employment market. Companies prefer to use terms such as streamlining, restructuring, rationalising, downsizing, rightsizing, or hollow-ing out rather than sacking people. Employees these days do not get re-trenched, phased out, or even made redundant; they are excessed, outplaced, transitioned, given a schedule adjustment, or offered voluntary severance. People are now described as disadvantaged instead of poverty-stricken. In all these expressions an inoffensive or more pleasant word or phrase is used instead of a more explicit or unpleasant one.

Drake Personnel's Career Outplacement Services brochure for June 1990 has this to say about some expressions that are useful in the current hard 'economic climate'.

> Relocation and Dehiring have become recent additions to business language. They are not euphemisms for firing. They are an attempt to describe the situation where long-term, valuable employees have been released from a

company due to factors that do not relate to their individual performance or ability, such as operational necessities, closures, or economic rationalisations.

A whole new industry, outplacement consultancy, has sprung up around a phenomenon which is described almost exclusively in euphemisms.

We do not unreservedly advocate the use of euphemisms in business writing. We do, however, recognise that they are socially necessary in sensitive areas such as job redundancy. While most people prefer to read words like 'budget' or 'economy' rather than 'cheap', by the same token they also usually prefer to see a spade called a spade, rather than 'a manually-operated, recreational, eco-unit maintenance tool'. Of course, there are others who prefer to see a spade called 'a bloody shovel'—but such colloquialisms are generally out of place in professional writing.

COLLOQUIALISMS

Colloquialisms are expressions that people use in casual conversations to create an air of informality. Restrict their place in business writing to informal memos between colleagues. Words like flak, hype, hitlist, and overkill appeal because they are evocative and accessible, and it is 'OK' to suggest to a colleague that 'If this organisation "is after" an effective communication system, it should...', but it is inadvisable to use expressions such as this in formal company documents. 'A lot of' and 'lots of' are also too colloquial; use 'much' or 'many'.

COINED WORDS

The informality of language that we see in colloquialisms has another manifestation in the evolution of words from one form to another and in the 'coining' of new words. A good example of this is the playful extension of hardware and software to firmware, groupware, shareware, vapourware, learnware, mindware, thunderware, and even to liveware (humans). Another example is the contrasting of 'user-friendly' with 'user-vicious'.

New words come into the language from quite varied origins and either drop out or become so accepted that they find a place in dictionaries. *The Oxford English Dictionary* added 5000 new words between 1986 and 1989. Among the new words were fax, fast track, lap-top, and plastic money. Words have varying life spans, depending on the need for them. 'Disincentivisation' did not last for long, perhaps because it was so difficult to pronounce. On the other hand, 'yuppie' is now not only in the *Oxford Dictionary* (1986), but it has spawned a couple of dozen variations including 'guppie' (a gay, green, or greedy yuppie) and 'slumpie' (a severely lazy and unhelpful male person). Yuppie may well have started its life as a 'stunt' word, but its acceptance is evidence of the relentless evolution of language and the enjoyment people get out of coining variations.

Will 'the churn factor', identified as the tendency of companies to 'retrench and recruit at the same time' become sanctioned by conventional use? It is too early to say.

How about the kind of 'advertisingspeak' seen in advertisements such as the following?

> A large population, its distribution and verifiable fast growth offers a genuine solid opportunity in a successful new 'Franklins' anchored neighbourhood Shopping Centre.

In this advertisement, the copywriter has used a noun, 'Franklin' to coin a compound adjective, 'Franklins anchored' (which should be hyphenated, by the way). Converting one part of speech to another is very common in this kind of writing. The belief that 'any noun can be verbed' has been acted upon enthusiastically by those who talk about maximising opportunities, prioritising goals, potentialising people, moduling problems, preambling meetings, respectabilising the game, pedestrianising the city, proceduralising manuals, energising the substation, and trivialising problems. Most of these verbs have evolved from nouns, and some are more acceptable than others. Few readers baulk at 'prioritising' these days, but not too many would be happy to 'preamble' meetings. How about 'carpet' and 'bucket' used as verbs? Or the description of public relations as 'trending towards...', and land 'densing to' thick rain forest? Other recent examples of coined words or words in a different form from their original include validatable, faxable, uploaded, and VCR-isation.

Acronyms

Another variety of coined words includes pronounceable words made up from the initial letters of words in a title or expression. These acronyms are a form of shorthand in the way that jargon is. For example, the acronym COIK is derived from the phrase 'clear only if known'. (If you already know the rule or the process, the explanation is clear. The implication is, of course, that if you do not, this explanation might not help much.)

ANZAC and QANTAS are well-known acronyms, and cause no pronunciation problems, unlike EFTPOS (electronic funds transfer at point of sale) which is barely pronounceable, and WYSIWYG (what you see is what you get), which just makes it if you think of the 'y's' as 'i's'. ASAP, FYI, VDU, and CIA cannot be classed as acronyms because they do not form pronounceable words. They are called initialisms.

Use only acronyms that most of your readers will instantly recognise. Always spell out in full each time that you use them any acronyms that would be new to your readers, and avoid gimmicky ones like MEGO (my eyes glaze over) and NIMBY (not in my backyard).

ARCHAISMS

In an era of acronyms, which attempt to make language more economical, it is surprising that so many archaisms remain, particularly in business letters. There are organisations which still use Latin to indicate the date: inst, ult, prox.

One organisation seemingly determined to do away with old-fashioned archaisms is the Brisbane City Council which, in 1989, announced a change of policy for their correspondence writers

- affix your signature—sign
- enclosed herewith please find—here are
- pursuant to our agreement—as we agreed
- duly note—read.

However, we question whether all sections of the City Council are following their advertised policy, as we have seen a recent council letter which started out with the archaic and impersonal 'Receipt is acknowledged' instead of the preferred 'Thanks for your letter'. The Council also distinguished itself by winning an inaugural, Australia-wide International Literacy Year Wooden Spoon Award in 1990 for their 'tortured' English.

Here are some further examples of archaic language from our consulting files.

Original: So we may effect cancellation of your membership.

Improved: So that we can cancel your membership.

Original: Your contribution book is returned herewith.

Improved: We are returning your contribution book.

Original: Membership would normally be deemed to have lapsed.

Improved: We would normally consider that your membership has lapsed.

Original: Your early attention to this matter is requested.

Improved: Please see to this as soon as you can.

WORDINESS

Wordiness in a document can involve verbosity (big, pompous words), redundancy (saying the same thing twice), and superfluity (using unnecessary extra words).

Verbosity

Verbose writers use facilitate (instead of ease), utilise (instead of use), initial (instead of first), prioritise (instead of rank), ascertain (instead of find out), endeavour (instead of try), transmit (instead of send), and fabricate (instead of build).

Language authorities such as George Orwell and Strunk and White (1979) favour the more familiar, shorter word. So do readers.

Redundancy

A redundant word or phrase is one that unnecessarily qualifies another word or phrase. Redundant expressions say the same thing at least twice, sometimes more than twice. For example, 'I myself alone was the only one there'. Note the pointless repetition in expressions such as co-operate together, absolutely essential, needs and requirements, goals and objectives, this particular instance, end product, end result, hands-on participatory experience, same identical, exact same, plan in advance, recur again, basic fundamentals, each and every, and close scrutiny.

Superfluity

Superfluity is the use of unnecessary extra words, which we have italicised in the following examples: on a daily *basis*, accounted for *the fact that*, through *the use of*, in view of *the fact that*, if *at all* possible, and until *such time as*. While it might be natural for superfluous expressions to slip into your writing in a first draft, there is no reason for them to remain after editing.

Writers sometimes feel that they need to inject variety (sometimes called elegant variation) into their writing, with the result that a word like 'because' has endless wordy variations: due to, as a result of, in view of the fact that, owing to the fact that, based on the fact that, for the reason that, etc. These expressions are padded out with unnecessary words that have no purpose.

Padding also occurs when a writer wants to 'hedge' or equivocate in sentences.

> I would probably suggest that maybe...
> May, under some circumstances, tend to...

Doubtless there are some occasions when you will need to be equivocal, but avoid being unnecessarily tentative if you want to create a positive tone. We have seen a book on equivocal communication which seriously discusses concepts such as 'strategic ambiguity', 'devious messages', and 'contradictory verbal and non-verbal signs'.

NEGATIVES

Most professional writing texts suggest that writers avoid negative expressions like against, avoid, bar, decline, deny, fail, forget, doubt, except, exclude, harsh, inefficient, lack, neglect, negligent, preclude, prevent, prohibit, refrain from, refuse, useless, without. Unless you have a good reason, also avoid double or multiple negatives because they are usually difficult for a reader to unravel. For example, a reader is going to have to think twice about 'This assumption does not seem inexplicable', 'Your reader is never unsure', 'It hardly went unnoticed', and 'I was not uninvolved with the process'. Do not universally avoid the double negative, however. 'It is not uncommon' is not equivalent to 'It is common'.

DOUBLESPEAK

Another type of evasive language is that which has become known as 'doublespeak', a blanket term for confusing or deceptive language which is a combination of the concepts of 'newspeak' and 'doublethink' featured in George Orwell's novel *Nineteen Eighty-Four*.

Government reports are often characterised by doublespeak. The *Quarterly Review of Doublespeak* publishes examples from business, industry, education, and government. The winner of one Doublespeak Award was the Exxon Corporation, which described fifty-six kilometres of beach in Alaska as 'environmentally clean' and 'environmentally stabilized' while the crude oil from the spill still glistened on the rocks. When challenged about their use of doublespeak, they announced that 'clean' 'doesn't mean that every oil stain is off every rock... It means that the natural inhabitants can live there without harm'.

A car company recalled cars with the following letter.

> Continued driving with a failed bearing could result in disengagement of the axle shaft and adversely affect vehicle control.

Why hide behind such doublespeak when it could be a matter of life and death?

Weasel words

Weasel words, yet another manifestation of evasion and whitewash deliberately used to conceal unpleasant facts, are a form of doublespeak. The term, which first appeared in America in 1900, is used to identify words that suck meaning out of other words in the same way that a weasel can supposedly suck out the inside of an egg without damaging the shell. Weasel words cannot be taken at face value because they are designed to obscure or skirt the truth. Weasel words undermine; they amount to semantic fraud because they evade a direct commitment. When you follow up the phrase 'in fact' with unsupported personal opinion, you are using weasel words. Other words that may be used as weasel words include mere, meaningful, arguable, marginal, relatively.

Other weasel expressions are 'can be' in the phrase 'can be of significant value', and 'as much as' in the phrase 'as much as 20 per cent more'. What does it mean to leave the environment in a 'close to wilderness state'? Watch out for weasel expressions in your own writing, as well as in the writing of others.

A related problem lies in using expressions such as 'consequently' and 'basically', which act as written forms of 'um', 'ah', and 'sort of'—in other words, they say nothing.

Foreign Words and Phrases

The *Style Manual* recommends that writers use foreign words and phrases only when there is no exact English equivalent, because they puzzle, confuse, and annoy readers. We include a list of common foreign expressions in Figure 9.3, not because we believe you should use them, but because many writers still do, and it is helpful to understand what they mean when you come across them. You will notice that most of them are in Latin.

Confusable Words

Mistakes in word choice can tarnish your professional image as a writer. Try to avoid problems with the confusable words in Figure 9.4, the meanings of which we have taken from *The Oxford Dictionary*.

Spelling

Many professional writers lament their poor spelling, but believe they can do little about it. The most reliable spelling aid is doubt. Never assume that you can spell a word, even if it is a word that you have been spelling a certain way for years. It is quite possible that you have been spelling it wrongly for years and no one has ever picked you up on it. An executive in one of our writing workshops discovered he had been spelling 'its' wrongly during his entire career. Other participants express great surprise when they see 'liaison' spelt correctly for the first time.

Here are some guidelines to help you to improve poor spelling.

- Always revise with a dictionary beside you. Have at least three dictionaries available to you—*The Macquarie*, *The Oxford*, and a good American dictionary like *The Random House* to cover differences between Australian, American, and British usage.
- If you are using a computer for your writing, always put your document through your spelling checker. A spelling checker will pick up most of your misspellings, but many spelling checkers are not 'context-sensitive'

a fortiori (Latin: stronger)—with stronger reason, still more conclusively

a priori (Latin: what is before)—previous to

à propos (French: plan to set forth)—with regard to, in respect of, as suggested by

ad hoc (Latin: to this)—to this end, for the particular purpose in hand or in view, improvised

ad nauseam (Latin: to nausea)—to the point of making ill

ad absurdum (Latin: to absurdity)—to the point of being absurd

ad infinitum (Latin: to the end)—on and on and on

au courant (French: in the running)—abreast of, in the know

bona fide (Latin: with good faith)—in good faith, authentic, sincere, genuine

caveat emptor (Latin: let the buyer beware)

c'est la vie (French: it is the life)—that's life

ceteris paribus (Latin: other things being equal)—other conditions corresponding

comme il faut (French: as it is necessary)

de rigueur (French: concerning/of strictness)—(a matter) strictly or rigorously obligatory, according to strict etiquette

e.g. (*exempli gratia*) (Latin: for the sake of example)—for instance

éminence grise (French: grey eminence)—a person who wields power unseen and unofficially, usually through another, official person

et al(ia) (Latin: and others)—and other people

et cetera (etc.) (Latin: and the rest)—and other things, the rest

ex parte (Latin: out of the part)–by myself

fait accompli (French: accomplished fact)—an accomplished fact, an action which is completed (and irreversible) before affected parties learn of its having been undertaken

hoi polloi (Greek: the many)—the majority, the masses

idée fixe (French: fixed idea)—fixed idea

i.e. (*id est*) (Latin: that is)—tends to explain, rather than merely list

ipso facto (Latin: does of itself)—of itself

in re (Latin: in respect of)—in the matter of

in situ (Latin: in the original place)—in position

inter alia (Latin: between others)—among, amid, in between, in the midst of other things

mea culpa (Latin: through my own fault)—it's all my fault

modus operandi (Latin: mode of operating)—way of going about things

modus vivendi (Latin: mode of living)—a working arrangement

ne plus ultra (Latin: not more beyond)—a command to go no further; a prohibition of further advance or action; also an impassable obstacle or limitation

per se (Latin: by/in itself)—intrinsically, essentially, without reference to anything (or anyone) else

prima facie (Latin: at first sight)—on the face of it

quid pro quo (Latin: something for something)—one thing in place of another

quod erat demonstrandum (Latin: which was to be demonstrated)

sic (Latin: thus)—*sic* is used to indicate that what appears to be a mistake is being quoted directly from the original

sine qua non (Latin: without which not)—indispensable, absolutely necessary or essential

status quo (Latin: state in which)—the existing state of affairs

sui generis (Latin: of its own kind)—in its own right

summa cum laude (Latin: with highest praise)—with highest distinction

ultra vires (Latin: beyond law)—beyond the powers of legal authority

verbatim (Latin: word for word)

vis-à-vis (French: face to face)—over and against, in comparison with, in relation to

viz (Latin: short for *videlecit*—namely)—used when listing items only mentioned or hinted at

Figure 9.3 Common foreign words and phrases

Activate (to make active) **Actuate** (to set in motion, to inspire, to motivate)

Advice (opinion given) **Advise** (to recommend, inform, notify)

Appraise (to evaluate) **Apprise** (to inform)

Affect (to influence, to pretend) **Effect** (a result or consequence, to bring about or accomplish)

Assume (to take as being true) **Presume** (to take or put on oneself)

Attain (to arrive at, to reach) **Obtain** (to get, to acquire)

Cite (to quote) **Sight** (to see) **Site** (a place)

Complement (that which completes) **Compliment** (a polite expression of praise)

Compose (to make up, set up, arrange) **Comprise** (consist of)

Continuous (connected, unbroken) **Continual** (always happening, very frequent)

Constant (unremitting, frequently occurring) **Incessant** (unceasing, continual, repeated)

Delegate (send as a representative) **Relegate** (transfer to an inferior position)

Deprecate (express disapproval of) **Depreciate** (reduce in value, disparage or belittle)

Discreet (prudent, circumspect, unobtrusive) **Discrete** (separate, individually distinct)

Disinterested (impartial) **Uninterested** (not interested, indifferent)

Effective (having an effect) **Effectual** (sufficient to produce an effect) **Efficient** (productive of effect, capable) **Efficacious** (sure to produce the desired effect)

Eminent (distinguished) **Imminent** (impending, about to happen)

Flaunt (to show off) **Flout** (to treat with contempt)

Home in (go in the direction of) **Hone** (to sharpen)

Imply (insinuate, hint) **Infer** (deduce, conclude)

Insidious (treacherous, crafty) **Invidious** (likely to give offence or ill feeling)

Lead (the metal) **Led** (past tense of the verb 'to lead')

Militate (have force against) **Mitigate** (alleviate, reduce the severity of)

Oral (spoken, by word of mouth) **Verbal** (concerned with words)

Practicable (feasible, can be done) **Practical** (useful)

Practice (the noun) **Practise** (the verb)

Principal (chief, main) **Principle** (fundamental truth or code)

Simple (not complicated, or elaborate, or highly developed) **Simplistic** (made unjustifiably easy, shallow, superficial)

Specious (plausible on the surface, but not in reality) **Spurious** (not genuine, not what it pretends to be)

Stationary (not moving) **Stationery** (writing materials)

Use (to put into use or operation) **Utilise+** (to make productive use of, to exploit profitably, to use something for other than its intended purpose)

+Many readers regard 'utilise' as an ugly piece of jargon, so use it only when you can legitimately do so. Many writers invent their own mnemonics (memory aids) to help them remember the differences between words that can be easily confused: for example, stationery equals envelopes; The principal is my pal.

Figure 9.4 Confusable words

so cannot pick up mistakes like 'casual' for 'causal'. Beware of totally relying on spelling checkers, as the perfectly spelt piece of writing shown in Figure 9.5 proves.

Catch That Spilling Error
by Norwood B. Gove

As an addled service, I am going to put this piece in the Spilling Checker, where I tryst it will sale through with flying colons. In this modern ear, it is simply inexplicable to ask readers to expose themselves to misspelled swords when they have bitter things to do.

And with all other time-saving features on my new work processor, it is in realty very east to pit together a piece like this one and get it tight. For instants, if there is a work that is wrong, I just put the curse on it, press Delete and it's Well sometimes it deletes to the end of the lion or worst yet the whole rage.

Figure 9.5 (Source: *Scholarly Publishing*, October 1989)

- Pronounce words correctly. Mispronunciation can lead to misspelling. If you have trouble correctly spelling words like asterisk, hierarchical, or disastrous, it could be because you are hearing them wrongly. Say words like 'environment' in your head, emphasising the second 'n'. Be careful of words that are similar in sound and form, for example, dependant/ dependent.
- Summarise and memorise the differences between simple but problem words. It is quite easy to make mistakes with such simple words as their/ they're/there, to/too/two, your/you're, whose/who's, and, the most universally common spelling mistake its/it's. Nothing is guaranteed to diminish your credibility so instantaneously and so thoroughly as making a mistake with its/it's. Check for this when you are revising/ editing/proofreading. All you need to remember is that if you have used 'it's', you have said 'it is' or 'it has'.
- There are spelling rules such as 'i' before 'e', except after 'c', but they are not foolproof, so you need to learn all the exceptions as well. In this case, weight, neighbour, leisure, forfeit, seize, weird, and science.
- Because spelling skills reside in the hand as well as in the brain, sometimes it can help to write a word out to see if it looks right. But do not rely on this method.
- If you have looked up a word in the dictionary because you could not spell it, write it out a few times to help you remember it for next time. Keep a list of words that you have misspelt in the past, words that you know you have trouble with. Devise mnemonics for troublesome words, for example, 'there's "a rat" in "separate"'.

achieve	elitism	organisation
accommodation	environment	parallel
accountability	emanate	perpetration
adjourned	exaggerate	portrayal
affect/effect	explanation	preferred
aggregate	existence	preparation
appearance	feasibility	privilege
business	focuses	prominent
campaign	formatting	propaganda
chronological	fulfilled	questionnaire
cite	gauge	receive/receipt
cohesive	hierarchical	recommendation
commitment/committed	impresario	reference
comparative	independence	relevant
comparison	indispensable	religious
completeness	infinitely	repetition
component	institutional	resistant
conciseness	integral	schedule
connoisseur	integrity	sentence
consciousness	irresistible	separate
consistent	leisure	sequence
contemporary	liaison	specific
definite	licence	statistics
dependent/ant	maintenance	substantially
derogatory	miniature	supersede
disappointment	noticeable	technological
discrete	occasion	ultimately
division	occurrence/occurred	weird
dossier	omission/omitted	writing
egalitarianism	opinion	

Figure 9.6 Commonly misspelt words

Problems with plurals

There is a growing tendency to form plurals of nouns by adding 'apostrophe s' instead of 's', but this is not acceptable. The plural of 'portfolio' is 'portfolios', not 'portfolio's'. We do not talk about waiting a few 'moment's'.

English nouns that end in 's', 'x', 'z', 'ch', or 'sh' are made plural by adding 'es'. For example, boss becomes bosses, box becomes boxes, lunch becomes lunches, and wish becomes wishes. Other nouns are made plural by adding 's'. Nouns that end in 'y' are a special case. If there is a vowel before the final 'y', add 's' only, for example, alley becomes alleys. If there is a consonant before the final 'y' or the noun ends in 'quy', change the 'y' to 'i' and add 'es', for example, ally becomes allies.

Some words derived from Latin have retained their Latin plurals

- medium is the singular; media is the plural
- criterion is the singular; criteria is the plural
- phenomenon is the singular; phenomena is the plural.

With other Latin-derived words such as memorandum, syllabus, and appendix, you have a choice between the Latin and the English plural.

Conclusion

We have looked at many aspects of language in these two chapters. We have warned you of the pitfalls, while highlighting the intrinsic interest that you, as a professional writer, should have in words. However, writing is not merely a matter of selecting the 'right words'; a love of language does not necessarily translate into a mastery of writing. You also need to be in command of all the other aspects of writing that we discuss in this book.

References

Bryson, B. (1984). *The Penguin dictionary of troublesome words*, Harmondsworth: Penguin.

Connor, J. J. (1987). 'Technical writing kits: Their origins, function and context'. *Journal of Technical Writing and Communication*, Vol.17(3), 233–242.

Fieldhouse, H. (1982). *Good English guide*, London: J.M. Dent & Sons.

Lutz, W. (ed.), (1989). *Beyond nineteen eighty-four: Doublespeak in a post-Orwellian age*, Urbana, Il.: National Council of Teachers of English.

Orwell, G. (1950). *Shooting an elephant and other essays*, London: Secker & Warburg.

Strunk, W. and White, E. B. (1979). *The elements of style*, 3rd edn, New York: Macmillan.

CHAPTER 10

DECIDING HOW TO PUNCTUATE

WHY PUNCTUATE?

Punctuation (the earliest form of which was the insertion of a space between words) is an essential ingredient in written communication because it clarifies relationships between words and groups of words by revealing the structure of sentences. This, in turn, increases the reader's understanding. Punctuation also controls the pace and rhythm of sentences.

Punctuation marks are often compared to traffic signals; for example, a comma is said to act like a yellow light or a speed bump to slow a reader down. Most readers will not particularly notice correct punctuation. However, they may notice idiosyncratic punctuation. (You may recall that three of the six most irritating sentences in the survey we mentioned in Chapter 7 caused problems because of their faulty punctuation.)

In this chapter we deal with the main punctuation marks: apostrophe, brackets, colon, comma, dash, ellipsis, exclamation mark, full stop, hyphen, question mark, quotation marks, semicolon, and slash. We also deal with other mechanical conventions such as abbreviations, bullets, capital letters, contractions, italics, and numbers.

PUNCTUATION PRINCIPLES

Only if you know how and where each punctuation mark can be used will you be able to punctuate in an informed and deliberate way. Some punctuation marks such as the semicolon have only a couple of main uses, whereas the comma has many. However, as with most other aspects of writing that we discuss in this book, punctuation cannot be totally reduced to rules.

In spoken English we can use the tone, pitch, stress, and volume of our voice, along with variation in pace and pausing, to help get our message across. In written English, punctuation has to substitute for these elements. However, writing is not merely speaking written down. Spoken and written language differ markedly in structure, and that is why we cannot solely rely on how sentences sound in our heads to guide us in our choice of punctuation. The old rule, 'Punctuate where you draw breath', is not applicable, let alone reliable.

Punctuation marks in writing *can* indicate where a speaker would pause, but they do not necessarily or always coincide with the pauses that a speaker would make. If writers punctuate solely according to how they mentally hear sentences, their punctuation will cause problems for their readers. A much more reliable strategy is to punctuate according to syntax (sentence structure), because punctuation has its own logic, based on the structure of written communication. To punctuate well, you need a good grasp of grammar and syntax.

In most instances, punctuation is a matter of individual taste and style rather than the strict application of a rigid rule. When in doubt, clarify whether a punctuation mark is necessary or optional in that spot, and then if you have a choice, decide which one you prefer. Some writers punctuate more heavily than others. Journalists traditionally use punctuation marks more sparingly than other writers because punctuation marks take up 'expensive' space in newspapers.

The most important principle to keep in mind when you are writing/editing any document is consistency, and the placing of your punctuation marks is no exception. For example, many writers are increasingly using a comma before the final 'and' in a list to ensure that the reader is always clear about whether the two final items are linked, as they are in 'stocks and bonds'. If you are not in the habit of doing this, how would you punctuate the following sentence?

> The committee the shareholders an old man eating an icecream and the auditors were present at the shareholders' meeting.

The Australian Government *Style Manual* suggests using the comma before the final 'and' only when this prevents ambiguity. We believe it to be useful in all cases.

Be aware also that punctuation constantly and fluidly evolves just as language evolves—particularly in the use of hyphens, capital letters, and commas. Note the tendency in contemporary business practice to use a full-block format which allows for 'open' punctuation in the opening and closing sections of letters. This punctuation can be left out because each section of the address starts on a new line so there is no need to clarify structure. (See page 69 for a letter which uses open punctuation.)

What follows is a discussion of the main punctuation marks and other relevant mechanical conventions. Consult the Australian Government *Style Manual* if you need a more comprehensive coverage of punctuation, because we could not include in this chapter all the uses of all the punctuation marks.

We have arranged the punctuation marks alphabetically so that you can refer to them easily.

THE APOSTROPHE

Use the apostrophe

- to show ownership
- to make contractions
- to form plurals—special cases.

To show ownership

English nouns show ownership (the possessive case) with a possessive apostrophe (') or a possessive apostrophe and the letter 's' ('s). For example, the phrase, the operator's desk, refers to the desk belonging to the operator; the phrase, the operators' desks, refers to the desks belonging to the operators.

Singular nouns

To make a singular noun possessive, add ('s) after the final letter. For example, the operator's desk (one operator).

For a singular noun that already ends in 's', you have the option of adding ('s) or the (') only.

We prefer to add ('s). The *Style Manual* recommends this also. For example, the report written by Harris would become Harris's report. Our reason for preferring this option is that we 'hear' the second 's' when we read it. We see no problem with applying this option, even when the next word begins with 's', as in the phrase Harris's submission. On the other hand, problems do arise when an apostrophe only is added to the word, for example, 'Dawkins' reforms'. Before long, this tends to evolve into 'Dawkin's reforms'. So we have 'the reforms of Dawkin'.

Some writers make an exception for words in which the final syllable of the ownership word both begins and ends in an 's' sound. Examples of such words are mostly classical or biblical: Xerxes, Moses, and Jesus. The argument is that it is too hard to pronounce three 's' sounds in a row. However, many writers are using 's in such cases. We have seen examples of this: the princess's new clothes.

Plural nouns

To make plural nouns that end in 's' possessive, add an apostrophe after the final letter. For example, operators' desks (more than one operator). For plural nouns that do not already end in 's' such as women and men, form the possessive by adding ('s)—women's and men's.

(None of the personal pronouns uses an apostrophe to form the possessive case: I becomes my, you becomes your, who becomes whose, he becomes his, she becomes her, we becomes our, they becomes their.)

To make contractions

An apostrophe is used when two words are contracted to one. The apostrophe takes the place of the missing letters. Don't, haven't, it's (it is), I'll, you've.

To form plurals—special cases

Apostrophes have also been traditionally used to form the plurals of letters, numbers, symbols, and words referred to as words.

> In the 1990's fewer writers are using +'s and -'s, p's and q's, to say nothing of but's in their writing.

The *Style Manual* no longer advocates that writers use the apostrophe in those cases. It recommends that you write that sentence as follows.

> In the 1990s fewer writers are using + s and – s, p s and q s, to say nothing of buts in their writing.

Problems with the possessive apostrophe

Writers have problems with the possessive apostrophe; they leave them out when they should put them in, and they put them in when they should leave them out.

Its/it's

The its/it's mistake is undoubtedly the most common error in all kinds of writing—and the one that, even though seemingly trivial, will generate the loudest groans from discerning readers. 'Its' means belonging to it; it is the possessive form of the pronoun it. 'It's' is always a contraction of it is; it can never be anything else. Although we have seen it in writing and so, probably, have you, its' is not accepted. When you are editing your work and find examples of it's, ask yourself if you intend it to mean it is. If you do, leave the possessive apostrophe there; if you do not, remove the possessive apostrophe.

Dropping of the apostrophe

Problems with the possessive apostrophe have caused a shift to adjectives substituting for them. For example, Drivers' Association has become Drivers

Association and Girls' High School has become Girls High School. But, organisations such as the Queensland Writers' Centre and many others are most particular about retaining their apostrophe.

The 'apostrophied plural'

Another problem with the apostrophe is its misuse in forming plurals—what some people call the 'apostrophied plural'. This probably happens because the plural and the possessive often sound the same when spoken. Signwriters seem to be very fond of the apostrophied plural, sometimes called the greengrocers' plural. We have all seen signs for Auto's, Tomato's, and Palm's. The plural of a proper noun is usually formed by adding 's' (but no apostrophe) as in the Browns. Plurals are also formed by adding 'es' or 'ies'. (Check Chapter 9.) There are exceptions to this, so always check in a dictionary if you are in doubt.

Making hyphenated expressions possessive

To make hyphenated compound nouns possessive, add ('s) to the final item. For example, editor-in-chief becomes editor-in-chief's. The plural editors-in-chief becomes editors-in-chief's in the possessive.

Making indefinite pronouns possessive

Make indefinite pronouns such as 'somebody' or 'anybody' possessive by adding ('s). For example, someone else becomes someone else's, anybody becomes anybody's, no one becomes no one's.

Making two subjects possessive

If you have two subjects, you must decide who is 'possessing'. For what is called 'joint possession', make the second element possessive. For example, Sam and Jack's office, if they share an office. For individual possession, make both elements possessive, for example, Sam's and Jack's offices, if they have an office each.

BRACKETS

The main use of round brackets (parentheses) is to set apart an 'aside' which is not essential to the meaning of the sentence.

The summary (see page two) should be helpful.

Inessential elements within sentences include explanations, examples, and small digressions.

Use round brackets also to enclose numbers or letters marking off items in a list.

> The most important parts of a report are as follows: (a) the executive summary, (b) the conclusions, and (c) the recommendations.

Square brackets are used to mark insertions in quoted text by someone other than the author of the original text. The most common use of square brackets is to insert 'sic' into quoted text. Writers use [sic] when there is an error in spelling, punctuation, grammar, or fact in the original text. Because a writer is not at liberty to correct an error in a direct quote, but wants the reader to know that the original error has been noticed, [sic] is a useful device. Note the following extract from a performance appraisal report of a junior employee by a section head.

> Jane needs to be much more meticulous when proofreading. I quote from one of her memos. 'The stationary [sic] was ordered last week'.

There is a growing tendency for writers, when quoting material from the days before non-discriminatory language policies were in place, to use [sic] in examples such as the following (if there is no indication of whether the manager is male or female).

> When a manager asks his [sic] staff for an evaluation, he [sic] is placing himself [sic] on the spot.

If you wish to highlight what you believe to be sexist language, this is a legitimate way to do it, although some readers may be irritated by this practice. Another way to handle the problem is to put [her] instead of [sic].

Square brackets can also be used to add clarifying words if there is ambiguity in a sentence.

> It is definitely established that she [Dr Sommers] signed the contract.

Bullets for Listed Items

There seems to be no consensus about whether the ends of lines of listed items should be punctuated or not. Whatever you decide to do, make sure that you are consistent. Bulleted lists have been presented using open punctuation in this book.

CAPITALS

Use capital letters to give importance and distinction to specific words. Your use of capitals is likely to vary with your perspective on the terms you use. However, generally speaking, be guided by the Australian Government *Style Manual*, which has around seventy rules for capitalisation. Some writers unnecessarily capitalise anything that seems important to them, for example, 'I attended the Conference'.

Note, also, the trend to 'minimal' capitalisation in titles of books and articles. Minimal capitalisation applied to the title of this book would result in *The professional writing guide: Writing well and knowing why*. Maximum capitalisation would result in *The Professional Writing Guide: Writing Well and Knowing Why*.

THE COLON

Use the colon to 'announce' or 'introduce' an explanation or clarification, an interpretation, an amplification, an illustrative example, or a formal list or quotation.

Here is a sentence in which the colon is used as an announcement mark.

> The software they chose had one advantage: it was easy to learn.

The colon is often used after 'following' or as 'follows'.

> We have used the following word processing packages: WordPerfect, Microsoft Word, Multimate, and Xywrite.

Misuse of the colon

The colon needs to follow an independent clause—in other words a full sentence. Avoid using it between a verb and its object in sentences such as 'Our favourite training films are: the films made by Video Arts'. Or between a preposition and its object, 'Please make a list of: staff eligible for leave', 'This course aims to familiarise participants with: the necessary terminology'. If your list is a formal, indented one, however, you may use a colon after a preposition.

The dash hybrid colon plus dash (:-) is becoming increasingly rare. A colon is sufficient; the dash is redundant.

THE COMMA

Many writers rely on a principle that they learned at school: use a comma where you would pause if you were speaking or reading aloud. This poor advice leads to the misuse of the comma in sentences such as the following.

His innate grasp of the world of finance, found him writing for the financial pages.

Both commands require that a tape created using one command, must be read using the same command.

A serious attempt on the part of management to remedy the state of affairs, demonstrates how importantly this is regarded by them.

In each case the comma inappropriately separates the subject of the sentence from its verb—thereby breaking up the structure of the sentence.

- Use a comma to divide introductory information from the main part of the sentence.

If you have any questions, please contact us.

There is a distinct break in the structure of the sentence after 'questions', so a comma is legitimate and useful.

To register, phone the secretary.

Even though the sentence is short, placing a comma after the word 'register' prevents possible disorientation for the reader.

Similarly, in the sentence 'Remember, the test is free!', placing a comma after 'Remember' prevents your reader from reading your sentence as if it were structured the same way as 'Remember the Alamo!'

The following sentence needs the comma after 'conferred' to prevent over-reading when your reader encounters your sentence for the first time.

> After they conferred, the delegates chose a leader.

If you omit the comma after 'conferred', your reader will infer that they conferred the delegates. This meaning will not hold once your reader gets further into the sentence. Your reader will then have to re-read your sentence and mentally supply your missing comma.

- Use a comma to co-ordinate and link two parts of a sentence.

> Please sign the documents, and we will lodge them.

In such a short sentence the comma is optional because there is little possibility of ambiguity. However, while a comma may not be necessary in this instance, it is certainly not incorrect.

There are only seven conjunctions that have this particular relationship with the comma: for, and, nor, but, or, yet, so. They are generally referred to by the mnemonic 'comma fanboys'. An alternative construction which is used in more complex sentences is the substitution of a semicolon for the comma plus fanboy.

> Please sign the documents; we will lodge them.

- Use a comma to insert information.

> We note, however, that you were late.
>
> My report, you will be pleased to hear, is finished.
>
> The senior partner, Ms Jackson, will meet you.
>
> You asked me, Mr Jones, to send copies to you.

The expressions between the commas are examples of non-essential elements. Each one could be left out without radically altering the meaning of the sentence. Make sure that you always enclose elements such as this within a 'comma pair'.

- Use a comma to separate items in a list (a list consists of more than two items). Use commas to separate items in a list, unless the items have internal punctuation, in which case use semicolons instead of commas.

> Remember to check your grammar, spelling, and punctuation.
>
> Remember to check your grammar, especially agreement of subjects and verbs; your spelling, especially tricky words such as 'liaison', 'separate', and 'accommodation'; and your punctuation, especially your use of the semicolon.

At the beginning of the chapter we mentioned that consistently placing a comma before the final 'and' in a list will help your readers. We have noticed that the use of the comma in this position is increasing in Australian and American writing. The advantage of using the comma here is that you will never confuse your reader about whether the two final items in a list are a unit or separate. Consider the following sentence.

> Original: Background, objectives, methods and timing and costs are major sections in our company's proposals.

Does the sentence above mean methods plus timing and costs? Or methods and timing plus costs? The meaning would be clearer if there were a comma in the necessary spot.

> Improved 1: Background, objectives, methods, and timing and costs are major sections in our company's proposals.
>
> Improved 2: Background, objectives, methods and timing, and costs are major sections in our company's proposals.

- Use a comma to separate parts of a sentence where there is a natural break in the structure.

> After the delegates conferred about the candidates who had been put forward, they chose a leader.

- Use a comma after the word that introduces a direct quotation.

> She said, 'Thank you for all your help'.

- Use a comma between adjectives if the adjectives could be joined by 'and'

> ...a large, expensive, glossy brochure.
>
> ...a good, clear, up-to-date manual.

Comma problems

The comma splice

Apart from the unnecessary or 'early' comma, which we mentioned at the beginning of this section, the most common comma problem is what is called the 'comma splice'. This occurs when a comma is used to splice (join together) two sentences.

> The comma splice is a common error, it is a fault of many writers.

Replace the comma with a full stop or a semicolon. We dealt with this problem in the survey at the beginning of Chapter 7.

Commas around a non-restrictive clause

Another comma problem occurs in the use of a 'comma pair' around a 'non-restrictive' clause. A non-restrictive clause adds information (makes a comment) but is not essential to the main message in the sentence. It must always be introduced by 'which' and always set off by commas.

> The taxes, which are reasonable, will be paid.

This sentence indicates that all the taxes will be paid. When the clause is essential (restrictive, defining) to the main message of the sentence it is introduced by 'which' or 'that' and not set off by commas, as in the following example.

> The taxes that are reasonable will be paid.

This sentence indicates that only the reasonable taxes will be paid.

Make sure that you use a comma pair to set off a clause that could be left out without radically altering the sense of the sentence. This is one of the six major problems identified in the survey we reported in Chapter 7.

Remember: use either no commas or a comma pair!

THE DASH

Use the dash to set off a distinct interruption (abrupt change in tone), new or unfinished thoughts, or to emphasise parenthetical expressions (particularly when the parenthetical expression contains commas), as in the following example.

> These three books—on speaking, interviewing, and negotiating—are very useful.

THE ELLIPSIS

Use an ellipsis (three full stops) to indicate the removal of a word or words from a quotation. The ellipsis allows you to quote selectively. If the missing element coincides with the end of a sentence, some writers use four spaced full stops, though the *Style Manual* recommends using three in all instances where you leave words out.

> Rituals that famous writers have followed include keeping rotten apples in a desk, working in a cork-lined room... and remaining bare-headed in the sunshine.

THE EXCLAMATION MARK

Use an exclamation mark after an expression of surprise.

> What a powerful computer this is!

The exclamation mark is not widely used in business writing—except in advertising copy, as this example indicates.

> To work a computer needs a brain. Yours!

The Full Stop

Use the full stop to end a sentence. It is the most frequently used punctuation mark. The only problem that writers seem to have with the full stop is where to place it when using brackets and quotes.

> The full stop is part of this sentence (not part of this aside).
>
> (This sentence is entirely within brackets.)
>
> His last words to me were, 'I'll contact you next week'.

Until quite recently, the full stop was used to indicate the shortened version of a word. For example, Doctor Lewis was shortened to Dr. Lewis. Increasingly, this full stop is being omitted when the final letter of the abbreviation coincides with the final letter of the original word. Most writers would end an abbreviation that does not end with the final letter of a word, for example, Jan. for January, with a full stop.

The Hyphen

The hyphen allows readers to distinguish between a 'man-eating tiger' and a 'man eating chicken' and between a 'little-used car' and a 'little, used car'.

Use the hyphen in numbers twenty-one to ninety-nine and fractions, for example, 'one-tenth the size'.

Also use the hyphen in compound adjectives in front of a noun. For example, 'a well-groomed employee'. They are not hyphenated when placed after the noun, for example, 'that employee is well groomed'.

Other examples of compound adjectives in front of the noun include a three-year-old computer, a hit-and-miss method, a standing-room-only crowd, a self-styled entrepreneur.

Words which may now not be hyphenated include uppercase, shutdown, and desktop. However, we still hyphenate un-Australian, all-inclusive, self-sufficient, a take-off, a go-between, anti-inflation, secretary-treasurer. The main problem with hyphens is maintaining consistency.

ITALICS OR UNDERLINING

Use italics for the titles of full documents such as books, newspapers, magazines, journals, television shows, films, and when you use foreign words and phrases that are not in common use, for example, *idée fixe*. If you are handwriting or using a typewriter without italics, underline titles.

THE QUESTION MARK

Use a question mark to ask a direct question or to indicate that you are unsure of your information.

> Example 1: Is punctuating your writing correctly a challenge for you?
>
> Example 2: The cost of the function was $35 (?).

QUOTATION MARKS

Quotation marks are also called inverted commas. Use quotation marks around directly quoted material. The current practice in Australia is to use single quotation marks in the first instance, then double quotation marks for a quote inside your first quote.

> Example 1: She said to me, 'Haven't you heard the expression "shop talk" used to refer to the jargon used in a particular field?'

An exception to this practice is if the material is longer than four lines or more than about forty words, in which case indent the material and do not use any quotation marks around the quote. The indentation does that for you.

The titles of articles from newspapers or magazines, chapters of books, episodes of television and radio programs, and speeches need to be placed inside quotation marks; the name of the newspaper, magazine, book, or television show should be in italics or underlined as discussed above.

You can use quotation marks to indicate that you are using a word or expression in an unusual way or to enclose an expression that you know is colloquial.

> Example 2: I think I know 'where you're coming from'.

However, do not overdo quotation marks. Some writers use them to add emphasis, but it can be distracting.

THE SEMICOLON

Use the semicolon to pull together and contrast two independent clauses that have linking subject matter. So, use the semicolon where you could also use a full stop.

> **Example 1: The comma splice is a common error; it is a fault of many writers.**
>
> **Example 2: Work when you play; play when you work.**

A variation on this pattern occurs when you have an independent clause followed by a co-ordinating conjunction such as 'however', 'in fact', 'nevertheless', 'therefore' etc. which is in turn followed by an independent clause. An example of this pattern follows.

> **Example 3: She had outstanding leadership qualities; consequently, the company promoted her very quickly.**

When items already have internal punctuation or when each item in the list starts off on a new line, use the semicolon between items.

> **Use figures for (1) sums of money—e.g. $100; (2) times—e.g. 7.30 a.m.; (3) weights and measures—e.g. 70 kg; and (4) percentages—e.g. 95%.**

THE SLASH

Use the slash to indicate appropriate alternatives (and/or) and to separate divisions in time (1996/1997).

MASTERING PUNCTUATION

A useful way to learn the correct use of punctuation marks is to go through well-edited written material and decide why each mark has been used. In some instances, the mark could be an optional choice, and you may prefer to leave it out or to use an alternative mark.

Finally, here are some sentences to test your mastery of punctuation. We have discussed these or similar examples in this chapter.

1: A hard-working group, these writers can produce a report in a day.

2: Proposals, a constant necessity, are a major problem for writers.

3: However, that doesn't mean that the business is finished.

4: His objection, therefore, was ignored.

5: I sat with my boss, and his assistant sat elsewhere.

6: It was damaged, but it is still usable.

7: This transport company provides its customers with safe, reliable, and comfortable service.

8: Travel should not be underestimated: it broadens the mind.

9: The operator ran the program; the disk drive was faulty.

10: Please make a list of staff eligible for leave.

11: The big advantages of the system are its versatility and its low cost.

12: The following contractors offered bids: Wilsons, Sydney; Jennings, Perth; and Sykes, Melbourne.

13: My report, you will be pleased to hear, is finished.

14: The taxes that are reasonable will be paid.

15: The taxes, which are reasonable, will be paid.

16: Most readers will not notice correct punctuation, and that's what you should aim for.

17: It's a wise dog that scratches its own fleas.

18: How do you know when its it's, and when it's its?

19: Whether hypertext becomes as widespread as word processing remains to be seen.

20: However, the process of successfully implementing these systems is extremely complex.

This is how we would punctuate these sentences.

1: A hard-working group, these writers can produce a report in a day.

2: Proposals, a constant necessity, are a major problem for writers.

3: However, that doesn't mean that the business is finished.

4: His objection, therefore, was ignored.

5: I sat with my boss, and his assistant sat elsewhere.

6: It was damaged, but it is still usable.

7: This transport company provides its customers with safe, reliable, and comfortable service.

8: Travel should not be underestimated; it broadens the mind. OR

8: Travel should not be underestimated: it broadens the mind.

9: The operator ran the program; the disk drive was faulty.

10: Please make a list of staff eligible for leave.

11: The big advantages of the system are its versatility and its low cost.

12: The following contractors offered bids: Wilsons, Sydney; Jennings, Perth; and Sykes, Melbourne.

13: My report, you will be pleased to hear, is finished.

14: The taxes that are reasonable will be paid.

15: The taxes, which are reasonable, will be paid.

16: Most readers will not notice correct punctuation, and that's what you should aim for.

17: It's a wise dog that scratches its own fleas.

18: How do you know when it's it's and when it's its? OR

18: How do you know when it's its and when it's it's?

19: Whether hypertext becomes as widespread as word processing remains to be seen.

20: However, the process of successfully implementing these systems is extremely complex.

References

Australian Government Publishing Service, (1994). *Style manual for authors, editors and printers*, 5th edn, Canberra: AGPS.

Carey, G. V. (1958). *Mind the stop*. Harmondsworth: Penguin.

Douglas, A. and Strumph, M. (1988). *Webster's new world guide to punctuation*, New York: Simon & Schuster.

Williams, J. (1989). *Style: Ten lessons in clarity and grace*, 3rd edn, Glenview, Il.: Scott Foresman.

CHAPTER 11

REVISING AND EDITING YOUR DOCUMENTS

WRITING IS REWRITING

Most writers and writing educators emphasise the importance of revising and editing by insisting that 'writing is rewriting'. They will tell you that writing is a process of discovering what you want to say and that you should write **with the intention of revising.**

Many people say that the only way that they can think is to jot their thoughts down. Writers who believe that writing is a matter of forming whole sentences in their heads and then capturing these sentences on paper are misguided. It is not easy to say what you want to say and say it in the best way possible at the same time. When beginning a sentence of more than a few words, it is usually impossible for most people to know how the sentence will end. That is why experienced writers rely on revising and editing.

Unfortunately, business writers do not usually have the luxury that creative writers such as novelists, poets, and scriptwriters have—the time to revise. Many creative writers will tell you that their writing–revising ratio is anything from one to four to one to ten, or even higher. Because revising is as unavoidable for business writers as for any other writers, you need to master as many workable revising/editing strategies as possible. This will enable you to efficiently apply them once you have written your first draft. Very experienced writers have their own strategies that they implement as they write.

You can be certain that any 'perfectly' correct document has been revised and edited by a highly-competent professional. You can be equally certain that an incoherent, mechanically inept document has not been revised and edited by a competent professional.

This chapter covers strategies for revising, editing, and proofreading that you can use to produce a well-written and mechanically-perfect document.

WHAT DO REVISING AND EDITING ENTAIL?

Revising (which literally means 're-seeing') requires the writer to consider the overall structure and content of the document. So revising takes place at the 'global' or 'macro' level of the document. Editing is the polishing and sharpening that takes place at the 'local' or 'micro' level after a writer is satisfied with the overall structure and content of the document. Because even the best writers do not necessarily 'get it right the first time', you should recognise the need to revise and edit all but the very shortest informal documents such as memos. Even then it is wise to double-check a memo before you send it. After you have written your first draft your aim should be to get as much distance as possible between you and your document. Not distance in the sense of sending it off for distribution—distance in the sense of time. Always try to get your writing task completed well in advance of your deadline so that you can take advantage of the benefits of an 'incubation' or 'cooling-off' period for a document.

Incubation

One of the most effective strategies for revising is to have a time gap between when you finish your first draft and when you revise it. The longer the incubation period, the more chance you have of simulating a reader's response to your document when you re-read it, because memories of what you have written fade quickly. A couple of days' incubation is desirable (particularly for a long and/or important document), but if you cannot afford that, then set the document aside for as long as you can. Even a couple of hours is better than no time at all. You can be sure that the weaknesses in your document will be more apparent to you the longer the time span between draft and revision.

You should set aside and consider important documents such as job applications or proposals as many times as possible—each time checking a different aspect. This process is called 'multistage revising' or 'the editorial loop'.

The editorial loop

The 'editorial loop' is a methodical strategy whereby you put your document through several 'pass throughs', looking at a different aspect of it each time. The first pass through considers the overall structure; the final pass through checks whether the pages are all there, the right way up, and in the right order. If you follow this suggestion you will revise at the global level and move down to the more mechanical micro aspects at the end of the process.

As you re-read your first draft, resist the temptation to tinker with micro-level problems such as punctuation, spacing etc. If you have to re-structure or scrap parts of your document, the time that you spend on minor changes in your initial run-through is wasted.

Writers who use a word processor know how much easier it is to do multistage revising and editing because they can keep working on a clean print-out as they put a document through the successive stages. Revising/ editing on a word processor is made even easier when you print out your text with wider margins than usual and double the line spacing of your document so that you have plenty of room to make alterations. You can also automatically print out the date of each specific draft to help you keep track of your revisions.

The realities of professional writing usually do not allow the luxury of unlimited multistage revising, but if you can manage to do it a few times on important documents and are impressed by its benefits, you can modify and use the steps we suggest below and practise a version of multistage revising that works for you. Nothing, however, can replace systematic revising and editing using the editorial loop. You will miss errors if you try to shortcut by looking at too many aspects in one pass through.

Writer-based Writing

If your writing situation means that your first draft must be your final draft, you need to be particularly conscious of the pitfalls of writing 'writer-based' documents so that you can avoid them. Writer-based writing (coined by writing researcher Linda Flower) results from a writer's desire to get out a message and/or pass on information, rather than a concern for what the reader wants and needs to know.

Writer-based writing contains content-based information from your point-of-view rather than reader-based information. When you write a covering letter to accompany your résumé in a job application it is highly likely that your first draft will be writer-based: 'I spent two years working for..., and then I got a job with ...' A potential employer is interested only in how significantly you can contribute to the organisation you are applying to. To write documents that are reader-based, try to put yourself in your reader's place as you re-read your draft. If you have written a writer-based rather than a reader-based document, you will mentally register a 'so what?' reaction at points where your document fails to be of relevance to your reader.

The Levels of Edit

In the late seventies, staff at the Jet Propulsion Laboratories in Pasadena, California, developed a checklist for an organised approach to editing which they called the 'Levels of Edit'. They identified the following nine points

- **co-ordination**—development of job specifications
- **policy**—verification of essential parts of the document such as page numbers, making sure that any comments that might be construed as

derogatory or as endorsements for products are brought to the attention of the authors

- **integrity**—making sure that all parts of the publication match up and that there are no gaps or repetitions in numbering
- **screening**—checking for incorrect grammar, misspellings, or missing text; typos; missing graphics; camera-ready graphics
- **copy clarification**—clarifying any illegible text for printing
- **format**—making sure that the document conforms to the appropriate format
- **mechanical style**—checking for consistency in aspects such as capitalisation, abbreviations, numbers, different typefaces, captions, and sequence
- **language**—checking usage, consistency of terminology, conciseness
- **substantive**—dealing with the content of the document, whether the content is accurately reflected by the title and summary, whether all the material is logical and relevant.

(Haugen, 1991, p. 61)

Because the first eight of these nine levels of edit are at a fairly mechanical level, many writers, recognising the power of such a strategy, developed their own versions of the levels of edit that give greater weight to more substantive matters such as content and structure.

The 'Levels of Edit' approach is valuable because it is systematic, not 'hit-and-miss'. Devising a checklist that suits you and applying it methodically and painstakingly will greatly increase your chances of producing a high-quality document. The headings that we and many other writers use are as follows

- structure
- content
- style
- format
- mechanics.

The structure and content loops are at the 'whole-document' or 'global' (macro) level, while successive loops move down to smaller details—at what we would call the 'local' (micro) level.

Once you become a reasonably experienced writer, and this will happen if your work has been constantly and competently critiqued by others, you will get to know your weaknesses. For example, you may tend to be less concise than is desirable. Make a list of your common faults and use this as a further reminder when you are putting your work through the editorial loop.

Following are some detailed questions which relate to each of the headings in the checklist above. These can be helpful to you at each stage of your revising and editing.

Structure—how your document is organised

An effective strategy for seeing the structure of a document is to construct an outline after you have completed your first draft. You can go through your document highlighting headings and important sentences with a coloured pen or use your computer to give you a print-out of the opening and closing sentences of each of your paragraphs because these usually contain the most important information. Or, persuade a colleague to construct an outline of your document. If the resulting outline does not flow and it is obvious that your structure is unbalanced or unfocused, you will need to restructure the document. (It is widely acknowledged that writing and editing are intrinsically iterative rather than linear.)

- What is the organising pattern (structure) of your document? (See arrangement patterns in Chapter 5.)
- Does this pattern help to make the document clear?
- Is this pattern clearly evident to the reader from the headings?
- Does your introduction clearly preview the structure?
- Does the document deal with all aspects outlined in the introduction?
- Is your document broken down into manageable sections which are signposted for your reader?
- Do all parts of your document flow logically from one to the next with ideas in an appropriate sequence?
- Are all related ideas together and clearly identified?
- Have you regularly summed up the gist of your argument if your document is long?
- Does the conclusion comprehensively summarise the main points of the document?

Content—what your document 'says'

Re-read your initial draft with your original purpose in mind and ask yourself whether your document says what you intended it to say and includes all the information that a reader would need.

- Is your title appropriate?
- Having read the document, what action will a reader take? (File it for reference? Base a decision on it? Act on it?) Do you think that your document will have your intended effect on your reader and generate the response you would like?
- Does the introduction clearly set the context or do you have preliminary 'warm-up' material that is unnecessary? For example, do you write letters that start out redundantly with 'We would like to advise you...'?
- Is your document convincing because your ideas are fully explained and your arguments proved by supporting details and illustrations?
- If your document is a strongly persuasive one, such as a proposal or a job application letter, are your persuasive strategies effective, for example, a convincing choice of words and an effective sequence of ideas?

- Have you identified the criteria that you used and qualified any tentative assertions you have made?
- Is there any evidence of unwarranted assumptions or bias that distorts your conclusions, or conclusions unjustified by the evidence?
- Have you included any irrelevant details or digressions?
- Is your material at the appropriate level for its readers—that is, not too specialised, nor too superficial, nor too pedestrian? (Do not underestimate or overestimate your readers.)
- If your document is one of a series, for example, a progress report, have you made sure that you have incorporated all the later developments that have occurred since the last report was written—particularly if you did not actually collect the information? (Clients are irritated by the inclusion of superseded material.)
- Have you checked to see that your document complies with company policy on the issues you have discussed?
- Did you consider opportunities for appropriate illustrations? (Check Chapter 12 on visual presentation.)

Style—how you say what you say

Check paragraph construction. (See Chapter 6.)

- Are your paragraphs adequately developed to support your major ideas?
- Are there too many ideas in any paragraph?
- Is there a new paragraph each time there is a shift in topic?
- Are there adequate links/transitions between paragraphs?

Check sentence construction. (See Chapter 7.)

- Can each sentence be understood on the first reading?
- Are any sentences too short and jerky or overly simple?
- Are any sentences too long and complex, with bits awkwardly tacked on or intrusively embedded?
- Have you varied your sentence patterns to add interest to your writing?
- Have you used more active verbs than passive verbs?
- Have you avoided expletive constructions?
- Have you avoided weak, linking verbs ('is', 'was')?
- Is the order of words in any sentence inverted with the result that the sentence is illogical or difficult to understand?
- Does every sentence coherently follow on from the one before?
- Have you avoided negative expressions, except where necessary?
- Have you generally avoided sentence fragments? Run-on sentences? Comma splices?
- Have you avoided inappropriate nominalisations and unwieldy noun strings?
- Is there parallel structure where you have parallel components?

Check the language you use. (See Chapters 8 and 9.)

- Have you used concrete and specific words rather than abstractions whenever possible?

- Are all your words used correctly and unambiguously?
- Have you used words economically? Have you pruned out verbose, superfluous, and redundant expressions?
- Are jargon words or technical words used appropriately and defined where necessary?
- Have you avoided 'elegant variation' and used terminology consistently so that your reader is never puzzled by varied terminology? For example, 'job openings' in one part of a letter and 'job vacancies' in another.
- Have you avoided indecipherable abbreviations or obscure acronyms?
- Have you avoided worn-out clichés? Out-worn archaisms?

Check tone. (See Chapter 8.)

- Is your tone appropriate for your subject?
- Is your tone appropriate for the level of formality of your document?
- Is your tone appropriate for your reader?
- Is your tone courteous and considerate? Not too pompous? Not too colloquial?
- Does the document read as if it is written by a human? Does your personality as the writer come through? (If so, is this appropriate, or does it jar?)
- Is the writing non-discriminatory?

Format

Format is the physical arrangement and appearance of the document. (See Chapter 12.)

- Have you used the appropriate format, for example, for a memo?
- Have you followed company style? If the company has a Style Guide or Quality Assurance Manual, has it been consistently followed?
- Have you followed guidelines for visual presentation with respect to typeface and type size, margins and white space, headings, graphic material, paper, highlighting, colour, and binding?
- Can your document be used for its intended purpose?
- Is your document visually pleasing?
- Is your use of headings and numbering consistent?
- Are the pages numbered in the right order and bound in correctly?
- Is the document complete? (Index, appendices etc.)
- Will your reader be able to find specific information easily?
- If your document is long (over five pages), have you included a Table of Contents?
- If a summary section is appropriate for this kind of document, for example, a report, have you included one?

Mechanics

- Are there any grammatical errors or syntax (sentence structure) problems? (See Chapter 7.)

- Are there any punctuation errors? (See Chapter 10.)
- Are there any spelling errors? (See Chapter 9.)
- Are there any typographical errors? (See section below on proof-reading.)

PROOFREADING

Proofreading is the final stage of the writing process and the one that, if neglected, can damage your professional image and cancel out all your efforts to produce a perfect document. You may have created the most cogently-argued proposal, but if there is a mechanical error in the covering letter, your proposal may be dismissed unread. Whenever you set out to proofread a document, consider the consequences of overlooking errors. Whether you have given your work professional attention will be immediately apparent to your reader. Competence as a proofreader will enhance your credibility as a writer.

Limit proofreading to the final stage of your writing process—after you have revised and edited. Premature proofreading, like premature editing, is time wasted. Read through the whole document one final time before proofreading to make sure that your overall flow is consistent.

To proofread well, you need to be meticulous, if not fanatical, about detail.

Because reading is usually a process of anticipation and prediction, avoid your normal reading process at the proofreading stage because you will see only what you think you wrote—and fail to detect the minor errors that mar your work. You can proofread effectively only if you suspend anticipation while you read and do not let your document lead you by the nose. Try to read as objectively as you can.

Modify your normal reading process of skimming, skipping, scanning, dipping, and browsing when you proofread **and concentrate 100 per cent on your task**.

Never set out to proofread if you are tired, bored, distracted, anticipating a telephone call, or are likely to be interrupted by colleagues. If you do not have the time to read the document critically and slowly, wait until you do.

Strategies for proofreading

Use these strategies for finding typographical errors (typos), irregular spacing, omissions, and errors in punctuation and spelling that you have missed at an earlier stage in the revising/editing process. Most of these proofreading strategies can help you reliably detect errors because they contravene your normal reading process, force you to be methodical, and force you to slow down.

First, use proofreading aids such as a pointer (pen or pencil) to force yourself to look at each letter, each word, and each punctuation mark—noting what is there, and what is not there. Or use a ruler and move it down your page line by line. Even photocopying your document onto different coloured paper can be useful in highlighting errors.

Second, allow time to elapse between writing and proofreading the document. The passage of time (the longer the better) will allow you to forget to some extent what you wrote originally, so your ability to skim over and predict what you think you have said is impaired, and you are more likely to see what is actually on the page, rather than what you think you wrote.

Third, read your document aloud—to yourself or to someone else who has a duplicate copy. Oral reading requires attention to each word, punctuation mark, and space, so the listener is able to check for accuracy word by word. This strategy is particularly useful for eliminating doubling up of words, and for picking up whole sections that have been left out.

Fourth, read in reverse order. Again, you cannot predict too easily when you are reading backwards. The process slows you down, and you cannot skip over bits, assuming that they are correct. Most editors baulk at this strategy because it is too painful to implement.

Fifth, always double-check if you have a doubt about the spelling or choice of a word, or any other detail such as dates, names, etc. Journalists who do not double check and cause their newspaper to print an apology soon learn the value of this. The greatest spelling aid is doubt.

Sixth, while spelling checkers are useful, they cannot be relied on to pick up much more than around 90 per cent of errors. It is impossible for them to flag 'charges' as an error for 'changes', 'on' as an error for 'of' etc. As you can see from Figure 9.5, correctly spelt but incorrectly used words can slip through.

Seventh, read your draft more than once, concentrating on a different aspect each time, for example, for consistency in your use of headings. You will find errors and omissions in second and subsequent pass throughs that you did not see on your first reading. To do this you need to construct a proofreading checklist—a companion to the one we have provided for revising/editing.

Eighth, get other people to proofread your document as you are often too close to your work to see errors. But do not rely solely on others. They lack the motivation that you have to ensure that your document is perfect. It has been said that a human's greatest urge is to change what someone else has written; our experience has been that this is most likely to take place when it is too late—after the document has been made public and the damage has been done.

Ninth, always double-check paired punctuation marks such as brackets to ensure the closing bracket is included.

Tenth, if possible, proofread word-processed material on a print-out because errors are much easier to spot on paper. If you need to proofread onscreen, scroll forward only one space or one line at a time, scroll rapidly all the way through to check spacing, or scroll backwards one line at a time. Another useful technique is to triple your line spacing so that your document takes on a different appearance, or create wide margins so there are fewer words on each line.

Use of proofreading marks

If your work is being edited by someone else or if you edit other writers' work, it may be helpful to learn the standard symbols used by professional editors. You will find them in the Australian Government *Style Manual*.

Strategies for reviewing other writers' work

If you find yourself in the role of editor for the writing of your colleagues, the following strategies should prove useful.

- Ask them what they would like you to do—for example, a full-scale revision of the whole document, a check for the accuracy of the content, or a mechanical check of a micro-level feature such as punctuation—and then ensure that you edit only at the level required.
- Ask why they have written the document and who their intended readers are.
- Be sensitive to their feelings when you assess their document and make your comments. It is a good idea to consider the document privately and talk to them later so that you can soften your comments if their writing is poor. We have found that while professional writers such as journalists are used to having their work critiqued and sub-edited, very few business writers handle criticism well. So, be empathic.
- Do your best to respect another writer's individual style when it differs from your own. If their style will not affect how the document is received, refrain from revising it. (If, however, their style is so idiosyncratic that they are not producing standard English, you will have to give them specific help in an attempt to remedy their problems.)
- Emphasise the good points of a document as well as its deficiencies. Be constructive.
- Generalities are not helpful, so make all your comments specific by telling the writer how the document can be improved. Refrain from making an arbitrary comment about a document such as 'I think your report's structure could be improved'. Instead, say 'You could improve the organisation of your report by considering altering the sequence in the way I've suggested in this re-ordered outline'.
- There are several methods of communicating feedback on a colleague's work: comments in margins, comments on a separate page, marking off a checklist. Use whichever method is suitable, in conjunction with an individual conference with the colleague.

Strategies for dealing with those who review your work

If you are fortunate enough to have a competent colleague who is willing to review your work, try the following strategies.

- Give them a good print-out, and label it as a draft. Handwritten material is not welcomed by most editors.
- Tell your reviewer what you want them to do. For example, you might want them to do a full-scale revision or merely to check some policy detail that you are uncertain about. Give them an editing checklist to help them systematically review your document.
- Explain to your reviewer the purpose and intended reader(s) of your document.
- Do not be over-protective or defensive about your work. Appreciate the potential benefits of having your work reviewed by others and be prepared to consider alternatives. You are not producing written documents for yourself; you are writing to communicate to a reader.
- Ask the reviewer to be as specific as possible in their comments. Do not let them get away with merely telling you that your writing is flowery, vague, disorganised, and unconvincing. Get them to point to specific instances of your problems.
- Do not blindly accept their suggestions. If you cannot agree with them, get a second opinion.
- Ask them to comment on your work in writing—if they have time.
- Be professional. Do not argue with your reviewer about points of style. Arguing makes them less enthusiastic about reviewing your work the next time.
- Let the reviewer's comments sit for a while before you implement them. If you need to compromise, do it in an informed and measured way—not in a rush.
- Keep personalities and politics out of the peer-editing process. The more you know about writing, the better you can weigh up the value of feedback.
- Try to become your own best critic, without forgetting the value of others as critics.

COLLABORATIVE WRITING AND EDITING

We used the above techniques for writing and editing this book. The problems we faced are ones that are shared by all professional collaborative writers

- achieving consistency in all aspects of the document—content, language, style, sentence and paragraph structure, and layout
- eliminating repetition
- smoothing over the transitions when different people write different sections.

Because collaborative writing is so prevalent in the workplace, time spent on refining techniques for collaborative writing can be very valuable.

References

Anderson, L. K. (1990). *Handbook for proofreading*, Lincolnwood, Il.: NTC Publishing.

Bernstein, T. M. (1967). *The careful writer*, New York: Atheneum.

Farkas, D. K. (1985). 'The concept of consistency in writing and editing'. *The Journal of Technical Writing and Communication*, Vol.15(4), 353–364.

Flower, L. (1989). *Problem-solving strategies for writing*, 3rd edn, New York: Harcourt Brace Jovanovich.

Haugen, D. (1991). 'Editors, rules, and revision research'. *Technical Communication*, 1st Quarter, 57–64.

CHAPTER 12

CHOOSING GOOD DESIGN

Appearance is generally the last thing writers tackle, but it's the first thing that readers notice, both consciously and subconsciously. (Mackh and Rew, 1991, p. 210)

Design is the sum total of the decisions which make a product serviceable and attractive. (Martin, 1991, p. 11)

The alternative to good design is bad design, not no design at all. (Martin, 1991, p. 12)

RESEARCH ON VISUAL COMMUNICATION

In this chapter we look at some of the research on visual communication that has been done in the USA, the UK, and Australia, to give you some guidance on design decisions for specific documents. Interestingly, the findings of the researchers do not always coincide on all aspects of design. The emerging consensus on document design, however, is that 'effective' documents are those in which the design reinforces the desired *use* of the document.

We have included this chapter to make you aware of the factors to consider in the design of your organisation's documents, but stress that you should consult a typographer/document designer for specialist advice.

THE ADVENT OF DESKTOP PUBLISHING

Until the recent exponential growth of desktop publishing, knowledge of typography and design was confined mainly to professional typographers, graphic designers, and those who briefed them. Now many professional writers circumvent the typesetter and design their own documents to take advantage of new desktop publishing technology. While this trend can dramatically reduce printing costs, it is not without its pitfalls.

The first desktop publishing software packages were released in 1984. By 1988, their output was of such high quality that the manufacturers of the software and hardware argued that the naked eye could not detect the difference between text produced on a laser printer and that produced by traditional offset printing. Desktop publishing software such as Ventura, PageMaker, and QuarkXpress, in combination with a laser printer, have the potential to greatly increase the quantity, economy, speed, and privacy of document production. Because writing and designing a document complement each other, writers who learn to use electronic publishing software have a distinct advantage because they can give an ordinary page a professionally-typeset look. Bowman and Renshaw quote Tilden, who says that 'most people read typeset documents about 27% faster than they read non-typeset documents. They also tend to view typeset documents as more credible, more persuasive, and more professional than non-typeset documents' (1989, p. 60).

As Martin points out, 'the gap between word processing and professional typesetting has narrowed in all dimensions from cost of equipment to ease of operation' (1991, p. 13). Some readers have complained that the availability of the technology has proliferated vast numbers of documents which do not warrant the credibility lent to them by their laser-printed professionalism. They argue that the higher presentation standards of laser-printed material are not always necessary. It has often been said that new inventions do not save time—they raise standards.

How many organisational writers using desktop publishing undertake training to learn how aspects of visual design influence readers' attitudes towards documents and the processing of them? How many realise that it is very easy to subvert communication out of ignorance of the principles and techniques that can enhance visual communication in written documents? How many of them learn what trained designers, compositors, and typographers do when putting documents together? What elements of the design of a document need to be considered? To what extent does the layout of a document affect readers' motivation to read it, their acceptance of it, their efficiency in reading it, their ease of comprehension of it, and their ability to use it in the way that the document designer intended?

Writers need to be aware of the answers to these questions.

DESIGN DECISIONS

Many Australian companies have a style guide or quality assurance manual which sets out protocol, formats, and stationery for all company documents—from internal, informal memos to major documents such as formal reports and proposals. When no style guide is available, a writer needs to make individual design decisions about specific documents.

Because words and visuals are interdependent, you will need to thoroughly integrate elements of visual design when you plan a document. Your visual presentation will be influenced by your knowledge of layout, your readers, your budget, and your time frame.

Aim to produce a consistently-designed document that does not distract your reader from your purpose. The best layout is like the best punctuation: your readers should not notice it. There are, of course, some exceptions; for example, promotional documents where design aims to draw attention to itself.

Visual style depends on the degree of formality of a document. While it is quite acceptable to scribble an informal handwritten memo to a colleague, anything less than a professionally-executed, laser-printed document is unsatisfactory in a formal document prepared for a client.

Charles Kostelnick in the *Journal of Business Communication* (Summer 1988) lists the range of visual factors that writer–designers of compulsory annual reports need to consider to help readers locate information and to provide a marketing tool for the company

- the company logo
- charts and graphs to display sales and production figures
- a plan and line drawing of a new plant
- photographs introducing board members
- textual displays of expenses, revenues, and earnings
- the size and number of pages
- graphic cues such as colour and line work.

The winner of a gold award in the *Australian Business* Annual Report Awards in 1990, Placer Dome, was particularly singled out in the judges' report for its design features—its 'very clear' tables and its 'checklist' for the investor at the start of the document.

Even in short documents like letters, many design decisions can be made. Choice of type style and layout are important considerations. For example, many companies have moved to full-block layout (everything on the left margin) and open punctuation (absence of unnecessary punctuation in the address, salutation, and closing parts of the letter) because it looks less old-fashioned than semiblock layout and because it is easier when word processing to automatically put every line on the left-hand margin of the page.

Before you begin to write/design a document, consider how your readers are going to use your document. They will have expectations about the content, structure, style, and layout. If used well, graphic design can reinforce the verbal message of your document. Remember your readers' expectations as you plan the major components of graphic design.

COMPONENTS OF GRAPHIC DESIGN

There are three basic components of graphic design

- the text (words and numbers)
- the typography (the appearance of the printed word) and its layout on the page

- the illustrative material such as graphs, tables, photographs, diagrams, flow charts, and maps.

Text

Overviews

Overviews 'tell readers what information to expect, how it will be presented, and why it is important, thus helping them to link new information with what they already know' (Mackh and Rew, 1991, p. 11).

Titles and headings

Titles of reports and submissions should be succinct but informative. An example was *The Tax Pack*, first published by the Australian Taxation Office in 1990. Titles of reports are sometimes supplemented with an explanatory subtitle, for example, *The Brisbane Plan: A Study in Strategy*. In letters, it is common to have a subject line at the beginning of a letter as a heading which is useful to the reader.

Titles are just one kind of heading that can 'signpost' parts of the document for a reader. Headings orient readers by flagging information that helps them navigate their way through your document. Headings can affect which parts of your text your readers will read and how well they will process and remember what they read. Design your headings to indicate the levels of your document—your hierarchical structure. Your headings help your reader to determine the relationships between sections of your document. Do your best to word your headings in parallel grammatical form, but do not strain to do so and end up with an effect that appears to be forced.

Your headings should be informative, clear, specific, and consistent. Poor readers are greatly helped by headings that are full statements or questions, for example, the question-headings in *The Tax Pack* such as 'Did you invest in the film industry?'.

Some researchers believe that headings should not be more than half a line in length. The research also suggests that headings placed out in the margin help more than those that are placed in the text, because they stand out better for a reader.

Another type of very useful heading for readers is what is called the 'running header'—a shortened heading which runs across the top of each page. (There are also 'running footers' that give the title at the bottom of each page.) They are particularly useful in long documents like reports or documentation manuals and are very common in books and magazines.

Lists

Lists 'condense information into related groups that help readers to understand, organize, and remember information' (Mackh and Rew, 1991, p. 211). Listing items vertically down the left-hand margin helps readers because the greater amount of blank (white) space focuses their attention on the material. Use bullets such as dots, squares, or asterisks to set off your individual points.

Numbering

Use numbers to help your readers locate information. Numbers are usually essential in documents such as procedural and documentation manuals and long reports, because readers need to be able to locate information quickly and efficiently. Place the numbers near the edge of the page—out in the left margin—so they are easy to find.

Use Arabic, not Roman, numbers, because not everyone is familiar with the latter, nor uses them consistently.

Although many writers use the Dewey Decimal System for numbering sections (1, 1.1, 1.1.1, 1.1.1.1), readers can feel intimidated by it, especially if up to five decimal places are used. This practice is not 'reader-friendly'. To avoid dividing the text up so much, it would be better to divide the material more at the top levels.

Retrievability or access aids

Retrievability or access aids include items that help readers retrieve information from a document

- **a table of contents**—lists major headings and sub-headings, along with their page numbers, enabling a reader to preview the contents of the document and access information
- **an index**—helps readers retrieve and cross-check information
- **a glossary**—defines terms and concepts for readers
- **coloured tabs and separators**—which are very common in manuals of all kinds, should be labelled on both sides so a reader can access sections from the back of the document as well as the front.

Summaries

Often called executive summaries or abstracts, they are a feature of most formal reports and submissions. Summaries usually occur at the beginning of a document, but can come at the end. Most business readers regard them as the most important part of the document because they give the main points of the document in a condensed form. A summary should, in fact, be a reliable substitute for the whole document.

A well-placed summary (perhaps on a page of its own or in a different typeface) can help your readers understand your document and recall your main points more easily than a summary that is indistinguishable from the bulk of your text.

Footnotes and appendices

Notes in a text can be handled in different ways. Traditionally, footnotes were placed at the bottom of the page. Current practice is to place them at the end of a chapter or an article. Footnotes are common in academic texts where it is assumed that readers will be interested in interrupting their reading flow to seek further information. However, they distract and may even irritate organisational readers because they interrupt the flow of text and the reader usually either cannot resist checking the note because of curiosity, or cannot ignore the note because the information it holds is necessary to fully understand the text. Try to minimise your use of footnotes by incorporating material in your text to avoid the above problems.

Writers also use appendices to include information that they cannot easily incorporate into the text. This may mean that that information does not get read or it gets read all at once after the reader has finished with the main part of the document.

Typography and layout

Page size

Research recommends using standard size A4 (210mm x 297mm) and A5 (148mm x 210mm) pages—based on the principle that a rectangle with sides in the ratio $1:\sqrt{2}$ can be halved or doubled in area without changing the ratio of width to depth. A4 is sometimes used simply because it is easy to reproduce on a photocopier, but it is common to put an A5 amount of information onto an A4 page to gain the maximum amount of white space.

Some computer documentation manuals are size A5 to reduce the amount of information that hits the reader at the one time and to reduce the space needed to fit the manual beside the computer.

Typography

The typeface creates a visual tone and should be chosen, along with the paper and ink colour, to complement the tone of the document. For example, special invitations often use elegant, old-fashioned lettering in gold ink.

The two main typefaces are serif and sans serif styles, but there are over 2000 specific variations of these.

Serif typefaces have long been regarded as highly readable because the thick and thin strokes and serifs—the finishing 'flicks' off the ends of letters—capture eye movement and create a horizontal flow from one letter to the next, making individual letters more easily distinguishable.

Sans serif typefaces have almost uniform strokes with no serifs. Whereas some typographers support serif very strongly over sans serif, research carried out by the Document Design Center, Washington DC, says that they are much of a muchness. Because the US research has shown that the legibility of serif and sans serif is so similar when the document is properly designed, many researchers and typographers suggest that document designers choose a serif or sans serif according to the visual texture they want the document to have.

Desktop publishing packages offer many different typefaces. Use them with restraint. The current trend seems to be to use only two typefaces: one for the body text and one for the headings. Sans serif is commonly used for headings and serif is used for the body text.

Research has also shown that legibility is adversely affected by

- reversed lettering (white on a black background—though it can be effective for headings)
- words set at an angle to the horizontal
- too much variety of type styles and sizes.

Headline type: Upper case versus lower case

When people read, they recognise letters by the shape of the upper half. The white space surrounding the upper half of lower case allows for easier identification than the solid rectangles formed by upper case, so readers can

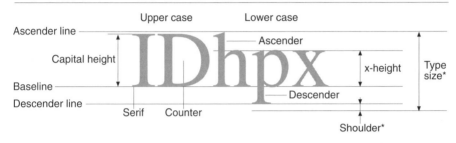

*The type size is a compound of two elements:
The total height of type (the distance between the *ascender* and *descender lines*) plus the *shoulder* (a fixed, additional space below the descender which prevents the ascenders and descenders of adjacent lines from collision).
In this example the type size is 60 points, the typeface is Times New Roman.

Figure 12.1 Basic typographical terms

Serif	Sans serif
Times	Helvetica
Palatino	Avant Garde
ITC Garamond	Futura
Plantin	Frutiger

Figure 12.2 Serif and sans serif typefaces

process lower case faster than upper case. Another reason is that lower case letters take up less space and more fit into the line, allowing readers to skim more words in a shorter time. Based on these findings, research suggests that writers avoid using all capital (upper case) letters for large chunks of text or long headings.

Upper case is useful if you restrict its use to short warnings such as 'CAUTION!' or 'URGENT!'

Highlighting techniques

Text can be highlighted by using bold face, italics, underlining, and colour, but overuse of these elements can make a document cluttered and confusing. Bold face is generally regarded as being the most effective signposting or emphatic device for small amounts of text, though italic is easier to read than bold if you need to highlight larger blocks of text.

Colour can be useful for drawing attention to a specific section of your document. However, there is a longstanding belief (sometimes attributed to Henry Ford) that colour gains in effect the closer it gets to black. In other words, text printed in coloured ink has lower readability than black type. Decisions about colour in brochures, for example, are strictly the province of the trained graphic designer.

Type weight

This is the degree of boldness of the type: light, medium, or bold. Bold face type is useful for highlighting headings, such as some levels of headings in this book, but do not over-use it, or it will lose its effect.

Research has shown that when readers can easily process a text because it is clear and logical, they notice changes in type weight more readily than changes in typeface. Make sure that your print is crisp and well-defined.

TORCH BATTERY
Torch Battery

Poor legibility
WORN OUT TYRES WITH LESS THAN 2 MM TREAD RECEIVE A RE-
PLACEMENT ALLOWANCE, OFF THE ORIGINAL PURCHASE PRICE, OF
50 PER CENT DURING THE FIRST QUARTER OF PERIOD

Better legibility
Worn out tyres with LESS than 2 mm tread receive a replacement allowance, off the original purchase price, of 50 per cent during the first quarter of period

---

Figure 12.3 Upper case letters versus lower case letters

Because advances in print technology such as laser printers have enabled writers to produce work that is very close to professional printing standards, material printed on a dot matrix printer now creates an undesirable impression and seems to be relegated to very informal intra-office documents in most organisations.

Point size

Point size is the height of each letter (see Figure 12.1). There are approximately 28 points to a centimetre.

The consensus about point size is that 9 to 11 points seems to be the most readable for general copy. This book is set in Goudy 11 points (with 1 point of leading—the space between the lines). Too big a point size results in laborious and inefficient reading because there are too few words to a line; too small a point size strains the eye. Typeface and point size need to be considered together because two different typefaces of the same point size will have different visual sizes.

		No leading (solid)	2 points leading
8 points	Goudy	Typefaces of the same size but different fonts can look entirely different	Typefaces of the same size but different fonts can look entirely different
	Helvetica	Typefaces of the same size but different fonts can look entirely different	Typefaces of the same size but different fonts can look entirely different
10 points	Goudy	Typefaces of the same size but different fonts can look entirely different	Typefaces of the same size but different fonts can look entirely different
	Helvetica	Typefaces of the same size but different fonts can look entirely different	Typefaces of the same size but different fonts can look entirely different
12 points	Goudy	Typefaces of the same size but different fonts can look entirely different	Typefaces of the same size but different fonts can look entirely different
	Helvetica	Typefaces of the same size but different fonts can look entirely different	Typefaces of the same size but different fonts can look entirely different

Figure 12.4 The same point size but different typeface can affect appearance

Line length

The generally recommended line length is 50–70 characters, or approximately twice the length of the alphabet of the typeface you use. If your lines are too long, the reader's eyes will have difficulty following the lines to their end. Short lines create awkward breaks in the text and the reader's eyes will be constantly jerking down to the next line.

Justification of lines

It is customary for business documents to have left-hand justification (all text flush against the left margin). However, there are differing opinions about whether the right margin should be justified. A justified right margin requires proportional spacing—the spaces between letters and between words vary so that each line ends evenly on the right margin. This can sometimes give words a distorted look which is disorienting for readers. It can also create 'rivers of white' within the text depending on the sophistication of the software being used (as demonstrated here).

When text is unjustified, the right margin is 'ragged' and words have consistent spacing between them (as shown in the following paragraphs). Research at the Document Design Center, Washington DC, has found that justified text is harder for poor readers to read and comprehend than ragged right. With a ragged right margin each line looks different, so the eye is less likely to stray to another line because the reader can quickly separate and identify each. Also, the eye does not have to adjust to the varying letter- and word-spacing of justified type. The US researchers argue that in justified copy readers lack visual cues.

The US researchers found that many readers also prefer a ragged right margin because it gives the document a more relaxed, contemporary look and seems more inviting. Ragged right gets the reader back to the start of a new line more quickly. Ragged right also removes the need for forced hyphenation. Another advantage is that it is more easily corrected, resulting in lower printing costs than justified text if traditional printing methods are used.

British document design expert John Hartley sees a further advantage in unjustified text: it is more flexible because it is possible to specify, for example, that no line should end with the first word of a new sentence, or that if the next-to-last word of a line is followed by a punctuation mark, the last word may be carried over to the next line. It may be important to have this kind of flexibility in documents.

Layout

Layout is the setting out of text on the page. To produce an effective layout you need to take into account the physiology of reading. Readers expect to start in the top left-hand corner and read across the page from left to right until they come to the bottom right hand corner.

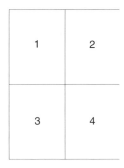

Figure 12.5 Readers expect to start reading from the top left-hand corner

White space

This is the portion of the page that is not taken up by text and illustrations. A rule of thumb in publishing is that textual material should occupy about 50 per cent of the page. Use white space, for example, in margins and between sections to make the document attractive and easier to read and to emphasise important text. There is no 'correct' arrangement of white space, but the amount of white space considerably affects the reader's ease of comprehension and retrieval.

Some writers check the visual appeal of their document by looking at a page upside down or holding it at arm's length. Ask yourself whether the negative (background) space balances with the positive space of text and visual material. White space can be expensive, however, because the more white space you have, the more pages you have in a document.

A further dimension of white space is the amount of space left at the bottom of a page. Hartley recommends having the flexibility of a 'floating baseline'—allowing content rather than page length to dictate the endings of lines and pages. This also avoids 'widows' (one line at the top of a page as a carry-over from a preceding paragraph) and 'orphans' (the first line of a paragraph on its own at the end of a page).

Paragraph spacing

The usual practice is to single space within paragraphs, and double space between paragraphs, so paragraphs can be distinguished from each other.

Indentation

Indentation is the practice of starting a new line a couple of spaces in from the left margin to indicate the start of a new paragraph. With very short paragraphs it is better to use line spacing between paragraphs rather than indentation. Otherwise, the middle of the sentence is more prominent than the beginning. In longer reports it is preferable to use indentation, particularly because it might be difficult to decide whether the start of a new page is the start of a new paragraph. Notice that in this book there is no indentation of the line after a heading, but that subsequent new paragraphs are indented.

Line spacing (leading)

Line spacing is the distance between the baseline of one line and the baseline of the next. Single, one and a half, and double line spacing are the most common. Whereas typewriters and basic word processors allow for single, double, or triple spacing, professional packages allow leading to be altered in fractions of points.

Margins

If you are binding the document, the inside margin or 'gutter' needs to be twice as wide as the outside margin to ensure that the text can be read and not obscured by the binding.

Use a smaller margin at the top of a page to get the reader going again on the new page and a larger margin at the bottom of the page to give the reader a break before going on to the next page.

Materials

The materials such as paper and binding used in your final document need to be carefully chosen.

- **Paper**—Choose paper of appropriate weight and quality. Get expert advice on this from your printer. Black ink on white paper is easiest to read, but a graphic designer will advise you on the use of colour. If you get documents professionally printed, make sure that you do not get 'show-through'—images from text or graphics on the other side of the paper—which happens if the paper is not of sufficient weight or opacity, or if the ink density is too high. Another problem which can occur with a poor 'print-job' is 'set-off'—the unwanted transfer of ink from one newly-printed sheet to another. Glossy paper is very glary—especially in artificial light, so use matt paper, if possible. Annual reports, however, tend to be done on high gloss paper, because it gives a more 'high-quality' look. Another consideration is the move to recycled paper.
- **Binding**—Leave a gutter margin for binding. Plastic comb binding (where a machine punches holes in the margin of each page and the pages are then collected up in a plastic comb binder) is preferable to other methods because it allows a document to open flat, rather than spring shut as soon as the reader takes a hand off it.

Illustrative materials

A great deal of research has been done on the most effective ways to present information graphically. The research strongly suggests that many readers can understand and use complex information more efficiently when the text is supported by devices such as graphs, tables, diagrams, photographs, and flow charts.

Use illustrations to motivate your readers, clarify your explanation, and help their long-term recall of your information. Computers can provide visual support in the form of graphs and spreadsheets.

The appropriate graph

Choose the graph most appropriate to your material

- line graphs are better than tables for showing trends
- bar charts are better than line graphs for presenting rough quantitative information
- bar charts are preferable because people find it easier to make judgements on the basis of relative length rather than relative area or volume

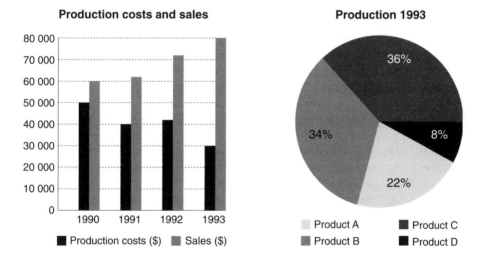

Mine A	1993	1992	1991
Production			
Gold—grams	42 322	50 781	62 095
Millfeed—tonnes (millions)	0.8	0.8	0.8
Grade—gold—g/tonne	0.065	0.090	0.105
Recovery—gold—%	73.23	68.97	70.08
Cash production cost—US$/g	$ 275	$ 233	$ 193
Total production cost—US$/g	$ 309	$ 274	$ 260
Reserves			
Ore—tonnes (millions)	5.4	1.3	0.7
Grade—gold—g/tonne	0.093	0.054	0.097

Figure 12.6 Bar chart, pie chart, and table samples

- pie charts are acceptable when there are no more than four or five segments, but it is difficult to judge proportions when the segments are small and it is difficult to include explanatory lettering
- flow charts should have clearly-defined flows that are easily discernible to readers.

Guidelines for graphic material

The guidelines on the use of visual aids noted below may help your design decisions.

- Visual aids must appropriately complement the message. Check to see that there is no contradiction between your graphic material and your text.
- Introduce your visual aid in the text before it occurs in the document. Try to avoid having your readers turn a page to find your visual aid.
- Help your readers grasp the significance of a visual aid quickly and easily by giving it an informative title and ensuring that the elements in the visual aid are simply and clearly labelled.
- Use only visual aids which your readers are used to interpreting, or which you can make understandable to your readers through your verbal explanation.
- If appropriate, sum up for your readers the conclusions you want them to draw from the visual aid.
- Round off numbers to help your readers make meaningful comparisons.
- Include averages because they not only summarise the data but they also allow your readers to grasp the spread between the above-average and the below-average values.
- Figures in vertical columns are easier to compare than figures across rows; after rows therefore, wherever possible, arrange items vertically.
- Order rows in columns by size to aid comparison. Larger numbers placed at the top help mental arithmetic. (This rule is more appropriate for single tables than for a series of tables where the order of sizes may vary. For a series of tables one must keep to the same order.)
- Use illustrations only if they are relevant to the text, only if they are of high quality, and only if they have a clear purpose.

Conclusion

We have given some practical advice which may be helpful to you when you use desktop publishing technology. However, reader perception of text and graphics is an extremely complex area, and we suggest that you read a selection of the material in the list below and contact a document design expert. The Australian experts in research on document design can be located at the Communication Research Institute of Australia in Canberra.

If you are interested in learning more technical detail about typography, refer to the extensive material in the Australian Government *Style Manual for authors, editors and printers* (5th edn), Canberra: Australian Government Publishing Service.

References

Benson, P. (1986). 'Writing visually: Design considerations in technical publications'. *Technical Communication*, 35–39.

Bowman, J. P. and Renshaw, D. A. (1989). 'Desktop publishing: Things Gutenberg never taught you'. *The Journal of Business Communication*, Vol.26 (1), 57–75.

Document Design Project. (1981). *Guidelines for document designers*, Washington DC: American Institute for Research.

Gottschall, E. M. (1989). *Typographic communications today*, Cambridge, Mass: MIT Press.

Hartley, J. (1986). *Designing instructional text*, 2nd edn, London: Kogan Page.

Mackh, G. E. and Rew, L. J. (1991). 'Using access aids to boost information retrieval'. *Technical Communication*, 210–213.

Martin, D. (1991). *Book design: A practical introduction*, New York: Van Nostrand Reinhold.

Spencer, H. (1969). *The visible word*. London: John Terceval.

White, J. V. (1988). *Graphic design for the electronic age*. New York: Watson-Guptill Publications.

Journals:
Information Design Journal.
Visible Language.

CHAPTER 13

THE IMPACT OF TECHNOLOGY ON WRITING

NEW TECHNOLOGIES FOR WRITERS

Word processing, desktop publishing, image-scanning technology, optical character recognition, fax machines, electronic mail, and computer conferencing have changed the terrain of the business writing landscape; the ongoing development of voice-activated computers that can recognise the human voice and stylus-based computers that can recognise cursive hand-writing will change it even further.

In this chapter we concentrate on the use of word processing, electronic mail, and computer conferencing in professional writing and speculate on the future impact of computer-mediated communication systems on the corporate writing culture.

Word processing

One of the most powerful and versatile writing tools in history, and regarded by many as second only to Gutenberg's invention of the printing press in the fifteenth century, the word processor has radically changed the processes and products of written communication. It is a rare business these days that does not rely on word processing. It is the process that many converts to it believe dramatically increases the productivity, accuracy, quality, and efficiency of written communication. The word processor is not merely a tool for stream-lining the writing process of individual documents within a workplace; it can be the organising tool that controls the production of all the documents in an organisation.

Since the introduction of the IBM personal computer into the workplace in 1981 there has been an astonishing growth in the use of computers for professional writing. Because it is becoming more common to put personal computers with word processing and desktop publishing software on the desks of executives, the executive practice of getting secretarial staff to transcribe letters, memos, reports, proposals etc. from dictated or handwritten notes is declining. Executives realise they can have much greater control over their documents when they personally generate the material and in some cases go so far as to design its layout with the help of desktop publishing software.

Few dispute the enhanced visual appearance of laser-printed documents produced by desktop publishing. Nor would anyone deny that using word processing software allows a writer to accumulate accuracy and eliminate the drudgery and cost of retyping as a document goes through successive 'editorial loops'. But there is still dissension in some circles about whether the word processing converts are right when they invariably testify that they write 'more, faster, and better' on a computer.

Current research on computer-generated writing in the USA has suggested that writing directly onto the computer may well provide even greater benefits than the long-recognised ones of assisting transcribing and revising. We tested the anecdotal claims of the word processing proponents that writing with a computer results in an improved product by investigating whether computers enhance the quality of the writing of university students. The results revealed that computers were of great benefit to student writers. Furthermore, we believe that these findings are applicable to business writers.

How can individual professional writers use word processing technology to its fullest potential by adapting their traditional writing strategies to the computer? By recognising and taking advantage of the following benefits of electronic writing.

Positive psychological effects

Many people feel compelled to write as soon as they sit in front of a computer, so 'writer's block' (inability to get started) is less of a problem than with traditional paper and pen composing. Writing on a computer makes it easier to get words onto the page because it seems easier to press keys than to pick up a pen—to engage in freewriting, to brainstorm freely, to follow associations, to indulge in uninterrupted 'satisficing' (making do) that can be tidied up and corrected later. When writers get the opportunity to make changes so easily, they learn that writing is often a strategy to find out what they know. This more 'open' experimental approach to writing (see Chapter 3) can provide positive reinforcement by helping writers think more and better.

Flexibility

Text can remain tentative for a longer time than when using secretarial help. Writing on a word processor enables writers to compose more freely and quickly, focusing first on what they want to say rather than on how they are saying it. Because writing rarely comes out right the first time, a writer can ignore correctness and coherence for later refining. Most writers agree that it is far easier to correct than create, as the right word or combination of words can easily be substituted in a later draft. Text on a computer is flexible and expendable. You can move blocks around; you can delete and substitute. You can use the computer to explore, shape, and refine ideas.

Ease of revising and editing

While first drafts on a computer are rougher, final drafts are smoother, because much of the resistance to finding one's errors disappears when revising and editing are so painless. As well, there is the positive reinforcement of seeing the revision happen. There is less tendency to make do with the less-than-perfect because text is so easy to alter, compared with that produced on a typewriter. (This can sometimes be a disadvantage in situations where executives dictate to or make notes for a secretary to word process documents. They can miss errors when reading drafts too quickly and the document goes through countless expensive cycles of correction and reprinting—often to the great exasperation of the secretary.)

Writing as mosaic/patchwork/jigsaw

Writers using word processors process words differently from writers with pen and paper. The computer short-circuits the linear approach that can inhibit the writing process because the writer can start at any point in the text—perhaps with a few headings or with the part that is easiest to write—without worrying about whether the first sentence will remain as such. Text can be inserted in fragments; documents can be built up incrementally by being constructed around notes and jottings. The computer can compile and shuffle scraps of headings, sentences, and paragraphs. The computer dissolves the distinction between writing and rewriting.

Ease of collaborative writing

Collaborative writing is commonly practised in the workplace, particularly in writing reports and proposals. Computers ease the burden of 'cutting and pasting' individual contributions because writers can append/merge their separate files so that the style can be unified and the transitions checked—absolutely essential when documents have been written by a team.

Power as a writer's helper

The computer is a powerful tool that supports the writer by carrying out massive and tedious editing tasks instantaneously. For example, a 'global search and replace' can automatically correct a misspelling or an inconsistently-hyphenated or capitalised word throughout a whole document.

The computer is without equal as a manipulator of text. It can automatically provide page formatting (margins, justification, centring); underlining; bold facing; italics; headers and footers; automatic page numbering; indexing; and documentation. Desktop publishing packages and some of the more sophisticated word processing packages now combine text with layout and graphics.

Other helpful features for writers include spelling checkers (very helpful for poor spellers, though unable to be totally relied upon), style checkers (useful for flagging problems, though also unable to be totally relied upon); onscreen outlining features (very helpful for structuring a text), and interactive heuristic programs that prompt writers by asking questions about a specific information theme. These programs are also called 'brainstorming programs' and include IdeaFisher, IdeaGenerator Plus, and WordBench.

For a busy executive or an intermittent writer, or even someone who writes all the time but who is not a confident writer, it might be worth while to investigate style analysis software such as RightWriter, Grammatik, and Correct Grammar.

Style analysis programs have the potential to flag problems in spelling, punctuation, word repetitions, potentially-awkward phrases, sexist phrases, abstract words, passives, acronyms, wordiness, vagueness, clichés, jargon, basic grammatical errors, and other elements. We do not recommend them, but we accept the fact that they could be useful in the absence of a human editor with finely-honed editing skills.

A new product is the 'writing-style replicator', which lets you develop your own 'ideal style' model based on samples of your own writing or the writing of others whose style you would like to emulate.

If you are writing a document that follows a standard format, your document can be written more efficiently if a 'frame', 'boilerplate', or 'template' is used. Be careful to avoid the pitfalls of a form letter by making sure that you individualise such letters.

Aside from these undoubted advantages, there are some drawbacks associated with using computers, but these should not be considered as serious obstacles.

Cyberphobia

The Computing Teaching Centre at Oxford University ran its famous *Computing for the Terrified* course for years, so you are not alone if you feel intimidated by technology. The way to overcome fear of computers is to get someone who knows more about computers than you do to help you get started.

Unlike Mark Twain, who was unwilling to share his experience with the 'new-fangled' machine on which he wrote the world's first typewritten novel, converts to writing on computers will usually be anything but reluctant to share with you their knowledge of this great leap in writing technology.

Learning curve

If you are prepared to take some time to become proficient, you will find that it is worth the investment. No one seems to know anyone who has reverted to using paper and pen, once they have mastered word processing. It is very helpful if at least one co-worker has more computer experience than you. The old adage, 'If all efforts to learn the software fail, read the manual', is unfortunately often accurate advice, although the usability of manuals is increasing.

Lack of keyboard skills

This is not as big a disadvantage as when using a typewriter, because it is so painless to correct mistakes. It is a good idea to learn to type by using one of the excellent software packages available for this purpose. However, it is not absolutely essential. The QWERTY keyboard, which was especially designed to prevent fast typists from entangling the keys on a typewriter, achieved this by placing the most frequently-used keys under the weakest fingers and as far away as possible from each other. Even though in the intervening years new keyboards have been designed that would allow touch typists to type much faster, they have never been widely implemented.

Planning on paper first

There is nothing to stop you from jotting your preliminary ideas down on paper, but move onto your computer as early in the writing process as you can. Using an outlining program that will hierarchise your headings in the planning stage of a report or proposal can be very useful.

Overwriting

Some writers get carried away and write too much. This is not such a bad thing. Once you have got it down, you can always cut it back if you have mastered efficient revising/editing strategies such as the process of multistage revising that we outlined in Chapter 11.

Premature editing

The temptation to tinker with the document before finishing the first draft is so irresistible to some writers that they compose with their screens turned off so they cannot see what they have written until they have finished. That way they do not waste time and effort in editing material which ends up not being in the final document.

The 'perfect page' syndrome

The print-out looks so good it disguises the fact that the document is deficient in content, structure, and other essential aspects. This problem will not occur if the revising/editing process is followed.

Problems with browsing onscreen text

Our advice—DON'T!

Run off a print-out of your draft and revise/edit on paper. Researchers (Haas and Hayes, 1986) have found that it is far more difficult to find errors in onscreen text than on paper. Writers also find it impossible to grapple with large chunks of onscreen text. It is far more efficient to run off a print-out of a document and revise it on paper than to try to juggle text in the computer.

FUTURE DEVELOPMENTS

Voice-activated computers and keyboardless computers will be very popular with those recalcitrant executives who have kept well clear of computers because of their lack of keyboard skills and possibly because of their perception that keyboarding does not fit their corporate executive status. Their belief that secretarial work is concomitant with transcribing their 'scribble and throw' notes and/or dictation is being challenged by the Australian Government's Structural Efficiency Principle, which has mandated that secretaries in the Commonwealth Public Service spend no more than 50 per cent of their working time doing routine 'typing'. It is highly likely that it will be necessary to master the keyboard to get an executive job in the future because of these and other developments.

The technology for computers that take dictation has arrived, and its potential is enormous. Computers that process voice input have been used for some time in assembly-line situations where vehicle defects are recorded. Designers are currently working on systems that recognise continuous speech output from specific individual speakers who have 'trained' their computer to do this by reading a specific document into the computer.

Voice-recognition technology will be ideal for professional writers—provided they have enhanced dictating skills—because they will be able to talk their first draft into the computer, run off a hard copy, revise it, then fix up their document through the keyboard.

Stylus-based computers, which are like notebook-sized electronic tablets, work with a special pen on a liquid crystal screen. They currently cannot recognise cursive handwriting, but research in this area goes on constantly because the potential for such a device is enormous—particularly out in the field where hand-held or palm-top units can relay important information to a central computer via a modem.

CHANGING THE WORKPLACE WITH ELECTRONIC MESSAGING

The writing process as well as the writing environment is changing through the use of linked computers. Two important developments in computer-aided communication are electronic mail and computer conferencing.

The 'paperless office' is part of the role that computers are expected to play in organisations. However, it has been noted that the possibility of an entirely paperless office in some organisations is remote. Hard copy documents are still valued in a number of organisations for two important reasons. First, they are more-or-less permanent. Computer records may be equally permanent, but the risks of disk failures and computer viruses that destroy information cannot be ignored. Second, paper documentation allows a number of people to keep records, rather than relying on this to be kept centrally. In some organisations, this dissemination of information in hard copy form means that a number of people will always have access to information. Some employees, for example, may worry that the paperless office may mean that information (as featured in George Orwell's novel *Nineteen Eighty-Four*), can be re-written to suit the powers that be. In the same way that Hansard is a 'clean' record of Parliamentary sittings, organisational staff may rewrite essential documents if problems with wording later arise. Until such concerns are addressed, hard copy documents will still be the norm.

Electronic mail

However, some changes from paper to computer messages on-screen are happening in organisations. The most common use of the computer for messaging is electronic mail, usually known as 'e-mail'. E-mail allows people to send and receive messages via computers which can be linked locally (for example, within the building), nationally, and internationally. Users with home or portable computers can receive and send messages even if they are not in the office. An e-mail facility is usually divided into message 'areas'. General announcements can be accessed from an area known as a bulletin board, and passwords or access codes allow private messages to be sent as well. It is also possible to send messages to particular groups, called CUGs (closed user groups).

If you are not familiar with e-mail, consider how your work would change if much of your information arrived via the computer. You arrive at your desk and turn on your computer. A beep lets you know that you have messages awaiting you. Some are from staff within the building, and others are from branches around the country and overseas. As you read, you decide how to deal with each. You can reply via the computer and also file the information in your electronic files on the computer. You can also decide if you want to destroy the file (the electronic equivalent of throwing it into the waste paper basket) or make a print-out.

Computer conferencing

Computer conferencing is another type of electronic messaging. It is like a discussion, or conference, but instead of talking face-to-face, people discuss via the computer. If you have not participated in a computer conference, here is a description. You arrive at work, and turn on your computer. Management has set up a computer conference to gauge employees' reactions to a proposed company move to another area of the city. Using specific commands gives you access to the conference 'area' of the computer network. You read the comments that others have already written. One person's ideas in particular appeal to you, and you decide to write a reply in support. You type in your views and electronically send it to the conference area. The next day, you check the conference area to read comments and see if anyone has responded to your ideas.

ADVANTAGES OF ELECTRONIC MESSAGING

Electronic messaging, whether by e-mail or computer conferencing, has several important advantages.

It saves time. Electronic messaging reduces the message path. For example, imagine how you respond in writing to someone else in your organisation. You may write or dictate information, which then goes to a secretary to be typed and then back to you for checking. If you accept the memo as a final draft, it is then put in an internal mail envelope and is left for the courier to pick up. In the mail room, the memo is directed to the recipient, who will probably get it the next day.

E-mail reduces the number of steps. By writing and sending messages yourself via the computer, you bypass both the secretary, in constructing the message, and the internal mail service, in sending it. This change does not always mean that people lose their job as a result. In many cases, secretarial staff who do not have to spend their time typing minor memos are then able to become involved in more complex writing and production projects.

It allows flexible work hours. Computers can store messages and present them when it is convenient for you. This facility to move from 'real-time' communication, called **asynchronicity**, is a plus for both e-mail and computer conferencing. In e-mail, asynchronicity means that messages from overseas staff written during their work hours can be read during your work hours. Having to place international telephone calls at odd hours to reach people is no longer needed.

Computer conferences have the same facility. You add your comments when it is convenient for you, and they are read by others when it suits them. Asynchronicity makes computer conferences more advantageous than video conferencing and telephone conferencing, as both require people to be available at the same real-time.

It allows mobility. If you have the right equipment, you can receive messages even when you are away from your office. Employees working at home or on location can use a modem to connect their computer to the workplace computer via the telephone line. This connection allows them to read and send messages (e-mail, fax, telex). They can also participate in computer conferences, as the essential ingredient is the computer, not the office.

It can support different types of communication. Conferences run by the computer, unlike traditional face-to-face conferences, can allow a topic to be discussed over weeks or months. With a good conference moderator on the computer network, participants are encouraged to explore ideas and offer more researched opinions. For example, participants can use the extra time available with a computer conference to confer with colleagues and check figures.

In some cases, computer conferencing is used to initiate discussion, and this is followed up with a face-to-face conference. The face-to-face one becomes more effective in both time and costs as participants have already established the basic issues. This combining of two modes of discussion is probably necessary when one considers the limitations of the computer. Research indicates that people find it difficult to discuss complex issues via the computer because of the lack of non-verbal cues. We understand the intent of someone's message not only from their words, but from their facial expression, gestures, and tone of voice. Such cues are simply not available via the computer.

Because of this drawback, computer conferencing is sometimes more informal or even humorous. Although some people complain about using the computer to 'horse around', this use often breaks down barriers between participants, and encourages them to want to communicate with others. A subsequent face-to-face conference may go more smoothly if participants have become familiar with each other through 'chatting' to each other via the computer.

Writing for the electronic media

Two famous researchers in computer conferencing, Hiltz and Turoff, suggest that any new technology is like a Rorschach ink blot: people relate it to what they already know and do (1978, p. 344). The car was first viewed as just a horseless carriage, and televisions were seen as radio with pictures! Only later did people come to realise that they had to think quite differently to use the potential of these inventions.

In the same way, computers are more than 'glorified typewriters'. When they are linked to messaging networks, they require organisational members to think about their writing process and the results of the writing in new ways. The following considerations should help you re-think what using a computer means to you as a communicator.

Decide whether you should communicate

Electronic information such as memos, announcements, and conference topics can inundate organisational members. This information overload can be countered in two ways. As a message sender, ask yourself if a conversation or a telephone call is more appropriate, if not easier. As a message receiver, ask yourself 'so what?' If your opinion does not really matter on a particular issue, do not give it!

Learn the discourse etiquette

You need to think about your communication in a much different way when you are using electronic media. The computer can allow the speed and 'chattiness' that you have in face-to-face conversations. But it can also allow your message to be read by more people, particularly those whom you may not usually have access to in the organisation. You need to consider what is acceptable in this new type of communication, which has both formal and informal attributes.

What usually happens is that an 'etiquette' develops for using electronic messaging in an organisation. This means that certain elements are considered acceptable or not acceptable, just as they are in other types of organisational communication. For comparison, consider that a business letter, as part of the written etiquette, is judged partially by its adherence to an accepted appearance, tone, and phrasing. A business meeting has certain conventions or procedures that make up the oral etiquette of communication.

Similarly, electronic messaging is in the process of developing a similar etiquette. Users of a computer network in one organisation may identify themselves by first and last name only, while users in another organisation may always use their formal title or position. Some organisations treat the e-mail facility as a type of electronic grapevine, while others restrict it to discussions of business-related topics.

If you are confused about what the etiquette of computer communication involves, consider these examples of inappropriate communication, that is, lack of etiquette.

Example 1: Sometimes writers on a network become so familiar with the topic or each other's style that they develop a kind of shorthand made up of jargon, abbreviations, and references to past events or jokes. This in itself is probably part of the etiquette of a Closed User Group. If the shorthand is impossible for others to decode, however, there is a problem. This can be relevant to newcomers or even regular contributors, who do not want to state that they do not understand. An example was a CUG for people interested in 'alternative sexual practices'. Unfortunately, the jargon, euphemisms, and colloquialisms were so cryptic that only a few users could decipher the messages to discover what the others were interested in. As part of the communication etiquette, confine your shorthand to your CUG, and if needed, provide definitions, explanations, or even an on-line glossary.

Example 2: An employee who did not learn this used his company's e-mail to threaten whoever moved his motorbike in the parking lot. He put his message as a general announcement because he wanted to make sure that the unknown culprit got the message. The person probably did—but so did everyone else, including the company boss!

Example 3: A participant in a computer conference was 'flaming', a term for electronic raving. The flamer ignored the usual give-and-take interaction of the conference to enter extremely long comments and abuse others. The result was that the person became isolated, as no one else sent messages to him.

The main point for a writer is to learn the etiquette. To understand the electronic communication etiquette of your own organisation, consider how others in the organisation are using the computer. This will enable you to be sensitive to what is acceptable in terms of topics, style, and recipients.

Cue your readers

Should you actually write differently for the electronic media? The answer must be 'yes', especially when you remember that your readers can only go on what is written, even if your message has a 'conversational' feel to it. People cannot always pick accurately the shadings that we place on our written words. Irony, forms of humour such as sarcasm, and other emotions are often 'lost' in print. The potential for receivers to mis-read your intentions is a problem you need to be sensitive to as you write. A study of one group of on-line users showed that even though they communicated more with each other, the number of misunderstandings also increased (cited in More and Laird, 1985, p. 129). The phrase 'You must be crazy', for example, could be written with a humorous intent, but read by someone else as an expression of anger.

As part of the communication etiquette, regular electronic correspondents often develop innovative ways to signal emotions and humour. They may include interpretative 'directions', such as '(irony)' or '(just joking)' after a sentence. Other ways that they get their meaning across

- exclamation marks to show emphasis
- adding spaces between letters to emphasise a word
- using capitalised letters to 'shout' to readers
- writing the result of an emotion to indicate it, for example 'grin', 'gasp'.

Gareth Powell, computer writer for the *Sydney Morning Herald*, gives other shorthand terms being used by writers using computers to communicate (6 August 1990)

- BCNU—be seeing you
- BTW—by the way
- BYE—signing off
- CUL—see you later
- FOO?—greeting
- RU THERE?—greeting
- FYI—for your information
- MtFBWY—may the force be with you
- OBTW—oh, by the way
- TNX—thanks
- TNX 1.0E6—thanks a million.

Do not go overboard

It is important not to let electronic messaging dominate your work or private life. Because messages can be read at any time (and almost anywhere), some computer 'addicts' spend too much time using e-mail or computer conferencing.

They become so compulsive that they interrupt more significant work projects, participation at staff development or professional conferences, and even activities in their private life to check for messages on the computer! In effect, they become 24-hour-a-day employees—which is not necessary or desirable.

Consider your timing

People often forget that paper-based writing in organisations has a 'built in' time-lag that is sometimes valuable to writers. For example, have you ever spontaneously written a curt memo which luckily sat in the tray for you to sign? During this time, the situation may have changed dramatically. Or, re-reading the memo before sending it, you realise that your facts are wrong or that the tone is inappropriate. This time-lag also allows ideas to incubate. Writing on a topic often means that we continue to think about it at the subconscious level—and return to the document surprised at how much more we have to discuss.

Electronic messaging makes writing 'immediate' by reducing the time between writing and sending a message. It is tempting to draft a reply, check the spelling, and then send it via the computer. As electronic mail catches on, people may be pressured to answer quickly and thus have much less time to think through their message or consult with others.

The solution? As a writer, you can combat the problem by consciously giving yourself a time-lag. Write a draft, then save it on the computer and return to it later for a second 'read' before you send it. Alternatively, some writers create a time-lag by jotting ideas down on paper, which they put aside. They then return to these notes to compose on the computer.

CONCLUSION

Predictions for a future in which written text will still predominate in the organisational sphere include increased use of networking and proliferation of hypermedia systems—where text, graphics, sound, video, and animation will provide 'virtual reality' for people working in the 'knowledge industry'.

References

Andera, F. (1989). 'Voice input to computers: How will it affect the teaching of business communication?' *Bulletin of the Association of Business Communication*, December 18–20.

Haas, C. and Hayes, J. (1986). 'What did I just say? Reading problems in writing with the machine'. *Research in the Teaching of English*, Vol.20(1), 22–35.

Hiltz, R. and Turoff, M. (1978). *The network nation*, Reading, MA: Addison-Wesley.

Matzkin, J. (1989). 'Grammatik III, Right-Writer 3.0: Grammar checkers get smarter, but not by much'. *PC Magazine*, 14 February.

More, E. A. and Laird, R. K. (1985). *Organisations in the communications age*, Sydney: Pergamon Press.

Strassmann, P. (1985). *Information payoff: The transformation of work in the electronic age*, New York: The Free Press.

CHAPTER 14

FUTURE DIRECTIONS FOR PROFESSIONAL WRITING

Writing practices are never static. Especially in the organisational setting, business and communication trends affect how, when, and why we write. Writing research also has an effect when research results are disseminated to the wider community of writers. This chapter examines some of the recent trends affecting our views of writing, as well as the current research interests relevant to professional writing. Noting these trends on the horizon can help you to assess their effect on your own written communication.

NEW DIRECTIONS

Effective communicators are flexible, able to incorporate communication changes in the business world. For example, when the issue of non-discriminatory language began to gain momentum in the 1970s, few of us predicted that it would lead to significant writing changes. Now, twenty years later (and with supporting legislation), it is becoming less common to insist on using 'he' as the common term for a human being and more common to address women as 'Ms' when their marital status is unknown. What was once considered trivial is now taken for granted.

What issues will you face in the future as a professional writer? Using Tom Peters's list of important 'emerging realities' for business in the 1990s (Paul, 1990, p. 172), we describe below how your writing in the workplace may be affected in five ways.

Markets are splintering into 'niches'

The result of specialist or niche markets will be higher expectations on the part of customers or clients. They will want more personalised communication, specifically, writing that demonstrates both by language and subject matter that it is specially geared to them. With a market place filled with similar products or services to choose from, customers will select according to how effectively they are addressed by the company. The documents that you write must be user-friendly, that is, attractively designed and easy to comprehend.

'Flat' organisations will prevail

Organisations will become less hierarchical (that is, have a 'flat' structure) and this will change traditional communication flows. How to maintain (or create) effective communication will be the challenge. Peters suggests that this new environment will require you to have access to more data, not just what is passed downward from the top. As well, you will need to be able to evaluate it and package it effectively for others.

People will work in self-managing teams

Instead of relying on a supervisor to delegate writing tasks, staff will be employed within an independently operating team and write in collaboration with others. To operate successfully in a team, you will need social interaction skills, for example, negotiating, team building, effective listening, as well as constructive criticism and assertive behaviour.

Specialists will disappear

Specialist writing categories ('technical writer', 'editor') may become less common, and more staff will be expected to know how to produce a variety of written material, from publicity releases to technical reports. As desktop publishing becomes widespread, organisational writers will increasingly be expected to supervise the whole publishing process, from first draft to final product.

Lifelong learning rather than training will be promoted

Staff development will be revolutionised to support lifelong learning. Writing education will be based less on the hypodermic syringe theory ('one-shot' immunises you for life) and more on long-term and regular writing courses to support you as you move to different levels of responsibility.

These five emerging realities suggest significant changes in the workplace which will affect your role as a professional writer. In addition, there is a major business trend which focuses on writing itself: the plain English movement.

The plain English movement

The plain English movement began in the USA in the 1970s. Its growth was spurred both by legislation which required government documents to be written more clearly and by court cases which were based on the failure of legal documents to communicate effectively. The movement is popular in Australia, with organisations like the Australian Taxation Office, the Law Foundation of NSW, and the NRMA simplifying documents geared to the public.

Proponents of plain English point out that greater comprehensibility of documents also benefits the organisation. When clearly written documents help readers understand what they need to do, such as filling in a form, the organisation saves time and money. Professor Robert Eagleson, Australia's leading specialist in plain English, gives as examples companies which saved personnel costs when they could dispense with additional staff needed to run help hotlines or check forms and other documents filled out by their clients. Training costs are reduced if information is clearer to new staff.

With these results, is there any reason to be concerned about the plain English movement? One problem is that there is a great deal of confusion about what constitutes plain English. In its most restricted definition, it is writing which uses a minimal vocabulary, short sentences, and an unadorned style. However, if these characteristics were followed, writers would be merely retailoring the traditional straitjacket of formulas and rules.

Plain English is better defined in terms of its final goal, which is to promote understanding. Focusing on the needs of readers means not only considering vocabulary and sentence length, but also more difficult decisions, such as how much explanation to give, how much information to cover within one document, and what arrangement of information will meet readers' needs. Plain English can include the objective of communicating ethically with readers and being accountable for what is written. Finally, the success of plain English depends not only on individual writers, but also on the organisation itself and its accepted communication practice.

Think of this wider context when you attempt plain English, rather than restricting yourself to word and sentence choices.

> Language and its users shape each other far more than other tools and their users. Words are not passive vehicles into which ideas might be deposited. The language is the thought... To speak and write plain English is to understand what sustains it, to appreciate when it should be used and in what degree.

(Crow, 1988, p. 94)

Another problem with plain English is the lack of research to substantiate whether, in fact, it does help readers. Plain English documents are often tested to establish their readability level, but the readability formulas themselves are not seen to be valid (see Chapter 2). More research into users' needs may be the answer to this problem.

One interesting experiment was conducted by Dr Robyn Penman of the Communication Research Institute of Australia (1990). Penman tested plain English and other versions of insurance policy documents to establish how well readers understood what they read. In some cases, the plain English documents were less successful. They seemed easier to read, but readers had trouble finding the information they needed.

Penman attributes the problem to the emphasis in plain English on communication as a simple transfer of information from writer to reader. This view suggests that there is one 'right way' to produce an acceptable document, and in fact the reader's needs and interests can be ignored during the document's creation. If trouble results, it is the fault of the reader. Penman suggests that communication involves negotiating meanings, that is, writers must think more about their readers and test documents to understand what readers think and need.

Research into workplace writing

Knowing these current and future directions of writing research and practice can help organisations become proactive, interested in staff improving their writing skills to meet changes in the workplace. But where should an organisation start? Instead of relying on out-dated writing formulas and traditional handy hints, writers can incorporate more recent information based on writing research.

Research about 'adult' writing has usually been conducted in universities, with researchers using the most available subjects, university students, to investigate the most common academic writing format, the essay. Then in the early 1980s, the focus of research shifted to business writing as organisations began to open their doors to writing researchers.

Writing research in the workplace is varied. It may focus on the types of writing common in an organisation, the writer's procedures in producing a document, or the ways that writers (and subsequently their writing) are influenced by organisational culture. Five major trends in writing research—social context, text analysis, process writing, collaborative writing, and intercultural communication—can affect the way we think about writing in the workplace, and particularly about new methods for training writers, new roles in the workplace, and new questions to be tackled by both writing researchers and business writers themselves.

The cultural context

Business writing researchers interested in the cultural context of writing (described in Chapter 1) study organisations in the same way that anthropologists study village life. An organisation has its own culture, its heroes and villains, its rules and taboos. To write effectively, you must be sensitive to what is acceptable and what is prohibited within the organisational culture, and be aware of the effect of external influences such as trade unions, government agencies, and competitors.

As the communication patterns of more organisations are studied, researchers will have more information about writing and can begin to differentiate those general writing standards from those peculiar to one organisation or type of organisation. This information, in turn, can make business writers more confident of exchanging formulas for guidelines for writing in the corporate culture, which can be attuned to the needs of the specific organisation.

The broad and neutral assumption that the purpose of organisational documents is to deliver information masks other motivations supported by the organisational culture. A study of one organisation, for example, indicated that its writers were motivated not only by an interest in delivering information, but also by the need to publicise their accomplishments and to 'mark' that they had originated specific ideas and activities (Paradis and others, 1985, p. 295). Being aware that writing is used and evaluated within the context of the organisational culture helps business writers produce documents that 'work' within their own organisation.

Text analysis

Studies of documents written by respected writers show that commonly accepted rules and formulas are routinely violated. These findings are redefining how we consider the more archaic of the grammatical rules which may have little to do with readers' ability to comprehend a document. There is also a growing realisation that these rules are almost impossible to teach to people with little knowledge of grammar.

Text analysis suggests that certain organisational patterns may be identified in documents, which in turn can provide guidelines for how information can be arranged effectively for readers. Of particular interest is systemic linguistics, which provides ways for researchers to consider how the writer's intention to communicate results in certain writing choices being made.

Writing as process

Research material on the process of writing is gathered by **protocol analysis** (Flower and others, 1983), which involves a researcher recording the thinking aloud comments of people as they write, to understand how they map their ideas. Studies using protocol analysis have yielded information about how writing is affected by the writer's knowledge and interest in the topic, the writing task, and the reader.

Protocol analysis has confirmed that writers do not write in a linear fashion, that is, in distinct, sequential steps: planning, writing, rewriting, and proofreading. Writing is recursive: we 'loop back' through the document as we create it, mixing planning, writing, and rewriting as we go. For example, the act of writing often triggers further thinking about planning. This research into writing processes can help writers understand their own individual processes, and perhaps become more flexible about methods to use, depending on the nature of the document, the time limit, and the readers.

Collaborative writing

Research in collaborative writing destroys the myth of solitary writers. In the corporate world, group writing is much more common. You may be placed in a group which collaborates from start to finish on the document, or more commonly, you may complete a document on your own but be expected to have it appraised by others.

To collaborate effectively, you may need to change your personal writing and editing methods, and become as skilled in group dynamics as in writing. You must be aware of behaviours that are constructive or destructive to the team project. Some writers, for example, effectively sabotage a writing project through disruptive tactics, such as not attending important group meetings, not having work prepared on schedule, being overly critical, or making meetings unproductive.

Intercultural communication

Skill in intercultural communication is becoming increasingly important for organisational writers, as Australian businesses realise that better language skills are needed to meet domestic and international trade demands. According to Joseph Lo Bianco, Chairman of the Australian Advisory Council on Languages and Multicultural Education (1990), Australia must learn to communicate more in the international marketplace.

> Germany is the biggest exporting nation and has the highest per capita trade surplus; Japan is Australia's fastest growing partner and a major source of tourism; European nations will form the world's largest single market... and the dynamic economies of Asia are growing at the fastest rate in the world.

Documents intended for international markets must be acceptable and understandable overseas. For example, occupational health and safety legislation in the European Community requires that exports have directions and warnings translated into the languages of the countries of use. The success of a translation depends on how simple and clear the original information is. Even when used in English-speaking countries, the product information may still need to be simplified to be understood by semi-literate users.

However, just simplifying the message is not enough to ensure that intercultural communication in writing is successful. You can no longer assume, even in Australia alone, that the so-called average reader comes from the traditional Anglo-Celtic culture. Cultural allusions and idiomatic expressions familiar to you (if you are Anglo-Celtic) can be misleading or incomprehensible to some of your readers. They may also not share your values, whether these be personal, organisational, or cultural. For example, what is considered assertive behaviour in the American business culture is sometimes considered aggressive in Australia.

To create culturally-acceptable documents, place yourself mentally with your readers and foresee possible difficulties. Learn more about other cultures, their interests and values. Just as a culturally inept speaker may not think of using different words or even non-verbal signs to communicate, writers may not realise how certain simple strategies can make a document more easily understood by readers of another culture. Below are five simple guidelines for reducing miscommunication with non-English speaking background (NESB) readers.

First, make the most important information easy to find. Bring the important information to the front of your sentences and paragraphs so that readers need not work to find it. Rely on the most simple and common sentence pattern, the subject-verb-object one (see Chapter 7). You can also highlight important information by using a different typeface (for example, bold face), placing the information in a box, or using lists.

Second, reduce the number of culture-specific allusions or expressions. Sometimes in an effort to be less formal or to provide a striking image, we use allusions. However, many are culture-specific. NESB readers might not fully understand a message with phrases such as the following.

> Example 1: Jack will need to carry the can on this project.
>
> Example 2: She was sent to Coventry after that incident.
>
> Example 3: He was given a red card.
>
> Example 4: It's a Clayton's budget.

You have a much better chance of understanding these expressions if you follow sports (1, 3), have lived in Australia and watch television advertisements (4), and have a British cultural heritage (2).

Third, limit your idiomatic expressions and slang. Idiomatic expressions are found more often in speech than in writing, but still crop up often enough to be problematic for readers from other cultures.

> Example 1: That's a dynamite idea!
>
> Example 2: It's right on the button.
>
> Example 3: I'm tied up at the moment.

Translations are especially problematic, for if the translator is not familiar with the idiomatic expression, it may be translated literally.

Fourth, limit technical vocabulary. Substitute more common words for technical ones when possible, or provide definitions. Even adding a small definition can aid comprehension. For example, the following sentence might be more understandable to non-technical readers if it were rewritten with a definition.

> Original: For easier transmission, set your modem at 2400 baud.
>
> Improved: For easier transmission, set your modem at the higher 2400 baud rate (baud rate is the speed that data is transmitted over the telephone).

Fifth, restrict humour. Humour is often culture-specific: what is funny in one culture may be misconstrued in another. Humour may depend on the type of document and the gender, age, and official position of both the sender and receiver. It is also important not to use irony or sarcasm, as both can be misinterpreted, even by native language users.

From Research to Practice

Changes in workplace writing will tie in with emerging business trends and developing areas of writing research. To ensure that business writers move with these changes, organisations must consider how staff will be trained or retrained. Executives already spend up to one-third of their time writing (this will probably increase) and it is safe to say that every professional in an organisation writes. However, individuals vary in how well they write, understand the writing process, and are aware of the role of writing within their organisation.

Effective writers have learned to integrate knowledge of text conventions, interpersonal goals, content, and language, as well as stipulations from the organisational culture. Their learning has probably happened by chance rather than by design, for writing is mistakenly considered a simple skill, that is, the writer 'just puts words down on paper'. Even on the job, it is hard to develop one's writing. For example, a study of one organisation found that writing was 'neither commonly discussed as a technique nor widely recognized as a key work activity' (Paradis and others, 1985, p. 286). Such a lack of concern about writing means organisational members are not being formally prepared to become good writers able to meet complex communication demands on the job.

People can improve their writing skills and knowledge on their own, but they may benefit more from working with a writing consultant. A good one is more than just a writing stylist. A consultant may design and run training courses specific to different levels of staff, undertake a writing audit to assess writing practices and needs, and develop a communication policy and style manual.

Training

Writing consultants can develop writing expertise within an organisation by designing training courses tailored to the specific needs of staff. A comprehensive plan of staff development not only provides long-term support for staff interested in writing improvement, but also highlights the organisation's commitment to effective writing. The long-term training can be easily integrated into the organisation, whereas one-off training programs may do little good. One study illustrates the problem of short-term courses failing to change writers' patterns, when participants in a writing seminar reverted quickly to the 'bureaucratese' because it was still promoted within their organisation (Charrow, 1982).

Testing writing skills

Because so many employees spend so much of their time on the job writing, it is desirable that you hire only those who can handle writing tasks well. Deducing an applicant's writing ability from a résumé is unwise, because so many applicants these days do not write their own. If you want to test the writing competence of job applicants, ask them to answer the following questions in fully-developed sentences and paragraphs. Their attitudes to writing will be evident in their answers, as will their writing ability. (The following questions would take half an hour to answer fully. You could also give applicants a hypothetical letter to write, based on details that you provide.)

- What proportion of your working time is spent writing?
- What is your reaction when you are asked to do some writing?
- Are you regarded as a 'good' writer by your colleagues?
- Have any documents that you have written ever, to your knowledge, been used as 'model' documents within your organisation?
- What kinds of documents do you most enjoy writing?
- What kinds of writing do you least enjoy doing?
- What do you see as your biggest problem in writing? Do you, for example, ever find it difficult to get started on a document and put off starting it for as long as you can? Do you ever feel bored with the thought of editing a document that you have written? How do you cope with these problems?
- How do you go about 'the business of writing'?
- Do you write on a computer? Revise/edit on a computer?

Writing audits

Writing consultants can undertake writing audits of an organisation. Audits scrutinise how much and what types of writing employees do and how effective it is. Consultants can check the number and kinds of documents that people at different levels are expected to write and the amount of time they have for writing. One company with the problem of poorly-written research proposals being rejected for funding found that staff were not being given enough lead-time to develop projects, write a submission, discuss it, rewrite, and submit.

The communication audit can be the basis of suggestions for the most appropriate writing practices and plans to meet the organisation's particular needs and interests.

Policy formulation

A writing consultant can help a company establish a communication policy as part of its mission and goals. Topics that could be included in a communication policy include

- the clearing procedure for making public statements

- appropriate use of communication technology
- emergency communication procedure
- co-ordination of information
- communication flow
- security of information
- storage of information.

Such a policy can prevent mistakes and miscalculations that range from the simple to the complex. For example, consider the employee who sent another organisation a draft of his personal views, but because it was on letterhead, the other organisation assumed that his ideas were officially recognised. The resulting confusion reflected poorly on both the employee and his company.

Style manuals

The writing consultant is often in demand to produce an in-house style manual as a guideline which establishes a house style for all written communication. A style manual is invaluable for new staff, as it identifies correct communication and frees other staff from having to teach 'This is how we do it here'.

The manual usually includes guidelines on both visual elements (formats, headings) and written elements, from how to abbreviate the word 'degree' on a chart to the appropriate tone for the first collection letter. It can include information about organisational values and culture that the company wants its written communication to reflect. Sample documents, which staff can use as writing models, are often included.

Selecting a Consultant

If your company wants to incorporate more writing, training, and development, consider hiring a writing consultant. Do not necessarily rely on your organisation's trainers, as they probably do not write enough themselves, have little knowledge of writing research, and are too 'close' to assess writing practices within their own organisation.

If you decide to employ a consultant, choose carefully by checking these essential points.

First, does the consultant have formal qualifications in writing or communication? You expect only a qualified dentist to work on your teeth and only qualified tradespeople to build your house. Why not expect the same degree of qualification from the writing consultant? If the consultant does not have formal qualifications, can knowledge of modern writing research and practices be demonstrated in some other way? For example, does the person subscribe to writing journals and belong to writing associations?

Second, does the consultant have writing experience? Does the consultant actually write and edit professionally, for example, reports, letters, technical articles, books, research submissions? The consultant's experience does not need to be in the same field as your company, as specialised types of writing still share the same basic principles.

Third, is the consultant able to develop a customised program? Some quick-fix writing trainers apply a standard training course to every organisation. The result is often disillusioning, resulting in companies questioning the value of any writing training. Writing consultants who can draw upon a wealth of writing experience and study can create a program customised to your company's needs.

Fourth, does the consultant have adult education or training experience? Learning patterns for adults differ from those of students. There is a big difference between handling a classroom of students regularly over a semester and a group of adults available for only a few hours. A trained consultant knows how to incorporate adult learning techniques to create relevant training programs that meet the needs of an organisation's staff.

Fifth, can the consultant prove training success? Consultants who are good trainers make the training program a learning experience, not a self-promotion lesson. They unify a collection of people into a supportive group, satisfy individual needs, pace the program well, and effectively handle disruptive or uninterested participants. Finally, good trainers give a professional presentation, from well-designed overhead sheets to time management.

To assess a consultant's training success, you can ask for evaluations from other workshops, but these 'smile sheets' are notorious for being unreliable indicators of quality. Instead, ask to see the consultant's planned program and materials, and interview the consultant to find out how the training session will be run.

CONCLUSION

Our views of professional writing are changing because of the influence of writing research and new directions in the workplace itself. To help connect business writers to these changes, organisations need to consider long-term staff development and planning about writing in the workplace. To ensure that their written communication remains (or becomes) effective, more companies are making writing consultants a part of their plans for developing and evaluating their corporate communication.

References

Crow, P. (1988). 'Plain English: What counts besides readability?' *The Journal of Business Communication*, 25, 1, 87–95.

Lo Bianco, J. (1990). Correspondence related to the Australian Community Language and Multicultural Education conference.

Paul, S. (1990). 'Communicating in the 1990s—Are We Ready? The simple answer is no—we are not'. *IABC Communication World*, May–June, 171–178.

Paradis, J., Dobrin, D. and Miller, R. (1985). 'Writing at Exxon ITD: Notes on the writing environment of an R&D organization', in L. Odell and D. Goswami (eds), *Writing in Nonacademic Settings*, pp. 287–307, New York: Guilford.

Penman, R. (1990). 'Comprehensible insurance documents: Plain English isn't good enough'. *Occasional Paper No. 14*, August, Canberra: Communication Research Institute of Australia.

INDEX